Third World Citizens and the Information Technology Revolution

The INFORMATION TECHNOLOGY AND GLOBAL GOVERNANCE series focuses on the complex inter-relationships between the social, political, and economic processes of global governance that occur at national, regional, and international levels. These processes are influenced by the rapid and ongoing developments in information and communication technologies, which are affecting numerous substantive areas, as well as creating new opportunities and mechanisms for participation in global governance processes and influencing how they are studied. The series encourages original scholarship on both the *global governance of information and communication technologies* (from the narrow issues of global Internet governance to the broader issues of global governance of the Information Society) as well as the *uses of information and communication technologies in the service of global governance* in a wide range of sectors.

Series Editor:

Derrick L. Cogburn, *American University/Syracuse University*

Associate Professor of International Relations
International Communication Program
School of International Service
American University

Associate Professor of Information
School of Information Studies
Syracuse University

Director: COTELCO The Collaboration Laboratory
American University/Syracuse University

Advisory Board:

Nanette Levinson—American University
John Mathiason—Syracuse University
Milton Mueller—Syracuse University/Technical University of Delft
Claudia Padovani—University of Padova (Università di Padova)
Priscilla Regan—George Mason University

Published by Palgrave Macmillan:

Third World Citizens and the Information Technology Revolution
   by Nivien Saleh

Third World Citizens and the Information Technology Revolution

Nivien Saleh

palgrave
macmillan

THIRD WORLD CITIZENS AND THE INFORMATION TECHNOLOGY REVOLUTION
Copyright © Nivien Saleh, 2010.

Cover Art: Sketch by Nivien Saleh based on a photo by www.jordanjubilee.com.

First published in 2010 by
PALGRAVE MACMILLAN®
in the United States—a division of St. Martin's Press LLC,
175 Fifth Avenue, New York, NY 10010.

Where this book is distributed in the UK, Europe and the rest of the world, this is by Palgrave Macmillan, a division of Macmillan Publishers Limited, registered in England, company number 785998, of Houndmills, Basingstoke, Hampshire RG21 6XS.

Palgrave Macmillan is the global academic imprint of the above companies and has companies and representatives throughout the world.

Palgrave® and Macmillan® are registered trademarks in the United States, the United Kingdom, Europe and other countries.

ISBN: 978–0–230–10364–1

Library of Congress Cataloging-in-Publication Data

Saleh, Nivien.
    Third world citizens and the information technology revolution / Nivien Saleh.
        p. cm.—(Information technology and global governance)
    ISBN 978–0–230–10364–1 (hardback)
    1. Information technology—Egypt. 2. Information technology—Political aspects—Egypt. 3. Information technology—Developing countries. I. Title.
HN786.Z9I566 2010
303.48′330962—dc22   2010013065

A catalogue record of the book is available from the British Library.

Design by Newgen Imaging Systems (P) Ltd., Chennai, India.

First edition: November 2010

10 9 8 7 6 5 4 3 2 1

Printed in the United States of America.

*For my parents Abdel Halim Saleh and Elfriede Saleh, and
for my brother Tilman*

Contents

Part II   The Rules of the Game are Enforced

Part III   Lessons

Illustrations

Acronyms

AFESD	Arab Fund for Economic and Social Development
ARENTO	Arab Republic of Egypt National Telecommunication Organization
ARPA	Advanced Research Projects Agency
AT&T	American Telephone and Telegraph
BBN	Bolt, Beranek and Newman
BTA	Basic Telecom Agreement
ccTLD	country-code top-level domain
CSI	Coalition of Service Industries
CSNet	Computer Science Net
DCA	Defense Communications Agency
DNS	domain name system
EARN	European Academic Research Network
EC	European Community
ECES	Egyptian Center for Economic Studies
ECMS	Egyptian Company for Mobile Communications
EIEF	Egypt's International Economic Forum
ETUF	Egyptian Trade Union Federation
EU	European Union
EUN	Egyptian Universities Network
FCC	Federal Communications Commission
GATS	General Agreement on Trade in Services
GATT	General Agreement on Tariffs and Trade
GBDe	Global Business Dialogue on Electronic Commerce
GDLC	Global Distance Learning Center
GDP	gross domestic product
GIIC	Global Information Infrastructure Commission
GNI	gross national income

gTLD	generic top-level domain
IAB	Internet Activities Board
ICANN	Corporation for Assigned Names and Numbers
IDSC	Information and Decision Support Center for the Egyptian Cabinet
IESG	Internet Engineering Steering Group
IETF	Internet Engineering Task Force
IIPA	International Intellectual Property Alliance
ILPF	Internet Law and Policy Forum
IMF	International Monetary Fund
IP	Internet protocol
IPR	intellectual property rights
ISE	Internet Society of Egypt
ISI	industrialization through import substitution
ISP	Internet service provider
IT	information technology
ITU	International Telecommunication Union
MCIT	Ministry of Communications and Information Technologies
MENA	Middle East and North Africa
MIT	Massachusetts Institute of Technology
MoT	Ministry of Transport and Communication
NGO	nongovernmental organization
NSF	National Science Foundation
OECD	Organization for Economic Cooperation and Development
PPP	purchasing power parity
PTT	post, telephone and telegraph
RFC	request for comments
RITSEC	Regional Information Technology and Software Engineering Center
TCP	Transport control protocol
TCP/IP	transport control protocol/Internet protocol
TNC	transnational corporation
TRA	Telecom Regulatory Authority
TRIPS	Agreement on Trade-Related Aspects of Intellectual Property Rights
UK	United Kingdom of Great Britain and Northern Ireland
UNCITRAL	United Nations Conference on International Trade Law
UNCTAD	United Nations Conference on Trade and Development
UNDP	United Nations Development Program

UNESCO	United Nations Educational, Scientific and Cultural Organization
USAID	U.S. Agency for International Development
USIPO	U.S. Investment Promotion Office
USIS	U. S. Information Service
W3C	World Wide Web Consortium
WIPO	World Intellectual Property Organization
WTO	World Trade Organization

Preface

Does the information technology (IT) revolution empower Third World citizens? If you answered "yes," you are in good company.

Most development experts and academics and most U.S. and European government officials sincerely believe that the IT revolution has brought enormous, unmitigated benefits to the people of the Third World.

Consolidating six years of research, this book challenges that consensus. It shows that First World governments and transnational corporations dominated the rule-making processes of the IT revolution. With this, they boosted their own economic competitiveness as they moved from the rigid production patterns of Fordism to flexible accumulation, emphasizing corporate mobility, organizational decentralization, and outsourcing.

After forging a new IT regime for themselves, these actors imposed it on Third World societies.

Examining how this process took place inside one Third World country, Egypt, this work documents how the World Bank, the European Commission, the U.S. government, and transnational corporations reconfigured power relations within poor economies with the allurement of technology and how they reinforced social injustice by denying ordinary citizens the right to choose their own political institutions. The book's analysis shatters the myth that the new technologies significantly diminish economic hierarchies.

The present study is written from the vantage point of critical realism, a philosophy of social science that specifically searches for power relationships and the play of power. Critical realism is vibrant in European academia but is still largely unknown in the United States, where positivism prevails. It is a premise of this book that positivism blinds scholars and policymakers to the destructive effects of First World power on human autonomy in low-income societies.

In sum, *Third World Citizens and the Information Technology Revolution* shows what happens when repressive Third World elites enrich themselves in cooperation with European and American corporations and governments. For those who wonder why some people in the world's periphery become attracted to violent oppositional visions, such as radical Islam, this study may be an eye-opener.

This analysis has been a long time in the making. The preliminary investigations began in 1999, when I was a PhD student at American University in Washington, DC, and scoured the field of comparative politics for a suitable dissertation topic. As every doctoral candidate knows, dissertation advisors exert strong influence over their students and often put their own mark on the works they supervise. I was lucky in that regard. As chair of my dissertation committee, Diane Singerman allowed me to truly follow my own intellectual inclinations while giving me the guidance I needed. Without her support, my work could not have become what it is today.

Edward Comor, who served on the dissertation committee until his return to Canada introduced me to the work of Gramscian international political economists, several of whom were affiliated with his alma mater, York University. Jon Anderson of the Catholic University of America contributed his expertise on information technology in the Middle East, read my chapters with a critical eye, and provided excellent substantive suggestions. Mireya Solis joined the committee after Edward's departure and helped me carry my dissertation to a successful defense.

Thanks are also due to over thirty policy experts in Washington, New York, and Cairo, who contributed their time and expertise by granting me in-depth interviews that complemented my archival research in the United States and Egypt, as well as the participant observations in Egypt.

Generally, I benefited from the heavy technology focus that prevailed at American University during my time as a graduate student there, and that manifested itself in faculty hires, technology-focused courses, and strong IT support for members of the campus community. I had the opportunity to work with Erran Carmel, an expert on the management of global information technology who taught me invaluable lessons about the economics of outsourcing business services. By offering me a position at the Social Science Research Lab, where I assisted students with their statistical research, maintained hard and software, and supported distance learning courses, Assen Assenov and Professor James Lee enabled me to acquire a very practical understanding of IT.

While I wrote up my results, my friends Tony Payan—now a professor at the University of Texas in El Paso—and Ayşegül Ateş—now a professor at Akdeniz University in Antalya—lived with me through the up and downs of writing a dissertation. So did Else Ward and John Hounsell of Washington, DC.

Over the last few years I have learned that writing an academic book is like a sculpture. You begin with a block of stone—the data you have gathered—and work to move it closer to the perfect shape that forms your vision. If you are an inexperienced sculptor—and I was—that vision itself evolves as you interact with your raw material. After weeks of labor, a figure emerges. You marvel at the progress you have made, see perfection in your sculpture, and put down your tools, afraid that further manipulation diminishes the beauty of what you have created. You then invite others to admire your creativity. If they are good friends, they will praise your effort but realize that your figure can be strengthened in its size, proportions, detail, or character, and tell you so.

I had many persons who did this for me by reading and commenting on my work: Mark Brawley of McGill University, Peter Katzenstein of Cornell University, Sheryl Lutjens, Cathy Small, Jacqueline Vaughn, Astrid Sheil, David Schlosberg, Zach Smith, Chris Gunn, and Susan Nyoka of Northern Arizona University in Flagstaff, where I worked as a visiting professor, Sandy Thatcher of Pennsylvania State University, and Elisabeth Muhlenberg, a doctoral candidate at the University of Illinois in Chicago and dear friend.

Since 2007 I have been an assistant professor at the Center for International Studies at the University of St. Thomas in Houston. My colleagues at the University—and especially the Center—have given me an intellectual home that allowed me to improve my manuscript. It saddens me that Gustavo Wensjoe, the director of the Center for International Studies and a wonderful, hospitable spirit, passed away a year ago in an accident. He would have been very proud of this book.

I met Jimmy Engineer, Pakistan's national artist, at an interfaith dialogue at the University of St. Thomas. Ever since our first encounter he has kept in touch, calling from Dubai, Karachi, or Berlin, to inquire into my progress. Amit Kumar, my Indian friend who works for the United Nations, has done the same.

Two persons remain to be named: Sandy Sheehy, a seasoned journalist and friend, helped me by suggesting edits to the manuscript that improved its flow. Terry O'Rourke, a creative attorney from Houston and adjunct professor of international studies at the University of St. Thomas, has read each chapter with enthusiasm and a sharpened pen. For this and the sketches that he has contributed to this book I am truly grateful.

I now place the sculpture on which I have worked for so long in your hands.

NIVIEN SALEH
September 2010

CHAPTER 1

A Human Rights Approach to Globalization

One Sunday in 2008 I visited Houston's Lakewood Church, the institutional home of America's popular televangelist Joel Osteen. A refurbished basketball stadium, the church has an average weekly attendance of forty-seven thousand followers. On the large speaker's stage the most prominent fixture is not a big cross, as one might expect given Osteen's commitment to the Christian faith. Instead, it is a giant, rotating globe. Once everybody had taken their seats, several rounds of rock music put the congregation into a celebratory mood. A few introductory remarks by Osteen's wife Victoria followed, and then her husband, the celebrity pastor himself, stepped into the limelight. At that moment, eight cameras started to roll and tape the show. Once the message was recorded, it would flood into the homes of millions of Americans and to viewers in one hundred other countries who tuned in to hear Osteen speak. Followers anywhere in the world could watch the famous preacher by podcast. While they listened to his message of self-love and wealth creation, they saw faint outlines of the globe, which turned quietly in the background.

Inside the Giant Globe

Although I had spent years studying the dynamics of globalization and had grown accustomed to their workings, my Sunday outing struck me on several levels. First, it showed me how potent the information technology (IT) revolution has become: Thanks to the advances in end user equipment and the improvement of the global communication network, Osteen's message spreads effortlessly into the corners of the world. In 1980, such rapid information transmission would have been unthinkable—partly because the hardware was not developed, and partly because the countries that were involved in cross-national data transmission had not yet agreed on rules for handing off network traffic or allowing foreign investment in their communication infrastructure.

Second, it demonstrated that the IT revolution is part and parcel of globalization, the integration of national markets worldwide. On the one hand, market integration has been driven by trade liberalization through international agreements negotiated at the World Trade Organization (WTO). They have made it easier for Osteen to sell his books to a worldwide audience, because he does not need to contend with the varying intellectual property laws that once impeded trade in knowledge products. On the other hand, market integration has been achieved through the IT revolution—the development of desktop and palm top computing technologies, the build-out of national communication networks, and the interconnection of all these components into a global communication grid. This has allowed Osteen to connect to audiences across the globe and alert them to his message. Thanks to trade liberalization and the IT revolution, Osteen has been able to sell over five million copies of his book *Your Best Life Now*, which was released in October 2004 and has been translated into twenty-five different languages (Dooley 2007).

Third, for those who have the resources and skills to play the game, globalization pays. For Joel Osteen, the funds to be gained from book sales are enormous. If we assume a conservative one dollar in royalties per book sold, his first publication earned him five million dollars.

Fourth, while theoretically the IT revolution allows for two-way communication, in practice, communication flows are often one-directional, originating from industrialized economies and flowing into the industrialized and the Third World. In the case of Lakewood Church, podcast recipients in foreign countries can choose whether or not to consume the weekly show "Discover the Champion in You." But their ability to speak back and engage in dialogue with church leaders is limited.

Fifth, my experience gave me a winner's perspective on globalization. When I was inside the church and a part of the crowd, I shared in the congregation's feeling of creating something great. In addition to receiving a chance at salvation, musical entertainment, and the permission to feel good about themselves, the faithful had an opportunity to help build the church's values—a uniquely American blend of capitalist and individualist ideas—and watch them take flight across the planet. At least for the time they were inside the church and actively supporting the message, they had the ability

to participate in forging the norms that would shape their lives. They experienced autonomy.

Turning the Globe

The air of elation and success that I felt at Lakewood is not part of the day-to-day American experience. Nevertheless, that Sunday service captured something typical of life in this country, although it intensified it and expressed it in heightened form: In a sense, U.S. residents are inside the command center of the global economy. We produce information, entertainment, and high-tech commodities that are exported to countries worldwide. The companies for which we work benefit from international trade and IT rules that the U.S. government negotiated on their behalf and in their favor. With a per capita gross domestic product (GDP) of forty-six thousand dollars purchasing power parity (PPP), we are sufficiently wealthy to buy and travel.

Let's walk up to the globe and turn it 125 degrees clockwise. This takes us to Egypt, a country of 81 million that is in many respects very different from the United States. While the United States enjoys the benefits of being the world's only superpower, Egypt's time as a hegemon passed several thousand years ago. While the United States is shaping world history, Egypt struggles to preserve the symbols of its ancient greatness from environmental degradation. While Americans are among the wealthiest people in the world, Egyptians have a very limited purchasing power of fifty-four hundred dollars PPP per capita—less than an eighth of ours. While American companies benefit from their alliance with a government that can negotiate trade rules in their favor, Egyptian businesses are aligned with a government of limited international stature that can gain them few benefits. While Americans are at the center of the global economy, Egyptians are at its periphery.

Egypt, like the United States, has popular television preachers who interpret the Qur'an for their followers. But it is hard to imagine that one of them might ever become a Joel Osteen. For one thing, Egypt has an authoritarian government that resents those who upstage it. But in addition they do not speak English, the language of the hegemon, the Internet, and global commerce; they do not have the technological resources to broadcast their godly message to the rest of mankind; and they do not preach values of capitalism and individualism that are aligned with corporate America. By virtue of living inside the center of the global economy, we have opportunities that those who inhabit its margins do not have. Being located in the world's periphery has negative consequences for a human being's autonomy. This is true even for the supposedly empowering IT revolution.

Meet a Nineteen-Year-Old Egyptian

If I asked Reverend Osteen whether he believed that the IT revolution enhanced the autonomy of people in poor countries like Egypt, he would probably answer in the affirmative. And in doing so he could count on the support of most development experts. The World Bank (2006), for example, defines empowerment similarly to what I call "autonomy," as "the process of enhancing the capacity of individuals or groups to make choices and to transform those choices into desired actions and outcomes." In 2002, the Bank's *Empowerment Sourcebook* explained that

Information and communications technology (ICT) is creating economic, social, and political empowerment opportunities for poor people in the developing world. Direct and independent access to information about prices and exchange rates can transform the relationship between poor producers and middlemen. Connectivity through telephones, radio, television, and the Internet can enable the voices of even the most marginal and excluded citizens to be heard, promoting greater government responsiveness. ICT can thus help to overcome poor people's powerlessness and voicelessness even while structural inequities exist in the distribution of traditional assets such as education, land, and finance. (Narayan 2002, 73)

According to this reasoning, deploying IT throughout the peripheral society will even out power differentials and render society more equitable.

To illustrate the World Bank's idea of empowerment, I'll use the story of Hisham, a composite based on several young Egyptians with whom I have spoken. The year is 1999, and Hisham is enrolled at Cairo University's Faculty of Commerce. His family of five lives in Shobra, an older and somewhat rundown Cairo district. They share one wireline telephone. Making long-distance calls from this phone is difficult, because Egypt's telephone infrastructure is poor. Making international calls from the apartment phone is impossible. If the family wants to call a cousin in Sydney, Australia, they have to go to a long-distance telephone station two miles from the apartment. Luckily, two international consortia have recently set up shop in Egypt and compete to provide customers with cellular phone service. Hisham just used up his personal savings to purchase a small handset and a cellular plan. He can now call or text his friends. He feels empowered.

From this perspective, which treats IT as external input into social actors' struggle for influence and status, IT is indeed empowering. This aspect of the IT revolution is real and must be taken into account. However, IT is more than ready-made pieces of hard and software, as the Bank suggests. Underneath the computing devices that people use are networks that connect the equipment. They are governed by rules of ownership, market entry, interconnection, data transmission, and the privacy of digital content that is sent across the infrastructure. The creation and enforcement of these rules is marked by a power struggle that puts Hisham and all other human beings at the periphery of the world economy at a disadvantage. There are two reasons for this. First, when it comes to forging the global rules of the game, those organizations that could possibly represent Third World citizens' interests in international negotiations have little bargaining power. Second, in implementing the rules, Third World citizens are at a disadvantage because their states must bow to the dictates of creditor states, development agencies, and corporations. If we want to fully understand the ramification of the IT revolution for citizens' autonomy, we have to consider this part of the story, too.

Delving further into Hisham's story illustrates this. Hisham is an idealist who regularly reads the newspaper. In the fall of 1999 a story announces the government's decision to inject the country into the global market as a software exporter. A few weeks later Hisham reads another story. It states that to implement the new strategy, President Mubarak has decided to establish a new ministry for IT, which will lure transnational IT corporations to Egypt. Hisham is disappointed. He has always believed that Egypt should keep foreign investors at arm's length and build on indigenous strength. More importantly, he is frustrated, because in drawing up this development plan his government worked closely with transnational corporations and development agencies. At the same time, it failed to involve the Egyptian people in its decisions. As a citizen who wants to take part in molding his own government institutions, Hisham feels powerless.

This book will attempt to counterbalance the one-sided understanding of globalization and the IT revolution that prevails among development experts. To do that, it will examine how the negotiation and implementation of IT rules affect the autonomy of Third World citizens. And since this book is about negotiating and implementing IT rules, the term "IT revolution" will serve as a shorthand for this process.

Ways of Looking at Information Technology

Hisham's two-part story points up the contrast between two research traditions that have examined connections between the situation of the Third World and the use of technology. The first part of Hisham's story treats technology as an external input into Third World politics. It does not to look at the rules that underpin technology, making it work in certain ways, and not in others, and committing its recipients to specific understandings of property rights, privacy, or trade. This is the perspective that is taken by the optimistic research tradition. Its early representatives were the modernization theorists, who treated the capitalist economies of Europe and the United States as models that poor countries should emulate. Moreover, they conceived of the development process that would bring the poor country into the state of prosperity, democracy, and industrialization as linear and divided into stages (Rostow 1960). The purpose of communications technology, which had been created in industrialized nations before being exported into the Third World, was to propel poor economies along this straight path, by diffusing "modern" social practices from the developed into the "backward" nations (Lerner 1958; Pye 1963).

Today, at least two strands of argument can be discerned within the optimistic paradigm. One emphasizes the impact of IT on culture. It argues that the diffusion of technology undermines authoritarianism, because it gives people in the developing world access to information that is independent of the government-controlled media. It also emphasizes that IT enables decentralized communication, and thereby evasion of dictatorial control by the dictator (Kedzie 1997; Pool 1983 and 1990; Taubman 1998).

The second strand examines technology as a factor of production that can improve economic efficiency (Saunders et al. 1994). J.P. Singh (1999), an expert on culture and technology at Georgetown University, has explained that these works often talk of "leapfrogging development." He describes the idea as follows:

> The phrase "leapfrogging development" reflects the belief, especially in the 1980s, among policymakers and theoreticians that information technologies, especially telecommunications, can help developing countries accelerate their pace of development or telescope the stages of growth. This results from the modernization and expansion of telecommunications infrastructures in developing countries. The infrastructure, in turn, feeds into demand for telecommunications services by other sectors of the economy...Often the word "leapfrogging" is used interchangeably in both technological and economic ways. (4f)

The second part of Hisham's story is aligned with the critical tradition of studying the relationship of technology and Third World politics, because that tradition examines the institutions that enable the workings of technology and investigates to what extent they express differences in wealth and are fraught with power.

The critical tradition aligned itself with dependency theory, an approach to development that combined Marxism with nationalism (Packenham 1992). Under the rubric "critique of cultural imperialism," this line of research argued that communication served advanced capitalism, the transnationalization of production, and a new business world order (Dan Schiller 1996, 88–105; Mosco 1993; Webster 1995, 74–100). Unlike the optimistic studies, these critiques treated communication technology not as ready-made pieces of equipment. Instead, they discussed how communication technology was made, regulated, and sold; and they showed that these processes were marked by a fight for control over the global communication network, in which the U.S. government and the U.S. service industry played leading parts (Comor 1998b; Dan Schiller 1999; Hamelink 1983; Herbert Schiller 1970; Mosco 1993). All in all, the critical approach to communication and its technologies has remained a weak undercurrent in the discussion of technology and development.

Embarking on a Dissertation

While optimistic and critical authors differ profoundly in their approaches to studying technology, all agree that IT is an integral aspect of globalization (Harvey 1990; Kellner 2002; Keohane and Nye 2000). A book that investigates the power relations marking the IT revolution would therefore have a great deal to contribute to our understanding of the struggles that characterize globalization.

That is why I dedicated my doctoral dissertation to this topic. The constraint that I imposed upon myself was that the specific topic I chose to investigate should somehow involve Europe and Egypt—the two shores of the Mediterranean from which I, with my German mother and Egyptian father, originated.

Although my choice of Egypt as model for how this social, economic, and political drama played out was influenced in part by my own advantages of familiarity and family connections, I also found that it made an ideal example in helping thoughtful North Americans and Europeans understand the issues surrounding the IT revolution. No two countries are the same, but Egypt shares significant qualities with many others in the Third World. It has a long history as a well-defined nation, during which it has been an active trading partner with its neighbors and other countries farther afield. It balances geographic advantages (position on the Mediterranean Sea and the Red Sea, its long and fertile Nile River valley) with disadvantages (vast expanses of Sahara Desert and limited arable land). It has had long periods under foreign control—most recently of France and England during the nineteenth and early twentieth centuries. Its economic growth has been largely fueled by foreign investment ($47.16 billion according to the 2008 CIA *World Factbook*), but little of that has trickled down to its rapidly growing population of eighty-one million. I concluded that what I learned from Egypt would illuminate the impact of the IT revolution on the rest of the Third World.

During my hunt for a good dissertation topic, I learned three things about the IT revolution that deeply puzzled me. First, the global telecom landscape had just undergone a profound overhaul in ownership. At the dawn of the new millennium, in country after country, the traditional state-owned operator had seen its administrative purview curtailed. Private companies had become the new, privileged operators. I wondered: Why did so many countries change a practice of administering telecom that had proven its effectiveness for more than a century?

Second, this wave of change appeared to have originated in Europe or the United States. Egypt and other Third World countries seemed to follow, and as they revamped their approach to providing communication infrastructure, they also established new government agencies that resembled America's Federal Communications Commission. This surprised me: Did Third World states seek to imitate their First World counterparts as scholars such as Martha Finnemore (1996) would suggest? Or were they pressured to create those agencies?

Third, the arcane topic of telecom sparked enormous interest among transnational corporations. Why were companies such as American Express and Sony so vested in the future of telecom? It dawned on me that great economic stakes had to be involved, and I concluded that it might be a good idea to get to the bottom of this.

Once I had reached this point, I decided to divide my research into two steps. In the first, I would investigate how global IT rules were made. In the second, I would examine whether the implementation of these rules led, in some way, to the creation of new state agencies in the Third World. I decided to arrange my research around one such agency, Egypt's newly established Ministry of Communications and Information Technologies (MCIT).

Only at this stage did I become interested in theoretical debates, and I searched the literature for concepts that would help explain what I had begun to see on my own.

From Fordism to Flexible Accumulation

While studies that fell into the optimistic paradigm offered interesting insights, none of them adequately explained the connections among the pieces of my jigsaw. Most importantly, they did not explain why corporations and the American government so eagerly persuaded Third World states to change their way of administering national communication networks.

Then I came across David Harvey's *The Condition of Postmodernity* (1990). Its attention to the motivations of actors from the core economies and its prophetic discussion of IT matched the data that I had gathered thus far. Harvey explained that between 1945 and 1973 the Fordist mode of accumulation dominated industrialized economies. Named after Henry Ford, its characteristic feature was assembly-line mass production. Fordism rested on a coalition among organized labor, corporations, and the state in the core economies. In this coalition, unions secured the cooperation of workers. Corporations invested in mass production and so provided employment. The state stabilized demand with Keynesian policies, and it protected the economy from negative external influences. Production happened in the industrialized countries at the core of the world economy, and peripheral economies delivered raw materials.

By the mid-1960s the hegemonic U.S. economy entered a crisis, and by the 1970s it was in full recession. American corporations drew their conclusion: to restore profits and take on the new Asian competition, they would change their operations and become flexible in production and marketing. They reorganized their operations. Horizontal networks based on teamwork replaced hierarchical chains of command, and production moved to cheaper locations at the periphery of the global economy, either through direct investment or through outsourcing. Corporations of countries at the world's economic center lobbied their governments to secure them access to these offshore sites by dismantling barriers to trade and investment. To obtain flexibility corporations also withdrew from the Fordist coalition. Supported by the governments of Ronald Reagan and Margaret Thatcher, American and British companies pushed labor unions—the former coalition partners—into retrenchment.

A new mode of flexible accumulation began to take shape. In the core economies it rejected stability and solidarity in favor of flexibility, and it expanded production across the world. Harvey predicted that IT would be central to this transition. Under flexible accumulation, corporations depend much more on communication and information processing than they used to. They need IT to gauge rapidly changing demand. They require it to maintain corporate cohesion in the face of operational decentralization. They depend on it to communicate with suppliers in the absence of large inventories.

Published in 1990, Harvey's analysis of globalization suggested that corporations would try to capture the IT rule-making process if they could and subject it to their needs, preempting input from those actors who might have had alternative visions for the IT revolution. Two decades of hindsight demonstrate that Harvey was prescient. Globalization is in fact the transition from Fordism to flexible accumulation.

The IT Revolution from a Post-Marxist Perspective

Harvey's study was unabashedly Marxist, and a Marxist perspective forms a helpful jumping-off point for this book. Like Marxism, my work attends to the ways in which economic resources influence the ability of humans to shape their environments. But my perspective on the IT revolution is anchored more securely within post-Marxism as defined by Tormey and Townshend (2006, 3–6). The philosophy of science position that guides it is critical realism.

This study departs from the Marxist legacy in a number of ways. First, whereas Marxists use "class" as their primary unit of observation, I opt for "organization." Marxist analyses regard class-based organizations, such as unions or firms, as direct expressions of class interest. That is, they view organizations as a mere extension of those individuals who own them. This assumption is problematic. Organizations may channel their owners' desires or be aligned with them, but they are also capable of violating them. Economic literature on the principal-agent problem supports this view: It stipulates that in cases when the interests of principal (the owner) and agent (the organization that is to carry out the owner's will) do not coincide, the agent is tempted to leverage its informational advantage to dodge the principal's interest in favor of its own needs.

Organizations also do not simply aggregate the interests of the individuals who staff them but have their own interests. They possess what Bhaskar (1979) describes as "emergent powers": abilities that are unique to the organization and cannot be reduced to its constituent parts, that is, the individuals that make up the entity. Consequently, organizational interest must be determined on a case-by-case basis, taking into account such factors as the institutional context that constrains what the entity can and cannot do (i.e., the external social structure) and the organization's internal, hierarchically ordered web of roles that determines its interest formation (i.e., the entity's internal structure). Organizational interest may, for instance, be environmental or religious, or—as in the case of corporations—it may come down to maximizing returns for shareholders.

Second, in traditional Marxist thinking, the state is the backdrop of social struggle (Miliband 1969, 5). In contrast, my approach emphasizing organizations views the state as an actor in its own right. Specifically, the state is a complex and potentially fragmented organization that insists on sovereignty and the legitimate monopoly on coercive power in a given territory (Migdal 1988).

The Social Construction of the IT Revolution

A third point that distinguishes this study's approach from traditional Marxist works is its focus on the idea that reality is socially constructed. That is, social actors first make common rules and then are bound to implement them. The best account of this remains Berger and Luckmann's (1966) landmark work *The Social Construction of Reality*. As it will form an important backbone for this book, an explanation of its concepts is in order.

Berger and Luckmann build a sociology of knowledge that draws on Marx's insight that humans produce the social world while the social world determines their consciousness. The two authors discuss how social rules and role expectations come about and then shape human awareness. They begin their discussion with an encounter between human beings in a state of nature—that is, prior to the formation of a society that could have imprinted its norms on these individuals. As these pre-societal human beings interact, they fill their clean slates with information about each other. They notice that one of them engages in a specific action: He washes clothes. They respond by doing something typically human: From the multiplicity of that person's actions, they extract those that take up a good part of his day (washing clothes) and assign a type to the person that engages in those activities. The individual therefore becomes the "clothes washer." As our human beings encounter other persons who engage in clothes washing, they also refer to them as members of the type "clothes washer." Over time these humans develop an encompassing set of types, or social categories, on which they draw as they make sense of their environment: "farmer," "woodworker," and so forth. Berger and Luckmann call this process "typification."

As time passes, our state-of-nature individuals begin to connect certain behavioral predictions with each type they have created. They see a person who belongs to the type "ruler" and predict that he will decide over harvest times and local disputes, and occasionally wear a crown.

Through the decades, impromptu typifications become institutionalized. That is, they become part of the nascent society's intersubjective memory. Types now cover entire groups of people, who accept the types into which they have been cast together, along with the behavioral expectations, and they typify their counterparts in turn. The end point of institutionalization is the formation of actual institutions. These are patterns of behavior that have acquired an existence independent of the actors who embody them at any particular moment. The patterns are no longer simple behavioral predictions that are associated with a type. Instead, they have reached the status of rules, and each formed society has a host of them.

An example of a behavioral prediction is the following: "Princes, before becoming king, are crowned." The following institution has emerged from it: "In order to become a king, a prince *must* be crowned." Because over the centuries coronation has evolved into an institution, it would be impossible for Britain's Prince Charles to demand the privileges of kingship without going through the crowning ceremony. Coronation has thus acquired an existence that is independent of Prince Charles or any currently living king. And no matter how little a coronation actually accomplishes, without it we would not accept Charles as monarch of England.

The complete web of society's rules (or, synonymously, institutions[1]) is called its "social structure." As Berger and Luckmann (1966) explain, members of society experience social structure as possessing a reality of its own, "a reality that confronts the individual as an external and coercive fact" (58). It has coercive power over the members of society, both by the simple fact that its institutions exist and call citizens into submission, and "through the control mechanisms that are usually attached to the most important of them" (60). A control or enforcement mechanism could be a police officer's act of making parents comply with their duty to send children to school, or a teacher's act of enforcing a dress code in her class room.

Social structure contains roles, that is, behavioral expectations and prescriptions that are associated with types of actors: "Roles share in the controlling character of institutionalization. As soon as actors are typified as role performers, their conduct is *ipso facto* susceptible to enforcement... The roles *represent* the institutional order" (74; emphasis in the original).

When a high school graduate enters college, she takes on the role of college student. As such, she must register for a certain number of credits, purchase text books, come to class on time, treat her instructors respectfully, and score above a certain minimum on exams. If an individual does not abide by these role prescriptions, she will be penalized. The web of hierarchically ordered roles—students, assistant professors, associate professors, administrative assistants—together with the associated enforcement mechanisms make up the "institutional order" of the university. Because role expectations and associated enforcement mechanisms have an existence that is independent of the individuals who embody them at any time, the institutional order that is the university perpetuates itself into the future, even as the individuals filling out this institutional order change. As Berger and Luckmann explain, this social structure constrains what human beings can do without penalty. However, it also shapes a person's identity by imprinting in him or her norms of desirability, success, and the good life.

For the purposes of this book, Berger and Luckmann's model will serve to conceptualize the IT revolution as a rule-making and rule-enforcement process. The individual human beings in their model become organizations, such as state agencies and corporations. Together, these organizations create specific rules or institutions. They determine how many operators a telecom sector may have, who legally owns digital property on the Internet, and who is allowed to register domain names on the web. The unconscious communication process that yields institutions as a by-product becomes an explicit rule-making process that actors consciously seek to dominate so as to shape the rules in their favor. Last, the actor to be pressed into role compliance is the Egyptian state, and enforcement mechanisms include World

Bank-administered structural adjustment and a trade agreement with the European Union.

On Regime Theory

Berger and Luckmann conceive of the institutional order as consisting of two basic components: specific rules on the one hand and inclusive social structure on the other. I will introduce an additional, intermediary component: regimes, that is, sets of rules that govern a specific issue area such as IT (Krasner 1982). Rules for IT are integrated into an IT regime. This regime, in turn, forms part of social structure—that is, the entirety of rules that govern the interaction among organizations at the global level and cast each one of them into specific roles, for example, those of "creditor state" and "debtor state."

This use of terminology points to the deep affinity of the present study for the literature on regime theory, in particular its constructivist or cognitivist strand (Hasenclever et al. 1997). A subfield of International Relations, regime theory emerged in the early 1980s. Since then it has analyzed whether and under what circumstances bodies of rules facilitate cooperation among states. Scholars such as Peter Cowhey (1990), Derrick Cogburn (2003, 2004, 2005), and Marcus Franda (2001) have successfully applied this literature to telecom and the newer information technologies.

This book speaks to the regime-theoretical literature. By systematically applying the concept of enforcement mechanisms it illuminates how regimes can alter state behavior. By causally relating the creation of Egypt's new ministry for IT to the IT regime, it supports the constructivist view that regimes in fact shape state identity.

At the same time this volume leaves the straight and narrow of the regime theoretical debate in at least three ways. First, it not only investigates state actors, as is common for regime-theoretical treatments, but organizations more generally.[2] Second, to fully understand the workings of the IT regime, it first studies politics at the international level, as regime theorists do, but then delves into the intricacies of (Egyptian) domestic politics—a realm where regime theorists seldom venture. Third, by querying the IT regime's impact on the peripheral state, it elucidates the IT revolution's impact on the autonomy of Third World citizens. Most fundamentally, perhaps, the present study diverges from regime theory in its explanatory intention. Its ultimate goal is not to illuminate the effects regimes can have under numerous sets of circumstances, at different times, and across a range of issue areas. Instead, it seeks to advance a new understanding of globalization.

Transformation of the State

So, how does the IT revolution impact the state? The present examination puts forth the following account: First, states and corporations at the center of the global economy worked to define an IT regime that would favor the transition toward flexible accumulation. This regime entered the global social structure and faced, in different ways, both state and nonstate organizations.

Second, in bringing this IT regime about, core states were motivated by the desire to situate *their* corporations so that they would capture the most lucrative niches in the global corporate struggle for competitive leadership. Means for doing so consisted of opening foreign markets and production sites. The hope was that corporations would invest abroad, sell their products, and repatriate their profits.

Third, peripheral states remained largely excluded from the negotiations that yielded the new IT regime.

Fourth, flexible accumulation had a role assigned for peripheral states: that of cheap production sites and consumption markets (Harvey 1990).

Fifth, as the case of Egypt will demonstrate, several enforcement mechanisms bore down on Third World states, prodding them toward role compliance. These mechanisms pressured the state to change its approach toward IT.

Sixth, in some cases—such as Egypt—the enforcement mechanisms had the combined effect of bringing about new state agencies for IT, thereby changing the composition of the state. The new agencies support their country's integration into the global economy.

This outline of how the Third World state is pushed into role compliance matches the model of state transformation that scholars of Gramscian international political economy have developed (Brenner 1999, 41; Comor 1998a and 1999; Cox 1996; Gill and Law 1993; Panitch 1996). Cox (1987) states:

> First, there is a process of interstate consensus formation regarding the needs or requirements of the world economy that takes place within a common ideological framework (i.e., common criteria of interpretation of economic events and common goals anchored in the idea of an open world economy). Second, participation in this consensus formation is hierarchically structured. Third, the internal structures of states are adjusted so that each can best transform the global consensus into national policy and practice, taking account of the specific kinds of obstacles likely to arise in countries occupying the different hierarchically arranged positions in the world economy. (254)

By exerting pressure on the peripheral state and changing its internal structure, the enforcement mechanisms associated with the IT regime thus help align the peripheral economy with flexible accumulation.

Autonomy

While this study examines the impact of the IT revolution on the state, its ultimate concern is the fate of human beings, particularly those in the world's periphery. An important motivation of this inquiry is the assumption that all human lives are valuable and equally so, no matter where in the world those lives are lived. This assumption is widely shared. It informed the work of Karl Marx, who sought to improve the condition of the most wretched members of society. It also lies at the heart of liberalism, a philosophical position that affirms foundational rights for all human beings, among others the right to freedom (Christman 2009).

Political theorists traditionally applied the tenets of liberalism to the national realm. However, under the mantle of cosmopolitanism an increasing number of scholars have recently transferred liberal ideals to the international arena. Philosophy professors Gillian Brock and Harry Brighouse (2005, 4) define the cosmopolitan position: "The crux of the idea of moral cosmopolitanism is that each human being has equal moral worth and that equal moral worth generates certain moral responsibilities that have universal scope."

David Held of the London School of Economics summarizes the cosmopolitan idea in eight principles:

1. Equal worth and dignity. All human lives are valuable and equally so.
2. Active agency. Individuals can and do shape their surroundings, and a flourishing life requires that human beings can make choices.
3. Personal responsibility and accountability. To the extent that human beings can make choices, they must take responsibility for the measures they take and can be held accountable for the consequences of their actions.
4. Consent. Interaction among human beings should be governed by deliberation and compromise, not coercion.
5. Collective decision-making about public matters through voting procedures. The principle of "consent" can be formalized in public decision processes that emphasize voting and majority rule.
6. Inclusiveness and subsidiarity. Those affected by social rules should have an equal opportunity to shape them. This may happen directly or indirectly through elected representatives.

7. Avoidance of harm and amelioration of urgent need. Policies that are implemented must not be harmful to human beings. Moreover, the alleviation of pressing human needs must be a priority concern.
8. Sustainability. Economic development must respect the world's fragile ecological system.

From these eight principles arises the metaprinciple of autonomy (Held 2005, 20). The *Stanford Encyclopedia of Philosophy* describes autonomy as follows:

> To be autonomous is to be one's own person, to be directed by considerations, desires, conditions, and characteristics that are not simply imposed externally upon one, but are part of what can somehow be considered one's authentic self. Autonomy in this sense seems an irrefutable value, especially since its opposite—being guided by forces external to the self and which one cannot authentically embrace—seems to mark the height of oppression. (Christman 2009)

For the purpose of this inquiry, autonomy is operationalized on the basis of Held's principles four through six as the human being's right to participate as equal in making the decisions that constrain his or her life.

Measuring Respect for Autonomy

The chapters in this book will evaluate how organizations, in their efforts to mold and enforce the IT regime, affected the autonomy of Third World citizens. This is easier said than done. To see why, consider the following ideal world scenario.

In an ideal world, each organization, at its founding, receives a mandate from its human originators, and it implements that mandate faithfully. In such a world, the company acts out the directives of its capitalist masters, the labor union does exactly what the workers want, and Marxists are justified in treating organizations as tools in the hands of their owners. If an ideal-world organization shuts Dan and Jane out of a decision process in which they have a right to participate, the organization's creators are morally responsible for the entity's action, and they can be said to have violated Dan and Jane's autonomy by giving their organization an unjust mandate.

Unfortunately, in the real word, organizations are not simple extensions of their creators' will. Some organizations actively avoid scrutiny by their owners or principals and subvert the mandate that they were given. Others—such as democratic states turned authoritarian—start out obeying their originators—the national body politic—but then become beholden to a narrow segment, for example, the military elite. Again other organizations, such as the Global Business Dialogue on Electronic Commerce (GBDe) that will be discussed in chapter three, have a highly mediated relationship to what might be considered human owners: The GBDe was founded not by humans, but by corporations. These are partly owned by other corporations or investment funds, which in turn represent a multitude of small investors (such as university faculty members who invest their monthly retirement contributions) and a small number of large investors.[3]

In the real world, there is a variety of complex relationships between organization and their human principals. That makes it difficult to assess which human beings have violated Hisham's autonomy when a certain organization injects itself into the process of making and enforcing rules. This is particularly true if the researcher does not possess precise information on the human beings whose interests the organization purports to represent.

Hence, this present study of the IT revolution will use an admittedly crude measurement to determine whose autonomy is disrespected. It will look at the organizations that are involved in rule-making processes and ask to whose feedback they are exposed. Those human beings who have the ability to provide their feedback to an organization, express displeasure with its actions, or engage in protest can be said to experience greater autonomy than those who are deprived of this feedback possibility.

Applying this measurement to the first part of this book, the formation of the IT regime, yields a clear picture. The organizations that were involved in the decision processes involving IT had strong roots in the core economies, and consequently they were exposed to the feedback of First World citizens. Few organizations with strong roots in the periphery were included in the bargaining process; hence, citizens from the periphery had disproportionately fewer opportunities to provide their feedback to the negotiation process. Consequently, their autonomy has been disrespected.

The second part of this study reveals that in the 1990s corporations and states from the core, as well as development organizations, insisted that peripheral economies opened their borders to trade, sold their state-owned enterprises, became wired, and created a transparent mechanism for administering the new technologies that were so central to flexible accumulation. If the presiding states did not have the bureaucratic capacity to administer the new technologies, they were pressured into creating the necessary capabilities.

This pressure disrespected the autonomy of the peripheral citizens, because they should have been the ones to determine their country's national policy and the shape of their government agencies.

In sum, this study, which covers a time period extending from the early 1980s to the early 2000s, suggests that our understanding of the IT revolution and globalization needs revision. Handing a human being a laptop with an Internet connection may be empowering, as the World Bank suggests. But negotiating the rules of the game without inviting peripheral citizens to the bargaining table accomplishes just the opposite.

Looking Ahead

Prior to the 1990s, countries across the world had administered telephony in a uniform fashion, which had been devised in Europe and then diffused into the European colonies. The sector was organized as a protected monopoly that the state owned and ran in conjunction with the post. Monopolists did their work in bureaucratic obscurity, and few people questioned their performance. In the 1980s this changed. A nonissue for so long, telecom administration became the object of great political activism in the core economies. Only ten years later a new "best practice" was in place, encapsulated in a small number of international agreements. They encouraged states across the world to privatize their telecom sectors and simultaneously open the service to competition. Monopolies fell, one by one.

Who stood behind this profound change, and why did it happen when it did? This question will be addressed in chapter two, which will trace the political battles that corporations and core states waged to obtain an improved telecom infrastructure. The chapter will show that these actors shaped the new telecom consensus. They did it to the exclusion of states and nonstate organizations from the periphery, which were only admitted to the bargaining table once the basic parameters were set.

Chapter three will take a close look at the Internet. Originally a technology developed for use by the U.S. Department of Defense, it opened its doors to the public in 1994. Shortly thereafter, new rules for encryption, electronic commerce, and the definition of intellectual property rights came into being, and supportive organizations that administered them emerged. This study will show that once again organizations from the core were the protagonists behind these processes and that they excluded organizations from the periphery that might have opted for a different set of institutions had they been consulted. In doing so, they disrespected peripheral citizens' autonomy.

Given that actors from the periphery were excluded from the decision processes of the IT revolution, were any attempts made to coax them into embracing the resulting IT regime? This question will be taken up in chapter four, which will explain how core corporations, states, and development organizations launched a concerted effort to persuade peripheral actors of their notion of the information society—that is, a market-driven information society that privileges the corporate desire for profit.

The World Bank and a number of other development organizations produced what can be called "IT-for-development narratives." These narratives took the desirability of globalization as an undisputable given, and they promised that Third World economies would leapfrog development if, and only if, they integrated into the global market. In producing their narratives, development organizations suggested that there was only one feasible vision of the information society. The IT-for-development narratives entered the global social structure where they joined the emerging international IT regime. The IT regime spelled out guidelines by which participants in the global economy were to abide. Supportive organizations such as ICANN, the Internet Corporation for Assigned Names and Numbers, enforced these guidelines. The IT-for-development narratives served as ideological frames. They encouraged voluntary compliance by detracting attention from alternative political possibilities.

In addressing the ideological aspect of the IT revolution, chapter four completes the discussion of how social structure was constituted. It then transitions to the enforcement of the IT regime, by introducing the mechanics of the case study that will fill out the second part of this study.

Substantively, part two investigates how peripheral states were socialized into the roles that social structure had produced for them. It will show that core actors and development organizations pressured Third World states to comply with social structure. The case that will serve to make the argument is that of Egypt, but the findings apply to other states occupying similar positions in the hierarchy of states.

Understanding Egypt's embeddedness in the world's social structure requires traveling back to the days of Gamal Abdel Nasser, who set the country on a collision course with those organizations that sought to advance flexible accumulation. As chapter five explains, Egypt had a troubled relationship with the global economy. By the late nineteenth century the country had come under de facto British rule, where it was used to safeguard the passage to India. In subsequent decades, Egyptians gradually regained their independence. Because of their imperialist experience, the Egyptian people, in the early twentieth century, became ever more assertive about their religious and national identity. In the 1950s, under President Gamal Abdel Nasser, the state translated this quest for identity into policy. It entered into a social contract with employed labor. In return for guaranteed social security, workers would commit their productive abilities to a nationalist development project.

This project consisted of a policy of industrialization through import substitution (ISI), which was designed to shield the Egyptian economy from the world market. But instead of freeing Egypt from foreign domination, as had been intended, the state over the following decades incurred rising levels of debt, raising its vulnerability to foreign pressure. In the early 1990s, when the Soviet Union collapsed and its influence on Middle East politics ended, Egypt's creditors from the core could leverage the country's debt, have the economy undergo structural adjustment, dismantle all remnants of the ISI policy, and lay the groundwork for globalization.

Freed from their Soviet rival, the core states of Europe and North America leaned on the Egyptian state, prodding it to embrace globalization and the tenets of the IT revolution. As chapter six will show, this pressure took a number of forms. Trade agreements that the European Union negotiated with Egypt called for trade liberalization and improvements in Egypt's capacity to utilize IT. Structural adjustment, administered by the World Bank, demanded that Egypt dismantle its barriers to trade, privatize state-owned enterprises, and float the exchange rate.

This pressure not only caused the state to seriously consider export-led growth as its new economic strategy, it also helped the emergence of a peripheral business elite, which favored the idea of globalization and demanded IT connectivity. Seeking to maintain its grip on society in the face of creditor demands for economic restructuring, the state entered into an alliance with this "globalization elite," while increasingly oppressing most other civil society groups.

Chapter seven will turn to Egypt's telecom sector. Like many other countries, Egypt in the early 1980s had a state-owned monopoly. The monopolist was part of the Ministry of Transport and Communication, which had been established during the presidency of Nasser. Rather than being market-oriented, the ministry's approach to infrastructure was motivated by a Nasserist commitment to social engineering. How did the ministry and its operator fare in the 1990s? As chapter seven explains, when the global economy began its move toward a new, market-oriented telecom arrangement, the monopolist and the supervising ministry fell out of favor with transnational companies, development organizations, and the domestic globalization elite. Together they nudged the telecom carrier to become more market-oriented.

Chapter eight focuses on Egypt's IT stakeholders: highly educated computer scientists, engineers, and managers whose social status was tied to IT adoption. A lower-level government agency, the Information and Decision Support Center for the Egyptian Cabinet (IDSC), channeled their desire for an improved, market-friendly information infrastructure. Tasked by the government with the informatization of the presidential cabinet, IDSC single-handedly expanded its mission to bringing IT to Egypt and making the country a software exporter.

The organization worked diligently to increase its domestic power base. Because its vision of a wired, borderless world economy was compatible with flexible accumulation, core actors provided abundant resources that IDSC used to expand its power base.

By the end of the 1990s, the network of IT stakeholders entered an alliance with Egypt's globalization elite and with a state that—thanks to pressure from creditors—embraced the notion that Egypt's future lay in globalization. Chapter nine will explain that in the fall of 1999, President Mubarak announced Egypt's new national goal of becoming a software exporter. A month later, he mandated that a new Ministry of Communications and Information Technologies (MCIT) be created. Telecommunications and postal operations were removed from the Ministry of Transport and assigned to MCIT. This curtailed the power of the Nasserist ministry, weakened the Egyptian ISI constituency, and improved Egypt's compliance with the role that the global social structure had created for it. The establishment of MCIT exemplifies the kind of state transformation described by Robert Cox.

Chapters five through nine show that Egypt's citizens were largely excluded from the decision-making process that opened the country to foreign trade and investment and that led to the establishment of MCIT. At the global level, Egypt's citizens were thus excluded from the formation of the IT regime, and domestically, they were excluded from shaping their own government institutions. Their autonomy was therefore disrespected twice.

Chapter ten will generate causal inferences from the case of Egypt to other poor economies. Chapter eleven, the conclusion, will draw general lessons from the preceding discussion. It will also address the question of what needs to be done, from a cosmopolitan perspective, on both the national and the global level, to work toward treating every human being as an end in her or his own right.

PART I

The Rules of the Game are Forged

CHAPTER 2

Telephony for the Global Economy

I n the mid-1990s Europeans had reason to marvel: Phone companies that had taken their customers for granted for decades now courted them with new services and fashionable brand names. Operators lowered their rates, emphasized customer care, and allowed them to attach equipment of their choice to the phone network. Why did they suddenly lavish their clients with attention?

Much of this change can be credited to the European Commission. In the late 1980s, it had become convinced that Europe's telecommunication services needed improvement if European companies were to remain competitive in the world market. Then it had used its power to change the rules of the game within the European Union (EU) by forcing member states to open their monopolistic telecom markets to European competitors. Carriers realized that their days as monopolists were numbered and that customers might soon migrate to other providers. In hopes of generating brand loyalty, they pulled themselves together and tried to impress their subscribers.

What happened in Europe was only the beginning. Having whipped its own operators into shape, the Commission now eyed monopolistic telecom markets in the Third World, where infrastructure was poorly developed, waiting lists for telephones were long, and call completion rates were low. If the Commission could open these markets to European investment, it would hit two birds with one stone: European operators would gain the opportunity to service unsaturated and therefore lucrative markets at the world's periphery, while European producers would gain telecom connections to cheap offshore production sites and new buyers for their products. Once its work in Europe was complete, the Commission therefore teamed up with the U.S. government, and both leveraged their bargaining power to abolish telecom monopolies worldwide. By the time the millennium turned, the global telecom landscape looked very different, and carriers played by an entirely new set of rules.

These institutional changes were an integral aspect of the worldwide transition from Fordism to flexible accumulation. Fordism had been marked by an alliance between the state, labor unions, and corporations. The state and corporations offered job security, while the unions guaranteed that their members would show up for work. This setup came under strain in the 1960s, when the postwar boom ended and demand for corporate output weakened. It crumbled in the 1970s, when world oil prices quadrupled. Depending on cheap energy, companies felt the pinch, and they reconsidered their commitment to their alliance partners. What they wanted was the flexibility to alter production decisions quickly, flatten their organizational structure, and move operations offshore. In their calculus, the unions had turned from partners into burdens. In Britain and the United States, the state took the side of the companies and cracked down on unionized labor. In the mid-1980s, the U.S. government went a step further, working toward a new deal on trade rules at the Uruguay round of trade negotiations in order to generate the flexibility its corporations demanded.

To ease the transition toward flexible accumulation for their respective enterprises, the EU and the U.S. government took on the rules by which telecom was administered. For the sake of global competitiveness, the time-honored telecom monopolies had to fall, and the provision of telecom services had to be opened to competition, for only competitive pressure could motivate operators to innovate.

The details of how the rules of the telecom game changed demonstrate the parts played by the core economies. As chapter one explained, societal rules and norms are the result of negotiation. And the telecom rules changed when they did not by coincidence, as optimistic accounts of the IT revolution suggest. Instead, core states deliberately sought transformation because they wanted to ensure that their corporations would occupy the most lucrative niches in the world economy. States from the core dominated the decision processes by which the new rules were made. States from the periphery were only admitted to the bargaining table once the outlines of the emerging model were clear. Because those organizations that provided access points to citizens from the First World were included in the decision processes that generated rules for all states, while those organizations that provided access points to citizens from the Third World remained excluded, the autonomy of citizens from the Third World was disrespected.

First things first, however. To appreciate the profundity of the overhaul that the telecom landscape experienced requires an understanding of the

Fordist *status quo ante*. How were national telecom sectors organized? Why were corporations dissatisfied?

Telecom under Fordism

The *status quo ante* that characterized Fordism dated back to the late nineteenth century. Since then, all but a few countries had administered their national telecom networks as state-owned monopolies.

Telephony was a public service. Like the police force or the fire brigade, it was considered a part of the state bureaucracy. Usually, the carrier reported to a specialized ministry that also oversaw postal and telegraph services in a so-called PTT (post, telephone, and telegraph). In many cases the services that reported to this ministry were not operationally separated. Therefore, instead of flowing back into the network, profits from the lucrative telecom service subsidized mail delivery. The ministry responsible for telephony did its work without external supervision. It determined what end user equipment could legally be connected to the network, and it limited the range of permissible equipment to those devices that had been produced by a few privileged manufacturers or by the ministry's own manufacturing plants. These devices were then sold or loaned to end users at high rates.

European states had invented this approach to PTT sector administration. In the late nineteenth century, during the second wave of imperialism, they introduced it to their colonial outposts. This is why telecom all over the world was administered in a remarkably uniform fashion.

Among the few exceptions to the state-owned monopoly was the United States. Here, American Telephone and Telegraph (AT&T) had the exclusive right to provide telecom services and manufacture lines and switches. Although the American sector shared characteristics with its European counterparts, it differed from them in that the carrier was privately owned.

A set of institutions that governed how telecom was to be operated existed at the global level. A central element of this worldwide telecom regime was the recognition that this sector was covered by national sovereignty. That is, a state's way of administering its national telecom sector was off-limits to interference from other states. De facto, however, the expectation existed that each country would be served by a monopolist. International transmission standards—a set of specialized, technical rules—were set at the International Telecommunication Union (ITU), an intergovernmental organization.

To enable voice and data transfer across national borders, the various national monopolists needed to cooperate with one another on a daily basis. That cooperation was institutionalized in the "international settlements regime," the body of rules under which monopolists connected to foreign networks and compensated one another for setting up international phone connection."[1]

To understand how international settlements worked, assume we are still living in the era of *status quo ante* and imagine a telephone call from Anne to Ben, who reside in different countries. Anne picks up her phone in A-Land and dials the number of Ben, who lives in B-Land. A-Land's monopolist, A-PTT, routes the call to the border of B-Land. There it connects to B-PTT, the monopolist servicing B-Land (figure 2.1). B-PTT then terminates the call by routing the signal to Ben, whose phone rings. Anne and Ben talk for two minutes. Since Anne has originated the call, she will pay for it. Through her upcoming bill A-PTT will collect the money by asking for the collection rate—the per-minute charge of making an international call to Ben—multiplied by the number of minutes Anne spent on the phone. Since A-PTT operates as a monopoly, it can charge Anne a high collection rate. After all, Anne cannot defect to an alternative provider.

Because A-PTT took advantage of B-PTT's network, B-PTT demands a share of the charge Anne has to pay. A-PTT therefore compensates B-PTT for call termination. It does so according to a contractual agreement between the two carriers, drawn up according to guidelines set by the ITU. The

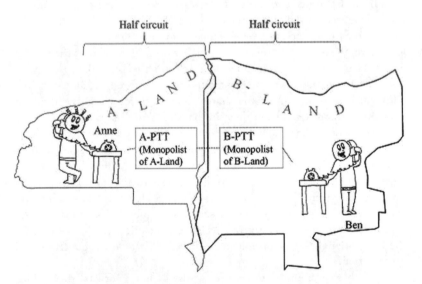

Figure 2.1 An international circuit.

agreement specifies two crucial items: The first is the so-called accounting rate, the assumed per-minute rate for establishing a telephone connection between users in the two countries. The second item is the "settlement rate." It is a fraction, usually 50 percent, of the accounting rate. The originating carrier agrees to reimburse the terminating carrier at the settlement rate (Stehmann 1995).

Importantly, the accounting and the settlement rates are negotiated between the two carriers, and they are completely detached from the collection rate, which each carrier determines according to national forces of supply and demand. Because it is a monopolist, A-PTT can charge a collection rate that far exceeds the accounting rate. It therefore charges Anne a long distance collection rate of $1 per minute. The accounting rate, according to the agreement that the carrier signed with B-PTT, is $0.6 per minute; and the settlement rate is half that amount, $0.3 per minute. Since Anne and Ben talked for two minutes, she will reimburse A-PTT in the amount of $2. A-PTT will settle its account with B-PTT by paying the latter $0.6. The remaining money, $1.4, is A-PTT's net revenue. This revenue will likely subsidize the postal service of A-land or the local telephone network. Anne depends heavily on international telephony, but she rarely uses her country's postal system, and it bothers her that she has to support other people's mailing habits by paying high long distance charges.

In this example, an individual is dissatisfied. In real life, however, it was corporations engaged in international business that paid the bill for countries' postal services and local telephony, because they used long distance communication most heavily. Yet in the years after World War II, they did not question the settlements regime or the monopoly status that made their telecom providers so powerful. Why was this?

At least two reasons offer themselves. First, competitive models of network administration did not exist at that time. Given contemporary theories of network economics, it was not clear whether alternative methods of telecom administration would work at all.[2]

Second, Fordist corporations had no incentive for destroying the monopoly system that was itself directly grounded in the Fordist mode of production. The relations between management and labor within the PTT reflected the dominant consensus that national economic progress rested on a coalition between labor, capital, and the state. Attacking the secure positions of unionized PTT employees would have soured relations among the coalition partners. As long as corporations put their faith in the Fordist mode of accumulation, they recognized that attacking their coalition partners within the PTT would undermine their position and incur possible retribution.

Change is in the Air

In the 1970s and 1980s, however, European and American corporations became increasingly insistent on excellent telecom infrastructure at low cost. This about-face in corporate attitude can be explained by environmental changes that these corporations faced, which altered their incentives in approaching telecom politics. Four changes rendered past practices obsolete:

1. The competitive telecom model was put to the test in the United States, and it succeeded, lowering the uncertainty cost of demanding an overhaul in other countries.
2. Technological developments brought new communication services within reach, and this raised the opportunity cost of leaving things as they were.
3. The 1973 recession convinced corporations across economic sectors that Fordism was no longer feasible. This lowered the costs of undermining unionized labor, specifically at the PTT.
4. After 1973 both traditional telecom and the newly emerging information technologies became more important for corporate cohesion and communication with suppliers and customers.

Here is how each of these major environmental shifts played out.

1. The Competitive Model is Put to the Test and Succeeds

Starting in 1982 when the U.S. courts stripped AT&T of its monopoly over local and long distance communication, the United States put a competitive model of telecom provision to the test. The court order marked the end of a decade-long struggle between AT&T and its would-be competitor MCI: In the early 1970s, MCI sought to enter the American long distance market. AT&T went out of its way to prevent this. In 1974 MCI and the Department of Justice responded with antitrust suits against the telecom giant. Eight years later, the trial concluded with the watershed Modified Final Judgment. It broke the monopolist into several distinct organizations. AT&T's local operations were split into seven regional Bell companies, each of which retained the monopoly on local telecommunications. Long distance traffic remained with AT&T but was opened to competition from other providers, barring only the so-called Baby Bells (Sterling 2005).

While the 1982 ruling maintained monopoly for providers of local telephony, it created a test case for competition in long distance communication, which showed that the long distance market could operate under competition.

The key to functioning competition appeared to be proper regulation of the carriers by the Federal Communications Commission (FCC): Independent of the executive branch, the FCC reported directly to Congress. Its mandate was to watch over the telecom sector for the benefit of customers. The key to functioning competition appeared to be proper regulation of the carriers by the Federal Communications Commission (FCC): Its mandate was to administer the frequency spectrum, license operators, and regulate interconnection and tariffs for the benefit of customers. What enabled it to properly fulfill this function was the fact that it reported to Congress—this freed it from becoming a political tool of the executive branch.

Analysts advanced the argument that other economies could have competitive telecom sectors as well, so long as they established an independent regulator to ensure the appropriate mix of cooperation and competition among operators. The American test case provided those who sought more sophisticated services in other national economies with the evidence they needed, and they began to hold this example up as a model to be implemented worldwide.

2. Technological Developments Bring New Communication Services Within Reach

In the age of the Internet, it is hard to imagine a world without computers, and yet it existed a short while ago. In the 1960s, large companies deployed a few closet-size mainframe machines, but smaller organizations were not computerized. By the early 1970s, more powerful minicomputers became available commercially, and large enterprises—especially financial service providers—inserted electronic data processing techniques into complex processes such as inventory control and sales analyses (Hamelink 1983). As a result, "islands of automation emerged, which corporations sought to connect by data communication networks; providing the potential for the fusion of productive activities into a single, flexible system of production" (Davies 1994, 102f).

Some corporations built private data networks on top of lines they leased from the telephone company. By the late 1970s, several transnational corporations (TNCs) managed worldwide data communications services in-house (McKenney and Nyce 1989, 245).

The adoption of computers by the private sector was a gradual process. As these machines became more powerful and less expensive, they began to permeate the production process, and demand grew for a telecom service that would allow the private sector to exploit the full potential of decentralized computing. Large companies desired the ability to transmit their data across the public telephone network, but monopolists that had sunk vast funds into their analog infrastructure wanted to hold on to their old equipment as long as possible. Generally, PTTs had no incentives to digitize their networks in response to customer demand. This caused growing dissatisfaction, giving the private sector a reason to call for the overthrow of the monopoly when that option became available (Davies 1994, 104–105; McKenney and Nyce 1989, 226f).

3. Recession Teaches Corporations that Fordism is No Longer Feasible

Corporations weathered the oil price shock of 1973 with difficulty. While the recession worked itself out, they began to withdraw from the Fordist coalition that had consisted of private sector employers, unions, and the state. Relinquishing the Fordist ideal, they lost interest in maintaining a working relationship with the unions. In fact, they wanted their erstwhile coalition partners to realize that they had to cut back on their demands for employment guarantees and compensation. Now that the Fordist alliance was terminated, companies no longer cared whether or not they antagonized the unions by jeopardizing the job security of PTT employees.

4. Corporations Have a Greater Need for Telecom and New Information Technologies

With the transition to flexible accumulation, the role of telecom and the new information technologies moved center stage. There are at least two reasons for this. First, corporations moved to decentralize and relocate portions of their operations to low-cost peripheral economies. This made them dependent on a telecom infrastructure that could support remote communication within the corporation.

Second, communication with suppliers became more important. "Just-in-time" production had established itself as a way of minimizing overhead costs, and corporations scaled back on inventories requiring costly storage space. Just-in-time production meant that relations with suppliers had to be managed with great care. In addition, companies increased their flexibility by concentrating on their core competencies and outsourcing other functions such as human resource management. For both purposes communication with business partners had to be instantaneous and flawless. This placed high demands on the communication network.

In sum, as a result of technological developments, macroeconomic changes, and a new approach toward the Fordist coalition, corporations had unprecedented incentives to pressure monopolists into fulfilling their service demands. They also had incentives to work toward the abolition of the monopoly.

Who Wants How Much Competition?

In the 1980s the administration of telecom became the focal point of policy discussions both in Europe and the United States. Global financial conglomerates, large manufacturers intent on relocating production facilities to low-cost sites, retail chains trying to enter new national markets—all desired competition, which they hoped would spur innovation and drive down long distance phone rates.

Telecom operators participated in the politics of their own reform. While the interests of corporate telecom customers were clear-cut, those of the carriers changed as their circumstances and incentive structure shifted. Operators with a monopoly over the national telecom network rejected the idea of competition, and so did their employees. However, once they lost their monopoly status, the ITU settlement regime became costly for them. Moreover, once state-owned carriers were privatized, they began to think like profit-oriented private sector firms and seek investment opportunities abroad. For those two reasons privatized carriers that had lost their monopolistic status insisted that foreign telecom markets be rendered as competitive as their home markets.

The U.S. example demonstrates this clearly. Prior to 1982, the year in which the Modified Final Judgment was passed, AT&T enjoyed monopoly status and therefore was satisfied with the international settlements regime. After 1982, however, it called for competition in foreign markets and the overhaul of the settlements regime. The reason for AT&T's policy shift was economic. The settlement mechanism functioned well for carriers in an international environment where no country had long distance competition. But once competitive carriers had to interact with a foreign monopolist, they could actually lose money from international telephony, because carriers had to offer low collection charges if they wanted to lure customers away from their domestic competitors. At the same time, carriers were bound to high settlement rates, forcing them to compensate the monopolist of the terminating half-circuit generously for its termination of phone calls. As a result, the profit margins of the competitive carriers dwindled.

This is what happened to AT&T after 1982. To avoid losing customers to MCI, AT&T lowered its collection charges, but it remained bound by high accounting and settlement rates. In 1988 the company was forced to hand over to the Brazilian monopolist 99 percent of the amount it collected from calls made to Brazil. Thus, AT&T joined the choir calling for competition in foreign telecom markets (Stehmann 1995, 261).

A 1993 communication from the staff of the House Subcommittee on Telecommunication and Finance reveals that Congress took demands for competition in the lucrative European markets seriously:

> Before the breakup of the Bell System in 1982, the U.S. routinely ran telecommunications trade surpluses. By 1989, that surplus had dissolved into a record $1.9 billion trade deficit. In the four years since 1989, the deficit has steadily dropped, down to about half a billion dollars…in 1992. While progress has been made, U.S. telecommunications companies continue to labor in a fundamentally unfair global marketplace. As a result of the AT&T breakup, the U.S. telecommunications market is the most open and competitive in the world. Many of the world's major industrialized countries, including France and Germany, continue to run government-held monopolies. (U.S. Congress, House. Committee on Energy and Commerce, Subcommittee on Telecommunications and Finance, and Subcommittee on Commerce, Consumer Protection, and Competitiveness 1993, 21f)

A European Telecom Infrastructure that Meets Business Needs

In the mid-1980s, long distance traffic in the United States was competitive, but the continental members of the European Community (EC) still administered telecom as a traditional PTT monopoly, in which the sector formed part of the state bureaucracy. Adamant about the need for a good telecom infrastructure, European businesses complained that monopolists exhibited a "civil service mentality." As civil servants PTT employees had secure positions, so the argument went, and therefore had no incentive to provide good service. Additionally, the private sector objected to the fact that customers were only allowed to attach terminal equipment[3] from licensed manufacturers and charged the privileged manufacturers with collusion (Thimm 1992).

In the European economies telecom liberalization was a controversial issue, pitting labor unions against the private sector. Alfred Thimm, who served as professor of business administration at the University of Vermont, reports that the German government signaled its intention to reform the postal and telecom monopoly as early as March 1985. German industry supported telecom liberalization—the separation of post and telecom operations, the opening of the market for terminal equipment, and, ultimately, the competitive provision of value-added services.[4] The Federation of German Industries, which represents the industrial private sector, publicly threw its weight behind the liberalization project. Not surprisingly, privileged German equipment manufacturers who had procurement contracts with the monopolist disapproved. However, Thimm (1992) notes, "the real losers were believed to be the post employees... and the postal union together with its ally the Association of Social Democratic Post Employees" (66f).

Those who wanted to hold onto the old ways advanced a range of arguments to appeal to the German public, including concerns with service quality and national identity. In other European countries, similar debates took place, preventing national governments from seriously exploring alternatives to the state-owned monopoly.

At the level of the European Community, all legislative branches—the Council of Ministers, the European Commission, and with some delay the European Parliament—embraced the view that telecom service needed to be improved, harmonized, and ultimately liberalized.[5] They all recognized that the competitiveness of European industry hinged on a good telecommunication infrastructure. In its 1990 directive, the Council of Ministers expressed this idea diplomatically:

> The Community attaches very great importance to... the contribution that telecommunications services provided by companies, firms or natural persons established in a Member State may make to the growth of the Community market, and to the increased participation of Community service providers in third country markets. (Council of the European Communities 1990)

The European Parliament recognized the importance of telecom for maintaining a competitive edge, as well. In 1993 it stated that "the creation of a Europe-wide telecom network is an urgent necessity to enable businesses in the EC to compete better with Japanese and American firms" (European Parliament 1993).

The crucial force in European telecom liberalization was the Commission. By 1987 it was convinced of the importance of telecom as a driver of European economic integration, which in turn was to boost Europe's competitiveness vis-à-vis the United States and Japan.[6]

To liberalize telecom, the Commission drew on several political resources. First, it argued that the Treaty of Rome contained provisions on commercial monopolies that assigned the Commission authority over telecom.[7] On the basis of these articles, it issued green papers (documents designed to prompt debate on a specific topic) that proposed general policy directions that the European Community should take. Second, it used its power to issue directives to be implemented by the national administrations. Third, to enforce its directives against the resistance of national monopolists, it took recourse to the European Court of Justice. The private sector and the Commission were thus pitted against national postal ministries, monopolists, and labor unions. The Council of Ministers and the European Parliament sided cautiously with business.

The Commission's strategy was one of rolling up the PTTs from the fringes. First, monopolists' control over terminal equipment had to go. In June 1987, the Commission issued a green paper for that purpose. It envisioned a more competitive environment for new services and terminal equipment and the provision of a wide range of value-added services, but it held on to the PTT monopoly on basic telecom. To justify the monopoly, the Commission argued that investment in these networks would result in economic growth and provide universal basic service for low-income areas (European Commission 1987).

In May 1988 the Commission followed up with a directive. It stated that under the Treaty of Rome a monopoly on the marketing and sale of terminal equipment was not justifiable and directed the member states to open up their markets (European Commission 1988). This sparked nationalist resistance. In 1989 the French government challenged the Commission's right to use the Rome Treaty to dismantle state monopolies before the European Court of Justice. In 1991 the European Court of Justice upheld the directive (Thimm 1992, 116).

In June 1988, the Council of Ministers issued a resolution supporting the objectives of the 1987 green paper (Council of the European Communities 1988). It said that strengthening European telecommunications was a major prerequisite for achieving an internal market for goods and services by 1992 and supported the liberalization of the terminal equipment market and value-added services. At the same time, it was content to leave basic services—that is, regular voice telephony—under monopoly control until a better solution could be found. A careful reading of the Council resolution reveals that it was only a matter of time before even basic telecom would be opened to competition.

By 1990 the Commission had all but won the terminal equipment battle. Now it mandated that value-added services be liberalized. To enforce competition rules, it issued a directive prescribing an independent regulatory board at the national level. Notably, the directive still recognized the necessity of having a monopoly on basic services (European Commission 1990). Basic telecom—voice telephony—was on the table next. In 1993 the Council stated as its long-term goal "the liberalization of public voice telephony services, while maintaining universal service" (Council of the European Communities 1993).

Finally, in 1996, the Commission directed the EU member states to open their telecom sectors to competition in voice telephony by January 1, 1998

(European Commission 1996). Between 1988 and 1998, the Commission had taken up the corporate cause for better infrastructure and had succeeded in opening the national telecom sectors within its territory to competition.

The European Union Enters the Race for Competitiveness

In 1993, the European Union was plagued by recession, increasing unemployment, and loss of competitiveness. In response to this situation, the Commission published the *White Paper on Growth, Competitiveness, and Employment* (European Commission 1993). It shows that the Commission was dedicated to promoting European corporations in the global race for strategic influence and that it was willing to subject telecom policy to these goals.

The recession, the Commission *White Paper* explained, had been underway since the 1970s. Since then, Europe's competitiveness had declined—both in relation to its traditional rivals, the United States and Japan, and with respect to new, technologically adept nations such as India. National and EU authorities therefore had to assist European companies in capturing high value-added niches in the world market:

> For the level of employment in the Community to improve, firms must achieve global competitiveness on open and competitive markets, both inside and outside Europe. It is the responsibility of the national and Community authorities to provide industry with a favourable environment, to open up clear and reliable prospects for it and to promote its international competitiveness.

The EU and its members were to negotiate access to foreign markets in return for opening the European market to foreign competitors. They were also to render labor regulations more flexible, thereby decreasing the cost for local semi- and unskilled labor. The telecom infrastructure played a prominent part in this agenda. The Commission pointed out that the United States led the world in deploying high speed digital infrastructure, and that two hundred of the biggest U.S. companies improved their competitive edge by using information highways. Europe was to follow this example, creating a European information sector and helping European businesses move into the increasingly strategic area of knowledge-based services.

The *White Paper* was ambitious. It goes without saying that its aspirations for information highways could only be realized if the European telecom carriers were willing to innovate. And the consensus was that monopolists had no such inclination.

Deepening Flexible Accumulation at the Uruguay Round

At home, Europeans reformed their telecom sectors. Abroad, the Commission and the U.S. government worked to open foreign markets to their exports and investments. Their vehicle for doing so was the Uruguay round of trade negotiations, which happened from 1986 to 1994 under the auspices of the General Agreement on Tariffs and Trade (GATT).

Signed and ratified shortly after World War II, the GATT aimed at liberalizing world trade. Toward that goal, it provided for regular trade rounds, which resulted in multilateral commitments to lower tariffs and cut back on nontariff trade barriers. However, with an underfunded secretariat and a weak dispute resolution mechanism, the GATT lacked the means for securing compliance. States took advantage of that by reneging on their commitments. The result was a world market that was more protectionist than the GATT had promised.

The Uruguay round changed this. One of its important policy innovations was the establishment of the World Trade Organization (WTO) in 1994. Endowed with a strong dispute settlement process, the WTO became the central repository and enforcer of a neoliberal trade regime that made national borders porous and transnational corporations mobile. When states reneged on liberalization commitments, the WTO prosecuted their violations swiftly and efficiently. As a consequence, states became locked into genuine trade liberalization that both deepened and expanded flexible accumulation.

The round produced three innovations that deserve discussion. First, it introduced trade in services into the GATT framework and assigned the WTO the task of advancing its liberalization. Second, it attacked the right of state-owned telecom monopolists to control who had access to their networks. Third, it defined telecom as a service in its own right and subjected it to the WTO's liberalization agenda.

The sections that follow explore these policy innovations one by one. They describe the dismantling of the traditional telecom regime and its replacement with a new "best practice" for sector administration that supported the corporate objective of deepening flexible accumulation. This best practice formed the telecom component of the new IT regime.

As will become clear, the formation of this new telecom framework was exclusive: Organizations with roots in the core of the global economy participated in the negotiations early on, while organizations with roots in the periphery were invited to the bargaining table only once the basic outlines of the framework were in place. In the words of Robert Cox (1987, 254), whose model of state transformation was introduced in chapter one, the Uruguay round negotiations on telecom were "a process of interstate consensus formation regarding the needs or requirements of the world economy that [took] place within a common ideological framework," and participation in the formation of this consensus was hierarchically structured.

1. The Uruguay Round Brings Services into the GATT Framework

The original General Agreement on Tariffs and Trade of the 1940s had concerned itself only with trade in goods. Services as they existed at that time had to be consumed where they were produced. For this reason, they were considered untradeable, and the GATT did not deal with them.

In the late decades of the twentieth century, this changed in two ways. First, the line between goods and services began to blur. What had been considered a traditional, immaterial service could now be integrated into a material good. Take the screening of motion pictures. Movies used to be shown in movie theaters. The showing of movies constituted an economic activity that was immaterial and therefore did not result in any kind of physical ownership. According to the classic distinction between goods and services, the screening of films therefore constituted a service. By the 1980s movies could be integrated into videotapes, which were physical, material devices and therefore goods. Integrated into goods, traditional services no longer needed to be consumed at a defined location. Instead, they could be traded.

Second, advances in telecommunications allowed services to be provided over great distances even without integrating them into physical devices. For example, it became feasible to stream a movie over the communication network into foreign economies. This activity did not result in ownership and therefore continued to possess the classic qualities of a service. Yet, because the screening could take place over great distances, the service was tradable.

Unlike most countries in the Third World, the European Community and the United States had competitive providers of knowledge-intensive services,[8] who produced, among others, digitized databases, films, market analyses, and computer programs. Many of these providers had already incurred the cost of producing these services for their home markets. If they were allowed to sell them in foreign economies, they could increase their revenue at little additional cost, thus raising their profit margins.

It is therefore not surprising that industry lobbies within the United States and the European Community spearheaded the drive toward pulling services out of the purview of individual states and placing them under the aegis of the multilateral GATT, which through its new dispute settlement mechanism could be held accountable to corporate demands. The agreement that resulted from this effort was the General Agreement on Trade in Services (GATS), which was signed in 1994. One of the lobbies most influential in bringing about this agreement was the Coalition of Service Industries (CSI). Its website explains that it played a significant part in bringing GATS about:

> CSI was formed in 1982 to ensure that U.S. trade in services, once considered outside the scope of U.S. trade negotiations, would become a central goal of future trade liberalization initiatives. It played a major role in shaping the General Agreement on Trade in Services (GATS) and in the advocacy effort leading to the 1997 WTO Basic Telecommunications and Financial Services Agreements. CSI actively engaged in services negotiations in the WTO, the Free Trade Area of the Americas, and free trade agreements with Chile and Singapore.
>
> CSI's ability to use services trade negotiations to advance the interests of its members is unmatched. (Coalition of Service Industries 2006)

The U.S. government was the driving force behind the GATS negotiations. In tune with its largest industry representatives, it had worked for the inclusion of services in the GATT trade negotiations since the early 1980s. During the substantive talks it applied both positive incentives and coercion (Comor 1998b, 142f).

The European Commission played a supporting role. It agreed with the overall agenda of service negotiations, but its approach was consensus-oriented, rather than one of carrot and stick. The explanation for its gentler tactic lies in the fragmented structure of the European Community's policy process. Within the institutional framework of the EC, the Commission was the agency in charge of trade negotiations. As such, it advocated for the best possible trading positions for European industry. However, it could not subscribe to trade deals without the approval of the EC member states, whose national interests varied. Reaching compromise was therefore a slow and bureaucratic process, diminishing the Commission's leverage in international trade negotiations.

While Third World states did possess service sectors, these tended to provide traditional services—such as medical, architectural, and repair services—that were not knowledge-intensive in the sense of requiring a substantial information and communication infrastructure. Third World economies were often unable to compete on quality. To realize their competitive advantage, which was low labor cost, they depended on "body shopping."[9] Therefore, peripheral economies had less to gain from international service liberalization, and their states resisted the inclusion of services into the GATT framework. In 1982, all members of the Group of 77, a large coalition of Third World states, voiced their opposition to the U.S. initiative for service negotiations. They looked toward United Nations Conference on Trade and Development (UNCTAD) as a forum for negotiation, because UNCTAD had traditionally heeded the interests of peripheral states (Sunsonline 1982a). Indian trade minister Shivraj Patil put this attitude into words when he said:

> Unlike trade in goods, trade in services is intimately linked with flows of factors of production—international flows in capital, labor and technology. Surely if one wants to discuss in a comprehensive manner issues related to trade in services, one has to discuss, among other things, issues related to immigration policies, technology flows policies etc....GATT has no mandate to discuss these issues...For many of them, there are other competent organizations such as UNCTAD which are doing excellent work in these areas. (Sunsonline 1982b)

As the results of the negotiations show, core states prevailed. The GATS was signed in 1994. It locked governments into service liberalization and gave those signatories interested in freeing services trade ample recourse to the dispute settlement mechanism. In doing so, it ensured that present and future national governments became increasingly accountable to the service providers of other WTO members. Over time, this tendency could lock in globalization and de facto reduce a government's accountability to its own electorate (Sinclair and Grieshaber-Otto 2002, vii).

Because it made national governments accountable to foreign service providers, the GATS presented a major achievement for transnational corporations, which are competitive providers of knowledge-intensive services. But to what extent did the agreement also heed the interests of peripheral companies, which might engage in service trade by exporting labor? To answer the question, we need to investigate the kinds of services that the GATS favored.

The GATS defines four different modes of delivering services. The first is delivery from the territory of one member into the territory of any other member. An example would be an architect located in one country providing a blueprint to a customer in another country by mail, phone, or via the Internet. Mode two is defined as the delivery of services in the territory of one member to the service consumer of any other member. Guide services supplied to international tourists would fall under this. Mode three captures delivery by a service supplier of one member through commercial presence in the territory of any other member. This mode includes all forms of foreign direct investment—for example, a health care company setting up a private clinic abroad, a fast-food chain establishing a franchise, or a bank setting up an overseas branch (Sinclair and Grieshaber-Otto 2002, 34). Mode four, finally, involves services provided by a supplier of one member through presence of its people physically located in the territory of any other member. Service provision through body shopping—that is, by exporting personnel to other economies where the personnel provide the services—falls under this mode. Mode four is therefore very attractive for Third World economies, as they usually have an abundance of low-cost labor.

A study by the WTO secretariat observed, however, that within a given service sector, trade conditions for mode four delivery tended to be much more restrictive than conditions for other delivery modes (WTO, Council for Trade in Services 1998). This shows that on average, the GATS rendered peripheral economies accessible to the digitized, knowledge-intensive products of core economies and facilitated delivery through various means, among them the telecom network. Peripheral economies, on the other hand, were not as capable of exporting low-cost, low-tech, labor-intensive services. The GATS agreement was therefore biased toward the interests of core states and businesses.

2. The Uruguay Round Attacks the Rights of Monopolists

The GATS formed the legal framework for liberalizing services trade, and it described four different modes by which a service could be delivered. Once trading states had adopted the GATS, they could delve into the substantive aspects of trade liberalization. In practice this meant that each state would draw up a schedule of commitments, in which it specified what kind of services it would allow to be imported into its domain and by what mode. For example, in its schedule of commitments, the government of Israel might stipulate that it allowed the import of architectural services by means of modes one and four. Architects from any other WTO member country were thus allowed to provide their architectural services via mail or Internet (mode one) or by sending their architects to Israel, where they would provide consultations on site (mode ffour). If a state committed itself to allowing mode one imports of a certain kind but then failed to open its telecom circuits to those imports, the WTO, through its dispute resolution process, had the power to force the telecom network open. And to positively prevent telecom monopolists from undermining services liberalization, negotiators produced the *GATS Annex on Telecommunications*. It stipulated that if a state, in its schedule of commitments, had allowed certain services to be imported into its domain via mode one, the foreign suppliers of those services had to be granted access to the country's telecom network.

This, of course, had direct implications for telecom monopolists. Before GATS, many state-owned operators enjoyed the prerogative of determining what kind of material could or could not travel across their network, and monopolists could simply bar foreign service providers from connecting to their infrastructure. With the *GATS Annex*, this was no longer possible. Negotiators had effectively curtailed the prerogative of telecom monopolists. The *GATS Annex* was the opening salvo against the traditional telecom regime. The full attack would begin in 1994.

3. The Uruguay Round Defines Telecom as a Service

U.S. negotiators spearheaded the drive for opening monopolistic telecom sectors to foreign competition. In March 1990, they introduced a draft proposal for a telecommunications annex that aimed at opening telecom as a service sector to foreign competition (Nicolaïdis 1995). Two months later the GATS Working Group on Telecommunications Services was set up. Its first order of business was to agree on the scope and rules of negotiations. The question to be answered was whether telecom as a service sector should be negotiated within the general GATS framework or whether it should be treated as a distinct sector with its own set of rules. U.S. negotiators wanted telecom to be part of the GATS overall definition of services trade (Comor 1998b, 144f). They were particularly eager to open the telecom markets of Europe and Japan to U.S. carriers, a goal that the executive branch and Congress had pursued since the late 1980s (U.S. Congress, Senate, Committee on Commerce, Science, and Transportation, Subcommittee on Communications 1988).

The initial U.S. proposal included the liberalization of long distance basic voice services, leaving the local infrastructure monopoly alone. The proposal met the opposition of the European Commission, which was joined by the majority of developing countries and Japan. Dissatisfied with the Commission's lack of enthusiasm, the United States in the fall of 1990 threatened to remove its own telecom sector from the negotiating table by taking a most favored nations exemption (Nicolaïdis 1995).

As William Garrison, the ICT director at the Kennan Institute for Private Enterprise, explained to me in an interview, the American long distance provider AT&T and a number of U.S. corporations were eager to see the negotiations proceed successfully:

> By the time the Clinton administration came in, AT&T was really hurting. So you had that special dynamic that took the largest carrier and put it firmly on the side of trade liberalization. However, most non-U.S.

carriers had a vested interest in maintaining the international settlements arrangements and the subsidies that flowed from them and consequently did not want competition or related trade liberalization. The service industry, people like Electronic Data Systems, and the money center banks, the insurance industry, the multinational corporations doing business in Europe, Japan, Southeast Asia, Latin America, really wanted competition and liberalization in telecom services, because their overhead costs were so high. As their business grew, they had more and more international data requirements, and they were paying more and more money to support that requirement, and they wanted competition in order to bring international rates down. So AT&T needed rates to come down in order to achieve symmetry in settlements. The multinational American service companies wanted rates to go down in order to lower costs. (Garrison 2001b)

In 1992 the United States tried to entice other governments, proposing to put its telecom sector back on the negotiating table by phasing out its most-favored nations exemption. As a condition it demanded that the EU and Japan open their basic telecom markets within three years after the GATS took effect. Under this pressure the EU accepted U.S. demands to include basic telecommunications in the negotiations and pursue an April 1996 deadline for reaching a compromise (Nicolaïdis 1995).

Thus on April 15, 1994, in Marrakesh, the ministers at the Uruguay round formally decided to enter negotiations on basic telecom under the auspices of the GATS. The Negotiating Group on Basic Telecom was to hold its first session before May 16, 1994, and conclude negotiations by April 30, 1996. Negotiators failed to meet the second deadline (WTO n.d.). The negotiations were wide-ranging. They included the basic telecom services that the United States had sought, but they also involved satellite and mobile services.[10] In fact, Kalypso Nicolaïdis (1995) of Oxford University suggests that the U.S. government was not eager to include mobile services in the negotiations. The inclusion of mobile services was a concession to European negotiators, who sought market access for their competitive cellular operators (288).

What explains the Commission's sluggish response to U.S. demands for negotiations? According to Nicolaïdis, the Commission had two motivations for being slow. For one thing, it sought to buy time. Its intention was to open European telecom sectors to the intra-European competition, thus enabling European carriers to consolidate their operations and become more competitive. Once this was accomplished, the Commission would be able to enter multilateral negotiations from a position of strength. Second, it gave political priority to European integration. The cognitive resources that Commissioners could spend on the Uruguay round were therefore limited (282).

Once negotiations were underway, the European Commission continued to leave the lead to the United States and contented itself with playing a supporting role. Three reasons account for this. First, the Commission had to broker consensus among fifteen governments that were in perpetual disagreement. It could therefore not present the image of a negotiator whose words would be backed up by action. Garrison makes that point when he refers to the EU process management nightmare:

> A lot of the policy assumptions in the WTO agreement on basic telecom were articulated, advocated, and ultimately the responsibility of the U.S. delegation. The European Commission in that process was in an ambivalent position. For the European Commission, any trade negotiation is a process management nightmare, because the Commission leads, but is not in control. They herd the national governments to make them agree what day it is and what shape the table will be. So even though they lead, the French etc. will torpedo them at the drop of a hat if there is an issue that they want to gain leverage on. So it's very difficult for the Europeans to manage these multilateral trade negotiations. Anything that is said or done by the Europeans collectively has always to be looked at through the filter of process management. (Garrison 2001a)

Second, because it was battling on two fronts, the Commission's organizational resources were strapped. On the one hand it was engaged in the WTO negotiations; on the other it had to overcome the resistance of the French and the German governments against opening basic telecom to European competitors by January 1, 1998. Having to choose between two policy arenas, the Commission opted to concentrate its resources on liberalizing its internal telecom market, an issue that it felt had strategic priority (Garrison 2001a). Finally, the colonialist past of several EU member states prevented the EU from pursuing a course of crude domination and forced it to seek agreement. Garrison explains:

> There is always a tension for the Europeans in these negotiations, because the developing economies tend to be the most difficult, and the Europeans have a very tense, often very difficult, relationship with their former colonies. This is especially true for France and England. As soon as they tell these developing countries: "you have to do such and such," they respond: "No, you can't tell us what to do." So the Europeans always tiptoe around very carefully, with everything that has to do with

getting the developing countries on board. In the case of the BTA [i.e., Basic Telecom Agreement,] negotiations, the US had pressed the hardest for reform. In order to reach the agreement, a more neutrally positioned advocate for the essential compromises was needed. Japan fulfilled that role with the quiet support of both the U.S. and the EU delegations. (Garrison 2001a)

During the Marrakesh discussions, the Department of Commerce lent ideological support to the U.S. negotiators. In 1995 it published the document *Global Information Infrastructure: An Agenda for Cooperation*. The paper evoked a united world, the different parts of which were interconnected by a seamless electronic nervous system. Information traveled freely from part to part, making the whole system flourish. Economic development would pick up pace, governance within countries would become more democratic, and an international discourse would emerge in which every country would have an equal chance at being heard:

> By interconnecting local, national, regional, and global networks, the GII [Global Information Infrastructure] can increase economic growth, create jobs, and improve infrastructures. Taken as a whole, this worldwide "network of networks" will create a global information marketplace, encouraging broad-based social discourse within and among all countries. (NTIA 1995)

Talk of democracy and equitable discourse, however, was only a varnish that placed a sheen of social justice over the *Agenda*'s real concern, sophisticated communication services for U.S. corporations intent on expanding. The document stated:

> The business community has become the principal force for the pro-competitive restructuring of telecommunications and information markets. Business users, whose commercial activities are becoming increasingly global, require access to advanced services at higher speeds and capabilities, and at lower costs, to manage their global operations effectively.

To realize the GII, the *Agenda* demanded the implementation of five principles for telecom on a global scale: private investment, competitive provision, open access for all information service providers to telecom networks, a flexible regulatory environment, and universal service. It then called for a successful conclusion of the GATS discussions on basic telecom so that markets for basic telecom services would be opened to facilities-based competition (NTIA 1995). The *Agenda* publicly chided the existing telecom regime, while U.S. negotiators revised it behind closed doors.

Another organization that supported the American push for the global abolition of the phone monopoly was the Federal Communications Commission (FCC). Through its rule-making authority, the FCC tried to force foreign governments to open their telecom markets to U.S. carriers. In the 1995 *Foreign Carrier Order*, it specified a new standard for deciding whether or not a foreign carrier would be granted permission to provide service to the United States. The relevant criteria included any "national security, law enforcement, foreign policy, and trade concerns raised by the Executive Branch" (FCC 1995; Spiwak 1998, 130f). Lawrence Spiwak (1998), who from 1994 to 1998 served as senior attorney with the FCC's Office of General Counsel, accused the regulatory commission of "acting as a wholly-owned subdivision of the U.S. Trade Representative and the Executive Branch" (137f). In 1998 the FCC issued an ultimatum, threatening that unless agreement was reached by the end of the year, it would unilaterally impose limits on the settlement U.S. carriers could pay foreign operators (Sunsonline 1998).

The Emerging IT Regime and its Organizations

In February 1997 three years of negotiations on market access for basic telecommunications came to a close. The results were laid down in the Basic Telecom Agreement (BTA), or, more formally, the *Fourth Protocol of the GATS*. It consisted of a reference paper that contained regulatory principles for the areas of competitive safeguards, interconnection, universal service, public availability of licensing criteria, independence of regulation, resource allocation and use. While not directly calling for sector privatization, the principles prepared the ground for it. Countries could subscribe to the reference paper in its entirety or in part. In addition, they could specify market access commitments for specific telecom subsectors. The protocol and its annexed documents came into force in February 1998.

Sixty-nine governments made commitments that were annexed to the *Fourth Protocol of the GATS*. Fifty-seven of these governments adopted the reference paper in whole or with some alterations (WTO 1997a). The sixty-nine WTO members that made commitments accounted for more than $550 billion or 96 percent of the 1995 telecom services revenue of WTO members (WTO 1997b). The BTA thus significantly altered the ownership rules in telecom. With its adoption, a new international consensus had formed. It said that telecom was ideally administered in competition.

For the U.S. government, the agreement was a resounding success. In March 1997, FCC chairman Reed Hundt told a subcommittee of the House of Representatives:

> Thank you for inviting me to testify before the subcommittee about an agreement that I believe will fundamentally alter the competitive land-scape in telecommunications in the United States and around the world. This agreement substantially achieves the objectives that are at the heart of the Telecommunications Act of 1996. In addition, it meets the goals that my colleagues [at the FCC] and I announced in 1995: promoting global competition; preventing anticompetitive conduct; and opening markets around the world.
>
> . . .
>
> I am also very proud that, under the able leadership of Ambassador Charlene Barshefsky [the U.S. Trade Representative], the United States has pioneered a new export industry—what might be called the 'competition in telecommunications' industry. For the deal that Ambassador Barshefsky negotiated on behalf of the American people accomplishes just that—it exports the American idea of open markets and fair rules of competition to 68 of our nation's largest trading partners. (U.S. Embassy Tel Aviv 1997)

The BTA did not prescribe that national telecom sectors be rendered competitive. Nevertheless, it suggested a preferable sequence for telecom liberalization:

1. Separation between state-owned operator and regulator.
2. Privatization of the state-owned operator.
3. Sector competition under the aegis of an independent regulator similar to the FCC.

The BTA formed the backbone of an incipient IT regime that was replacing the old telecom regime and began to enter global social structure. In the words of Berger and Luckmann (1966), the BTA possessed coercive force by its sheer existence. Washington and Brussels based development specialists embraced the agreement as the new status quo and based their policy recommendations to Third World states on it. The effort to theorize a link between telecom liberalization and economic development intensified, and peripheral states began to learn that sector liberalization was ultimately unavoidable. To these weaker elements in the international hierarchy the new telecom consensus represented a set of norms in whose making they had been marginally involved. Now they had to espouse it if they wanted to maintain the goodwill of actors from the core.

To ensure that the BTA would have maximum impact, the advocates of the new IT regime worked to reconfigure those international organizations that had upheld the old telecom regime since the end of the nineteenth century. The organizations in question were the International Telecommunication Union (ITU), Intelsat, and Inmarsat. As enforcers of the old regime, they would either be neutralized or turned into enforcers of the new regime.

Within this trio the ITU was most prominent. Established in 1865 as the International Telegraph Union, it set technical standards for international telecom and administered the international settlements regime. Intelsat was founded in 1964 and oversaw a global network of geostationary satellites on behalf of the national member governments. Inmarsat had been founded in 1979. Based in London, it was an intergovernmental organization that owned and operated a global satellite system for commercial and safety maritime communications services.

Now, each of the three organizations was put through reform. As ownership rules in telecom had changed, the ITU had come under pressure to allow for private sector representation and to support the notion that telecom services were a trade issue for which the WTO shared responsibility (Sunsonline 1998).

The ITU faced the choice between adapting to these demands and being marginalized. In 1987 U.S. officials made clear that if the ITU failed to promote a free trade agenda, an alternative telecommunications regime based on private sector proprietary standards might replace the Union. From 1989 to 1991, the ITU had a specialized committee review its mandate. In 1993 the ITU announced that it would undertake fundamental changes to become more "market oriented" (Comor 1998b, 137, 147, 148). A 1998 ITU meeting in Minneapolis featured a debate on how, in addition to meeting the demands of member states, the ITU could accommodate private sector interests (Sunsonline 1998).

Intelsat was to be reformed as well. As early as 1984, the Reagan administration had fought the organization over admission of privately owned, U.S. based satellite systems. It had also complained about the high prices for satellite communications that made it hard for U.S. companies to expand overseas (Komiya 1990, 63–65). In 1999 Intelsat was moving toward privatization by creating a spin-off company by the name of New Skies. In 2000, a fundamental overhaul of Intelsat's organizational structure followed: The organization's executive organs vowed to turn Intelsat from an intergovernmental organization into a private corporation with a fiduciary board of directors. Stripped of its intergovernmental status, it would no longer enjoy the attendant privileges and immunities (Abelson 2000).

Inmarsat was also transformed. In April 1999, the organization transferred its assets to a newly created private company incorporated in the United Kingdom. This new company provided commercial, maritime, aeronautical, and land mobile, and safety services (Abelson 2000).

In a Nutshell

To summarize, the telecom regime that existed under Fordism treated telecom as a state-owned monopoly, recognized the right of monopolists to determine who could connect to their networks, and regulated interconnection among national networks through the ITU settlement regime.

Under Fordism, European and American companies accepted this regime as one aspect of their coalition with labor and the state. In the 1970s, however, they found that they required flexibility, and they revisited their commitment to the Fordist coalition. Supported by the governments of Britain and the United States, they began to make the transition to flexible accumulation and demand a better communication infrastructure. In the 1980s pressure on telecom monopolists built. The European Commission identified with the fate of European corporations for which it wanted to secure the most lucrative niches in the global economy, became concerned with the quality of the European telecom network, and promoted intra-European sector reform.

In addition, the Commission and the U.S. government worked on opening telecom markets outside their respective borders. Not only was this necessary for providing corporations with the full mobility they desired; it would also improve their access to new consumer segments in overseas locations that were once considered remote.

In the context of the GATS, the core states negotiated an incipient IT regime, which replaced the rules by which telecom had been administered under Fordism. The regime suggested a new best practice for administering telecom, which culminated in sector competition. Once this had been accomplished, the intergovernmental organizations that had supported and enforced the previous regime—ITU, Intelsat, Inmarsat—were either neutralized or pressed to support the new regime.

The process of renegotiating the global rules for telecom was dominated by organizations of the core economies. Meanwhile, organizations to which citizens from the periphery had access were far less involved. Using the framework for translating organizational involvement in rule-making processes into personal autonomy, the overhaul of telecom rules may have disrespected the autonomy of many disenfranchised citizens in the core economies. What is certain, however, is that it disrespected the autonomy of peripheral citizens disproportionately.

CHAPTER 3

Introducing the Internet

In 1994 the Internet became available to the nonacademic public. Since then it has impacted human interaction profoundly. It has allowed individuals who have never met in real life to strike up lasting relationships in cyber space. It has increased the velocity of money by enabling point-and-click purchases. Thanks to the Internet, the exchange of data files between remote locations has become a matter of seconds, and geographic proximity is no longer necessary for companies that seek to execute commercial transactions or cooperate on the production of a good. Because the Internet has transformed the concept of distance as a factor in economic decision-making, it has made the corporation more mobile than ever before.

This chapter will show that companies and states from the core economies anticipated the transformative potential of the Internet when it was still dormant and there were few norms that governed online communication. They then steered the capability of the Internet toward supporting the corporate desire for flexibility. In doing so, they effectively controlled the decision processes that yielded rules for online communication. To ensure that these rules would support corporate needs, they surrounded the decision processes with specialized organizations that would engage in advocacy for the private sector. Organizations that embraced noncommercial concerns played a much smaller part in the formation of Internet rules.

As companies and states from the core economies dominated the making of rules for the Internet, those core citizens whose interests were not aligned with corporate intentions were deprived of their autonomy. Citizens from the peripheral economies were in an even worse position. While core citizens could claim a measure of access to these core organizations and voice their protest, citizens of the periphery had no such opportunities. Consequently, the processes that augmented the existing IT regime with rules for the Internet disrespected their autonomy disproportionately.

What is the Internet?

To understand how this exclusion of peripheral citizens came about, it helps to understand, first, that the Internet was an evolving data network. The Internet of the early 1990s used the physical infrastructure built by telecom providers, but it differed greatly from traditional "plain old" telephony, which used to be the telecom providers' mainstay. Roughly speaking, the difference lay in the way this physical infrastructure was put to use. To create a telephone connection, operators established a circuit between two users or "end nodes." For the duration of the call, the circuit was dedicated to the communication between those end nodes. Plain old telephony was therefore said to be "circuit-switched."

By contrast, during an Internet data call—this could be a request for a web page or the sending of an e-mail message—only a small piece of the telecom network was dedicated exclusively to the caller. This piece was the local telephone line leading from the user's modem to her Internet service provider (ISP). There the data call was offloaded to a part of the telecom network that the ISP had bought or leased from the telecom operator for the Internet traffic of its clients. This part of the telecom network was governed by the TCP/IP communication protocol.

Unlike a plain old telephone call, which occupied an entire circuit, an Internet call was broken up into small data packets. Each of these packets was tagged with sender and recipient information. Then it was routed along the least congested path to its destination. Here the packets were reassembled into one complete message. During their travel, data packets that came from different senders and were destined for different recipients shared bandwidth. For this reason the Internet was referred to as a "packet-switched" network. Thanks to packet-switching, the Internet made more efficient use of the physical infrastructure than did circuit-switched telephony.

To compare the two networks, we can draw the analogy of a four-lane divided highway with two lanes in each direction. In this analogy, a voice telephony call occupies one entire lane of the information highway. The call can be pictured as a presidential convoy that keeps the lane entirely to itself. On the second lane travel numerous Internet packets from varying origins and with varying destinations. These packets resemble a large number of small coupes. Coming from different locations, they have entered the highway at different junctures. Pieces of routing equipment are stationed at each juncture of the Internet lane, resembling traffic cops. The equipment examines the tag of each packet for the address of its recipient. The destination address consists of an eight-to-nine digit number, separated by periods. This number is the so-called IP address (short for Internet Protocol address). After examining the IP address, the routing equipment sends the packet on that path that leads closer to its destination.

This routing method is called redundant, because it does not depend on any single circuit, as is the case for telephony. If one segment of the information highway is destroyed, the presidential telephony convoy is stuck and the call will not be completed. The coupes on the Internet lane, however, will reach their target. This is because the various pieces of routing equipment (the traffic cops) communicate with one another. If one piece of the highway is out of order, surrounding routers are notified of the failure. They respond by sending the packets along a different, second-best path. It was this redundant network architecture that allowed e-mail communication with New York on September 11, 2001, when reaching Manhattan by phone was next to impossible.

Three Major Phases of Codification

Although universal access to the Internet was granted only in the 1990s, the technology itself was fairly old. Its history can be broken down into three phases, each of which corresponds to a distinct organizational coalition that administered the Internet and controlled its rule-making processes. The coalition that marked the first phase consisted of a research agency under the U.S. Department of Defense, a small number of American universities with defense contracts, and their commercial spin-offs. The coalition that controlled the Internet during the second phase consisted of an independent government agency that funds scientific research, as well as an increasing number of research universities. The third phase began when the gates of the Internet were opened to the nonacademic public, including commercial users of the network. Now corporations, which had long demanded access to the network, entered a coalition with the U.S. Department of Commerce. In Europe, this was paralleled by a coalition between the European Commission and European corporations. Together, core governments and corporations worked out rules that would govern online communication as the Internet expanded from an American into a global phenomenon.

Phase 1: The Defense Coalition

The organizational triangle that conceived the Internet was united by its interest in defense research. It consisted of the Massachusetts Institute of

Technology (MIT); the company Bolt, Beranek and Newman (BBN), which two MIT professors had founded in 1948; and the Advanced Research Projects Agency (ARPA). ARPA was an agency under the Department of Defense, formed in 1958. Its purpose was to help surpass the Soviet state of technology by funding basic research.

Joseph Licklider linked the three organizations together. In 1950, he joined the MIT faculty. Seven years later he became the vice president of BBN. In 1962 he spent a two-year period working for ARPA. During this time Licklider instilled in the agency an interest in computer research by launching the information processing techniques program (Titus 1967). In 1964 he returned to MIT.

In 1967, ARPA asked the Stanford Research Institute to write the specifications for a new communications network. Based on the institute's report, the agency awarded contracts for implementing the network. One of the contractors was BBN. Its task was to build the routers for what would be the ARPANET (Hauben 1997).

ARPA then selected a handful of university computing centers in the West as first sites for the network.[1] By 1969 BBN had built the routers, and each of the chosen universities received an ARPANET node. In 1970 BBN added nodes on its own premises and at MIT.[2] The physical lines over which the ARPANET ran were obtained on lease from AT&T.

Car traffic is impossible without rules of the road—signs, speed limits, turning procedures, and others. The same is true for data traffic on communication networks. To flow properly, it requires a set of standards that determines how routers respond to the data that pass their way. These standards were developed by programmers of the first ARPANET hosts. Under the leadership of UCLA graduate student Stephen Crocker, they cooperated in the loosely organized Network Working Group. The group communicated through RFCs, "requests for comments," documents that explained the nascent technology, recorded agreed-upon rules, presented technical problems that arose, and solicited comments and input from other members of the ARPANET community.[3] In 1970 the Network Working Group produced the network control protocol, which governed the ARPANET for roughly a decade.

Among the members of the Network Working Group was Robert Kahn, an MIT professor who would later work for BBN, then ARPA. Another member was Vinton Cerf, an ARPA scientist with degrees from Stanford and UCLA. In the 1970s the two men cooperated on a new set of standards, the transport control protocol (TCP), and in 1978, they added the Internet Protocol (IP), which would take over the routing of messages. This was the birth of the TCP/IP protocol suite, the set of standards that has since come to define the Internet (LivingInternet n.d.; Zakon 2002).

By the 1980s the academic computing centers that were connected to ARPANET had a sustainable interest in the networking endeavor, and the Department of Defense withdrew from the project. It did so in four stages. In July 1975 ARPA transferred responsibility for ARPANET to the Defense Communications Agency (DCA). In 1983 DCA split the ARPANET network into the "ARPA Internet" and MILNET (Roberts 1999). The former continued to include universities, but the latter became a separate network, exclusively for communication among military installations. In 1988 the Department of Defense decided to adopt a different protocol as its communication standard and ultimately give up TCP/IP. Finally, in 1990, the ARPA Internet infrastructure was taken out of service.

Phase 2: The Research Coalition

The withdrawal of ARPA from the project that it had spawned weakened the defense coalition. Meanwhile, the National Science Foundation (NSF), an independent government agency for funding nonmedical research in natural and social sciences at universities, became interested in networking efforts. With its support, a new coalition that defined the Internet as a research network emerged.

What gave rise to the research coalition was a widespread sense of exclusion from the defense coalition. Only a few university computing centers with an interest in networking research had access to the ARPANET project. Those who remained outsiders responded by creating their own networks. One example was USENET, which college students created in 1979 as a network among UNIX machines, powerful mainframe computers.

To gain support for their alternative networking efforts, universities turned to the National Science Foundation (NSF). In 1980 the NSF approved funding for the Computer Science Net (CSNet), a network that ran the new TCP/IP protocol suite and connected university computing centers nationwide. In 1982, CSNet and ARPANET established a physical connection. This enabled nodes on one network to communicate with nodes residing on the other. With this connection two networks, both using the TCP/IP protocol suite, had joined to form a first network of networks, an inter-net, or simply "the Internet."

Still, the Internet was only one of several networks, each of which ran its own distinct protocol. Among the Internet's more prominent competitors was BITNET, a network that connected IBM mainframe computers.

It emerged in 1981 and ran a rather unwieldy store-and-forward protocol.[4] Another was FidoNet, a store-and-forward email network developed in 1984.

In 1986, however, the Internet received a boost. In that year, the NSF established its Internet backbone, which it called NSFNet (Mills and Braun 1987). It was connected to the ARPA Internet and allowed all university and regional networks to connect. So enticed, universities joined rapidly, and the TCP/IP protocol suite came to govern ever increasing swaths of infrastructure, pushing alternative protocols to the margins of the networking community.[5]

The first and second phase of the Internet differed from one another in the way technical rules were created. In phase one, the small number of ARPANET nodes had used an informal rule-making procedure. Here, RFCs were requests for comments in the truest sense. The writer of an RFC saw himself as contributing to an ongoing debate, not as finalizing a regulatory framework. In phase two, however, when more and more nodes were added to the network and the number of participants in the rule-making discourse widened, the Internet community created small organizations that oversaw the Internet standardization process as a whole and also the specific processes by which standards were devised. A peer review process was established. RFCs stopped being invitations for discussion and instead evolved into fully fledged standards that concluded rule-making debates. Passed in 1992, RFC 1310 describes this formalized decision process:

> The Internet Activities Board (IAB) is the primary coordinating committee for Internet design, engineering, and management. The IAB has delegated to its Internet Engineering Task Force (IETF) the primary responsibility for the development and review of potential Internet Standards from all sources. The IETF forms Working Groups to pursue specific technical issues, frequently resulting in the development of one or more specifications that are proposed for adoption as Internet Standards.
>
> Final decisions on Internet standardization are made by the IAB, based upon recommendations from the Internet Engineering Steering Group (IESG), the leadership body of the IETF. IETF Working Groups are organized into areas, and each area is coordinated by an Area Director. The Area Directors and the IETF Chairman are included in the IESG.[6]

Even though the standardization process became formalized, it remained open to any person who was interested in joining in the deliberations. Excerpted from RFC 1310, the following passage attests that in phase two, individual human beings, rather than organizations, drove the setting of standards:

> Any member of the Internet community with the time and interest is urged to attend IETF meetings and to participate actively in one or more IETF Working Groups. Participation is by individual technical contributors, rather than formal representatives of organizations. The process works because the IETF Working Groups display a spirit of cooperation as well as a high degree of technical maturity; most IETF members agree that the greatest benefit for all members of the Internet community results from cooperative development of technically superior protocols and services.

Where, in all of this, was the private sector? During phases one and two, only universities participated in networking efforts. With a few exceptions—one of which was BBN—businesses were not a part of the early networking community and did not participate in its decision processes. Their absence can be explained by the as yet immature state of the technology. In phase one, only research organizations had invested funds into the first and second generations of computers, each of which usually filled out a room. Computing technology served the purposes of basic research but was not sufficiently user-friendly to serve the needs of the private sector. As the technology evolved and machines shrank to the size of a cabinet, corporate actors began to integrate them into their operations. That is when they became interested in the possibilities for communication that the Internet offered.[7] Xerox exemplifies this trend. By 1976 it had a network connecting various company sites. Parts of this network used the TCP/IP protocol suite.[8]

The real breakthrough for the private sector occurred, however, during phase two. In 1983 desktop computers became available. In comparison to the older and larger main frames, these systems were cheap, if less powerful, and they enabled companies to disperse computing power throughout the organization.[9] As the number of companies that adopted computers grew, private sector interest in connecting computers with one another intensified. In the 1980s, commercial providers of electronic mail and other services came into being. They did not use TCP/IP, but in 1989 two relays to the Internet were installed.

Companies now wanted to communicate commercially with users of the NSFNet, and they demanded access to it. This, however, was not possible under the acceptable use policy of the NSF, which funded the backbone. As an independent agency whose mission it was to promote scientific research, the NSF could not subsidize commercial undertakings, and therefore—says

RFC 1192—it confined access to the backbone to "scientific research and other scholarly activities." Commercial information was not permitted to cross the NSFNet. Displeased, companies mounted pressure on the agency to change its mind. The pressure worked. In 1990 the beleaguered foundation allowed the contractor in charge of the network to establish a parallel network, which used the excess capacity of the leased lines. Allowed to connect to this parallel network, the private sector could now reach nodes on the NSFNet, provided these nodes also agreed to connect to the parallel network (Heywood 1992).

At last the private sector had gained access to the Internet. Now commercial ISPs emerged on the scene, offering end users the ability to dial into the network using a telephone line and a modem. "Fortune 500" companies were the earliest customers of commercial Internet services. Among them were the AT&T Bell Laboratories, as well as Procter and Gamble. In Europe, BP Research, BASF, and Alcatel signed on (Cook 1992; Heywood 1992).

By 1993, the Internet had established itself as communication technology. Demand for its services was so high that NSF support was no longer needed to keep it afloat. Consequently, the NSF withdrew from Internet provision.

Phase 3: The Corporate Coalition

The demands that hardware manufacturers, software houses, and corporate giants placed on the Internet differed from those of the Internet's academic clientele. Academics had sought to increase the capacity of the Internet so that it would accommodate data of any kind. Corporations were eager to expand the technological capabilities of the network, but at the same time they wanted to control what kinds of data were permitted to travel across the electronic grid. Kathryn Kleiman (2003), who directed the Internet Governance Project at the Association for Computing Machinery, put the matter as follows:

> When commercial use developed on the Net, it was small and it was welcome. Its first form was access. Entrepreneurs created dial-up networks and pay-as-you-go commercial accounts for those who had left universities and longed to return to the Internet dialogue. Its second form was new services. Entrepreneurs experimented and created new services unique to the Internet medium, such as Yahoo! (indexing Internet content to allow people to search) and ClariNet (taking a person's favorite keywords and running them against news feeds for the first email delivery of personalized news) . . .

Large companies were late to join the Internet…Large companies quickly came online and became concerned not only with communication, but with control.

An example of the way in which commercial interests differed from those of academics revolves around domain names. Before the Internet became commercialized, domain names such as BBN.com, Think.com, or rice.edu had simply served as heuristics for the numeric IP addresses of remote hosts. IP addresses were the true addresses that servers used to identify host computers on the network. But they were hard to remember, so to make the lives of Internet users easier, programmers had come up with the idea of generating unique domain names, each of which would be matched up with one specific IP address. When users wanted to communicate with a remote host on the net, they could simply address their message to the host's domain name. Specialized root servers then translated the domain name into the corresponding IP address. Once the IP address was obtained, the message was forwarded to the remote host.

It was a simple and effective approach to online communication. Domain names were given out on a first-come-first-served basis, and users were satisfied with this way of assigning domains. However, once businesses went online and hoped to attract customers to their websites, things changed. Suddenly, domain names became commercially valuable property. By matching existing brand names, as in the case of Cocacola.com, these names could support the brands of brick-and-mortar businesses. Corporations therefore sought to define domains as intellectual property and limit the public's ability to purchase domain names that were reminiscent of existing brands.

Companies had many additional concerns that they wanted Internet rules to address. According to Cook (1992), they worried about preventing hacker attacks and industrial espionage. Furthermore, their desire to move from paper-based to paperless commercial transactions brought up a number of legal questions they wanted answered: Would it be possible to sign contracts digitally, without paper or ink? How would a paperless contract stand up in court? How could payments be made over the Internet? How would sales be taxed—especially in cases when both payment and delivery took place online and no packages were shipped across state borders? How could firms authenticate parties to online transactions and ascertain that they were who they pretended to be? How could corporations communicate with branch divisions and customers without risking interception of their data transmissions?

Complicating the matter was the fact that many of the new transactions were not only paperless but also crossed national borders. This meant that many potential disputes would be international in nature, and U.S. companies wanted to ensure that they could at least co-determine the venue in which such a dispute would be adjudicated. In short, companies wanted certainty, and they desired the kind of certainty that would favor them.

The absence of preexisting rules that established rights, duties, and entitlements in cyber space held advantages for those who acted fast. The first movers in the Internet's regulatory scene could enter virgin territory, promote their preferred framework of rules, and create a regulatory *fait accompli*. As subsequent sections of this chapter will show, large companies of the core economies realized this and worked to fashion rules that would affect online communication worldwide and shape the face of global capitalism.

It was not long before large American companies found champions within the U.S. government that shared their concern with global competitiveness. One of them was Senator Al Gore, who in 1991 secured the passage of the *High Performance Computing and Communications Act*. It promised federal support for high-performance computing in order to secure the U.S. lead in this increasingly crucial segment of the global economy. The act stated as much:

> The United States currently leads the world in the development and use of high-performance computing for national security, industrial productivity, science and engineering, but that lead is being challenged by foreign competitors...
>
> The purpose of this Act is to help ensure the continued leadership of the United States in high-performance computing and its applications.

As the research coalition matured, a new coalition took shape and soon surpassed its predecessor in financial muscle and political influence. It consisted of American corporations, on the one hand, and the U.S. government at its highest level, on the other. Across the Atlantic, this pairing was paralleled by a coalition between the European Commission and European corporations. Both corporate coalitions knew that the future of the Internet would depend on the regulatory framework in which it became embedded. Both shared the goal of putting the Internet in the service of flexible accumulation, and each coalition wanted to dictate the terms under which this happened.

As soon as it took office in January 1993, the Clinton-Gore administration made IT deployment a policy priority. It established an Information Infrastructure Task Force, headed by the secretary of commerce, which evaluated and developed IT policy. In addition to the task force the administration established the National Information Infrastructure Advisory Council.

The council was to channel input from civil society and advise the task force on strategy. Apparently, "civil society" was interpreted as meaning primarily the private sector, as two-thirds of the council's members were chief executive officers of major corporations (Anderson 1995). They would ensure that U.S. trade interests guided policy.

The council and the task force produced the document *The National Information Infrastructure [NII]: Agenda for Action*. Published in September 1993, this document launched the government's National Information Infrastructure initiative. The initiative aimed at creating a high-speed communication network that enabled Americans to access databases and applications remotely, and it sought to boost American competitiveness. In that spirit, the *Agenda for Action* promised that "[a]n advanced information infrastructure will enable U.S. firms to compete and win in the global economy" (NTIA 1993).

While the U.S. government set the pace, Europeans played catch-up. A reason for this was that Europe had a feebler networking history. European universities had engaged in networking efforts, just like their American counterparts, but with only limited success. From the time it was established in 1983, the European Academic Research Network (EARN), which linked European university computing centers,[10] suffered from several disadvantages. The network's communication protocol was unwieldy, communication was slow, and overhead costs were high. Strapped for money, participating computing centers migrated to the much cheaper NSFNet as soon as the opportunity presented itself. This made it more expensive for the remaining organizations to share the overhead cost, and this in turn accelerated the rate of defection. In this way TCP/IP became the dominant communication protocol for European networking, but Internet projects received no government funding (Grier 2001; Heywood 1992; Zielinski 2001).

In the early 1990s attempts at creating commercial Europe-wide data networks ran into difficulties with the fragmented and monopolistic organization of telecom in Europe.[11] European industry realized that faster development of the IT revolution in the United States would render their rivals on the other side of the Atlantic more competitive. To prevent this, they collaborated with the European Commission (Hedblom and Garrison 1997, 502). Under the leadership of Commissioner Martin Bangemann, a panel of high level representatives of industry and government issued the 1994 report *Europe and the Global Information Society: Recommendations to the European Council*. Frequently referenced as the *Bangemann Report*, the document is the European equivalent of the *Agenda for Action*.

The *Bangemann Report* marked a break in EU policy, which so far had focused narrowly on telecom infrastructure and neglected the newer information and communication technologies. It introduced the concept of the information society and conceived it as an ideal society, based on the convergence of information and communication technologies.[12] According to the report, human knowledge that was stored in databases would be accessible to a large section of European society through the public data network. The information society was to be achieved through partnerships between the public and private sectors. In this partnership private industry was to provide the driving force for change (High-Level Group on the Information Society 1994; Hedblom and Garrison 1997, 491).

The U.S. government and the Commission moved remarkably in tandem. The *Agenda for Action* was published in 1993, the *Bangemann Report* appeared in 1994. Both documents were concerned with the convergence of information and communication technologies, as embodied in the Internet. Both conceived of a range of societal applications of the new technologies that would be rooted in the worlds of engineering and academic research. But commercial uses and concerns for competitiveness were moving center stage.

By 1997 the Commission and the U.S. government zoomed in on the regulation of e-commerce. In that year, the Commission published the *European Initiative in Electronic Commerce*, and the U.S. government published the *U.S. Framework for Electronic Commerce* (Clinton and Gore 1997; European Commission 1997a). Both documents called for creating the regulatory and legal conditions that would facilitate use of the Internet as a medium for online trade. The U.S. framework defined the Internet as an online marketplace while also emphasizing its democratizing effects. The document recognized that many of the information services in which the United States was competitive could be traded internationally over the Internet. It assumed that such international free trade was desirable. It called for standards, regulations, and policies that maximized the ability of the Internet to function as a global market place. The U.S. framework specifically addressed the policy areas of taxation, electronic payment, privacy and data protection, and protection of intellectual property.

The Commission and the U.S. government viewed each other as competitors, but their interests were aligned in that both sought a global regulatory context that created the terrain on which they would compete for leadership positions in the global economy. As a result, they cooperated to obtain a core consensus that they would then carry into the more inclusive multilateral fora in which trade negotiations took place. The rules emerging from this process would enter the global IT regime and become part of global social structure.

One such example of narrow consensus-building involved the G-7 or Group of Seven Nations. It consisted of the world's major economic powers:

United States, United Kingdom, France, Germany, Italy, Canada, and Japan. In 1995 these governments held the G-7 ministerial conference on the information society. In a preparatory message to the European Commission, the Information Infrastructure Task Force of the United States explained that the U.S. government wanted the global information infrastructure to reflect a number of distinct principles: encouragement of private investment, competition, a flexible regulatory framework, open access to the network for all information service providers, and universal service. It continued to explain the strategic importance of reaching a narrow consensus before entering multilateral negotiations:

> A key objective for the United States is to achieve support among the G-7 countries for the five principles as the foundation for the global information infrastructure. We believe that commitment by the G-7 members to advancing these principles would constructively create a shared "vision" of the global information infrastructure and would be a critical step in building a broader international consensus on the emerging global information infrastructure. (Information Infrastructure Taskforce 1994)

The goal was thus to achieve consensus among the most powerful states before others would be invited into the deliberations. Large corporations were carefully included in the search for a narrow consensus. The agenda of the G-7 conference provided for a roundtable of business leaders. Meanwhile, other societal groups remained shut out, a fact that prompted criticism from civil society groups, who responded by organizing a counter summit (Communet 1995; Reuter/Tabor Griffin 1995).

Once a narrow coalition was built among the G-7 states, their consensus was carried into more inclusive fora such as the United Nations Conference on International Trade Law (UNCITRAL). In 1996 UNCITRAL adopted the Model Law for Electronic Commerce. It contained rules for validating and enforcing contracts that were concluded electronically. The model law served as a template that could be adopted by the various national legislatures. In providing the model law UNCITRAL sought to minimize legal conflict arising from cross-border transactions among jurisdictions that applied different rules. Since then, numerous economies have adopted this model law in its entirety or with modifications. It had the effect of enhancing legal clarity among jurisdictions and reducing transaction costs. This has helped to ease cross-border electronic trade and make corporations more mobile.

The World Trade Organization (WTO) was another inclusive forum. In 1998 it adopted the *Geneva Ministerial Declaration on Global Electronic*

Commerce, which urged the creation of a work program on electronic commerce and imposed a temporary moratorium on customs duties for all products delivered over the Internet.

By appropriately leveraging the regulatory void that surrounded the Internet, it was thus possible to turn the technology into a facilitator of flexible accumulation. Recognizing that their corporations could benefit enormously from well-specified Internet rules, governments of the core economies encouraged their corporations to lead the way in the rule-making process. Meanwhile, engineers, academic researchers, and civil society organizations with an alternative economic agenda were elbowed aside.

Areas of Internet Governance

A regulatory framework for the Internet was taking shape, which would become part of the global IT regime. While governments played a role in negotiating the new rules of the game, it was the private sector in the core economies—and here specifically transnational corporations, technology companies, large providers of digital content and information services—that took the lead in shaping the regulations. These actors dominated the development of the three main aspects of the Internet regulatory framework: (1) Technical standards surrounding the Internet; (2) strategic vision for the Internet; and (3) governing domain names.

Technical Standardization

During phase two of the Internet's development, when the research coalition was in the lead, a number of smaller organizations came into being that supported the network. Among them was the Internet Engineering Task Force (IETF), which was responsible for the Internet standardization process. It was based on individual participation: "The IETF is not a membership organization (no cards, no dues, no secret handshakes :-) The IETF is a large open international community of network designers, operators, vendors, and researchers concerned with the evolution of the Internet architecture and the smooth operation of the Internet. It is open to any interested individual" (IETF n.d.).

In 1994, when phase three began and the Internet opened its doors to the private sector, the World Wide Web Consortium (W3C) came into being. Its members were organizations—mostly private sector companies—that developed software and IT products or that used the web as an enabling platform for sales, research, or intraorganizational communication (W3C 2001).

Both the IETF and the W3C set technical standards. When the W3C was created, it took over certain areas of IETF activity, such as html or "hypertext markup language," the code that instructed web browsers how to display a webpage. Other areas of activity, such as http or "hypertext transfer protocol," the protocol governing communication between a personal computer and a web server, remained with the IETF (Khare 1998).

The organizations represented in the W3C were primarily technology companies from the core economies. They paid substantial membership dues that smaller technology firms from the periphery could not afford.[13] In 2002, the W3C had over 450 members, and the overwhelming majority came from the private sector of the core economies, giving these organization a disproportionate input into the shape of emerging standards (W3C 2002).[14]

Strategic Vision

In the early 1990s the Internet as a new communication medium attracted a great amount of interest from companies, scholars, students, governments, and citizens who were curious about the possibilities this network offered. It appeared capable of supporting a variety of social agendas, and much depended on the strategic vision that would be brought to bear on it. Core governments opted to leverage the Internet for deepening flexible accumulation, and they invited corporations to help them chart this course.

When the G-7 states held the 1995 ministerial conference on the information society, they issued a challenge to large corporations, urging them to become more vocal about their needs and provide input into future policy. Accepting this invitation, global corporations established several specialized advocacy organizations. Three of them—the Global Information Infrastructure Commission, the Internet Law and Policy Forum, and the Global Business Dialogue on Electronic Commerce—exemplify the emerging coalition between core states and large companies.

Created during the 1995 G-7 meeting in Brussels, the Global Information Infrastructure Commission (GIIC) was the oldest among the three organizations. Describing itself as a confederation of chief executive officers of corporations that developed and deployed, operated, relied upon, and financed information and communications technology infrastructure facilities, it explained that "together as GIIC commissioners, these executives are dedicated to speeding the spread of information infrastructure throughout the world" (GIIC 2002a). That membership in the GIIC was by invitation only ensured that the organization remained a club of almost exclusively large corporations. Through its secretariat, which was located in

Washington, D.C., the GIIC published policy papers, held business conferences, and provided input into intergovernmental fora such as the World Summit of the Information Society, a conference held in 2003 in Switzerland by mandate of the United Nations.

Founded in 1995, the Internet Law and Policy Forum (ILPF) was an international business association made up of companies that developed and deployed the Internet. Member companies were large corporations. The Forum's goal was to support the "sustainable global development of the Internet." It did so by involving itself in the public policy process:

> Through its conferences, working groups, and expert workshops, the ILPF provides a neutral forum and international perspective in order to discover best practices and develop practical solutions for the multi-faceted challenges posed by the Internet in the realms of law, policy, technology and business. In the seven years since its founding, the ILPF has gained a leadership reputation for helping to shape the laws and policies on issues vital to the Internet in many jurisdictions around the world. (ILPF [2002])

A more recent creation was the Global Business Dialogue on Electronic Commerce (GBDe).[15] In 1998, EU commissioner Martin Bangemann invited business leaders from around the world to participate in a round-table discussion on global communications issues. In response to the event, the GBDe was founded. Consisting of senior business leaders, its credo was to improve business coordination at the global level and to prevent conflicting policies and legislation. The GBDe worked with governments to develop business-led regulatory frameworks. It explained: "Conflicting policies, rules and regional patchwork-regulations are obstacles to our business. Therefore, strengthened coordination between industry, governments and international organizations is required" (GBDe n.d.). The GBDe developed recommendations in policy areas affecting e-commerce, such as intellectual property rights, online payments, authentication, personal data protection and tariffs (GBDe 2002). Mann et al. (2000) make the point that in less than two years, the GBDe had become an influential vehicle to communicate industry perspectives to governments (165). Andrew Pincus (2000), general counsel for the Department of Commerce, confirms this. In an essay on policies for a legal e-commerce framework, he bolstered his ideas by stating that the GBDe issued a recommendation to governments that strongly embraced his approach (13). Table 3.1 contains membership lists for both the ILPF and the GBDe.

Table 3.1 Members of the Global Business Dialogue on Electronic Commerce (GBDe) and the Internet Law and Policy Forum (ILPF)

GBDe members in 2002	GBDe members in 2002, continued	ILFP members as of 2002
ABNAmro *	Indra	Bell Canada
Accenture	KT Corporation	British Telecom
Alcatel	LG Electronics	Deutsche Telekom AG
AOL Time Warner	Masreya	DoubleClick, Inc
BCE Inc.	Matsushita Electric	Fujitsu Limited
Bertelsmann AG	Industrial Co., Ltd.	MasterCard International
Cable & Wireless	Mediaset S.p.A.,	MCI
Cisneros Group*	Microsoft*	NEC Corporation
CxNetworks	MIH	NIFTY Corporation
DaimlerChrysler*	Mitsui & Co.	NTT Communications
DB Software Systems	Multimedia Development	Corporation
Dentsu Inc	Corporation	NTT Data Corporation
Deutsche Bank	NEC	Oracle Corporation
Deutsche Telekom *	Nihon Unisys, Ltd.	Schlumberger
Disney*	NIIT	Telus Corporation
EDS (Electronic Data	Nokia	Time Warner
Systems Corporation) *	Nomura Research	VeriSign
Equitable Card Network	Institute	Visa International
France Telecom	NTT Data Corporation	Yahoo! Inc.
Fujitsu Ltd.	Sesame Workshop	
Fuji Xerox Co., Ltd.	Sharp Corporation	
Hewlett Packard	Siemens AG	
Hitachi, Ltd	Sumerian Networks	
IBM*	Telecom Argentina *	
Toshiba Corporation	Telefónica, S.A.	
VeriSign, Inc.	TEPCO	
Vivendi*		
WorldCom*		

Sources: For GBDe: Global Business Dialogue on Electronic Commerce (2003) except: * Orts (2001).
For ILPF: Internet Law and Policy Forum ([2002]).

These were not the only specialized organizations representing the private sector. Another was the Internet Alliance, a U.S. based advocacy organization for the online industry. Its membership included AOL Time Warner, e-Bay, IBM, Microsoft, and WorldCom. Yet another, the Global Internet Alliance, was founded in 2000 and specifically represented Internet service providers. All these organizations concerned themselves with policy issues such as data protection, encryption, taxation, tariffs, liability, intellectual property rights, and ways of promoting electronic commerce. The membership lists of these organizations frequently overlapped, reducing their effective constituency to a small number of highly influential companies. Together they developed a strategic vision for the Internet that promoted corporate mobility and flexibility. The core states of Europe and the United States then propagated this vision internationally. In doing so they endowed it with the legitimacy that stems from having been democratically elected by their respective citizens. While serving the desires of their corporations, these elected governments chose to disregard alternative visions of a world society and of the contributions that the Internet might make to bringing these visions about.

Governing Domain Names

In the 1990s the corporate private sector worked to remold the institutions of Internet governance to ensure that their marketing concerns received priority consideration when it came to assigning domain names. To see how, it helps to understand how the Internet naming system is organized.

Domain names are arranged hierarchically. At the highest level are the top-level domains, indicated by the last few characters of the domain name. For example, the website of Northern Arizona University can be found by entering "www.nau.edu" into a web browser. Of this expression, the last three characters indicate that Northern Arizona University is located in the .edu, or education, top-level domain. To access the website of the World Bank, a user would type "www.worldbank.org" into a web browser. The last few characters show that the World Bank is at home in the .org, or organization, top-level domain. The expression "www.lemonde.fr" would lead us to the website of the French newspaper *Le Monde*. It is located under the top-level domain .fr, which stands for "France."

By the early 1990s two different types of top-level domains existed. The first type included country-code top-level domains (ccTLDs). With few exceptions, each country had one top-level domain, and so the overall number of ccTLDs approximated the number of nations that had been recognized by the United Nations Organization. Each ccTLD consisted of a two-letter combination that specified a country. Examples are .de for Germany, .eg for Egypt, .tv for Tuvalu. Each country administered its ccTLD according to its own national rules.

The second type of top-level domains included generic top-level domains (gTLDs). Seven gTLDs existed: the .com, .edu, .gov, .int, .mil, .net, and

.org domains. Four of them—.edu, .gov, .int, and, .mil—were reserved for educational, U.S. governmental, international, and U.S. military organizations, respectively. The others were open to the general Internet public. Thus, anyone who chose to do so could register a domain that ended with .com or .net.

To appreciate the hierarchy of the domain name system, it makes sense to conceive it as a warehouse of websites. Each warehouse needs order, and the same is true for the web. The hierarchy of the domain name system creates order. Imagine that the warehouse contains two large file cabinets. One is reserved for gTLDs; the other is the ccTLD cabinet. Each file cabinet contains drawers, one for each TLD. The gTLD cabinet thus contains seven drawers. The ccTLD cabinet contains over 150 drawers, one for each country. Each drawer is maintained by an organization that serves as registrar.

Once a customer creates, or registers, a domain, the registrar creates an index card for that user and files it in the appropriate spot in its drawer. The index card contains the contact information of the person who registered the website, the IP address of the server that hosts it, and the full domain name, which must be unique. For instance, there may be one www.oxford.edu and one www.oxford.com. But there must not be two sites with the name www.oxford.edu. Once it has that information, the registrar will pass it on to the root servers, which translate domain names into the corresponding IP addresses. Thanks to this system, it is possible to find a website over the Internet without knowing its "real," numeric IP address.

Corporations tried to control the rules by which these domain names were assigned. A central dispute turned around the question of which domains individual users should be allowed to register. Corporations sought to limit access to domains that sounded like their brand names. They were pitted against free speech activists who rejected such limitations.

To see why domain registration was such a contentious issue, imagine a hypothetical example: The cigarette maker Philip Morris has a domain called www.philipmorris.com. According to the Agreement on Trade-Related Aspects of Intellectual Property Rights (TRIPS) that was negotiated during the Uruguay round of trade negotiations, Philip Morris was entitled to protection of the sign that it registered as its trademark. Article 16 of the agreement said:

> The owner of a registered trademark shall have the exclusive right to prevent all third parties not having the owner's consent from using in the course of trade identical or similar signs for goods or services which are identical or similar to those in respect of which the trademark is registered where such use would result in a likelihood of confusion.

Owners of trademarks that were considered famous were granted a number of additional protections.

The agreement did not specify that domain names were to be considered "signs...which are similar to those in respect of which the trademark is registered." Consequently, it did not say whether or not it was legitimate to curtail access to domains in order to protect trademarks. Should a person be denied access to a domain name because it sounded like a famous brand? Should antismoking advocates be kept from registering a domain reminiscent of a tobacco company and using it to explain the health risks of smoking? Alternatively, should it be illegitimate for a political scientist with the name Phillip Morris to register the domain www.phillipmorris.org, because it sounds like the name of the famous cigarette maker? These questions were at the heart of the quarrel over domain registration that unfolded in the late 1990s.

Free speech activists were on one side of the dispute. They answered all these questions in the negative. They wanted to grant as many actors as possible access to as many domains as possible, and they favored the old practice of assigning domains strictly on a first-come-first-served basis, no matter whether the first in line were antismoking activists, individuals that launched a consultancy, or a large corporation. Corporations took the opposite stance. They vehemently objected to granting others access to what they viewed as their property.

How did the struggle between these two sides unfold, and who won out? In 1993 the National Science Foundation gave the company Network Solutions a contract to act as the sole domain name registrar for the nonmilitary top-level domains (NSF 1992). In May 1996 IANA, the organization that since the days of the ARPANET had administered the Internet's IP address and domain name system,[16] proposed that Network Solutions' monopoly over registration in the gTLDs be ended. IANA suggested the creation of 50 competing domain name registries. Each of these would have the exclusive right to register names in up to three new top-level domains (Paik and Stark 2000). This suggestion would have resulted in up to 150 new gTLDs (Kleinwächter 2001, 26). Trademark owners cried foul. They feared that Internet users could now register names resembling their brands in over 100 different top-level domains, thereby diluting the impact of their famous signs.

In response to these concerns, the International Ad-Hoc Committee was formed. It consisted of the ten individuals from the private sector, universities, the International Telecommunication Union, the National Science Foundation, and the World Intellectual Property Organization (WIPO), a specialized agency of the United Nations (Internet Society 1996). The committee proposed the creation of seven new gTLDs. A number of private registrars would administer them under the supervision of a consortium of stakeholders. With 7 instead of 150 new gTLDs, the risk for diluting brands was reduced. But the community of trademark owners protested again. They insisted that before any new gTLDs were created, safeguards for their trademark interests had to be in place. In 1997 the committee and others issued a memorandum of understanding. It assigned the task of dispute resolution between trademark owners and domain owners to WIPO (Froomkin 1999, 12 and 20).

This time free speech advocates protested. They argued that the memorandum privileged trademark owners and that WIPO, with its mandate to protect, or advocate, the interests of the intellectual property rights community, would not be neutral. Consequently the memorandum failed (13).

Now the Department of Commerce stepped in. It asked WIPO to draw up recommendations for a dispute resolution process that would involve both trademark holders and those members of the Internet community that did not own marks. The process was to protect famous marks in the gTLDs (11). WIPO therefore designed a dispute resolution process, and in April 1999 it issued a final report.

Michael Froomkin, a professor at the University of Miami and expert of Internet law, explains that WIPO's report received mixed reviews. Several trademark advocates argued that it was too timid. Others approved. Some objected on technical grounds. The free speech advocates were dissatisfied because the report was not sufficiently specific and left too much open to interpretation. Froomkin adds:

Another very controversial issue was the special protections proposed for famous and well-known marks. Famous and well-known marks are particularly recognizable trademarks that are entitled to additional legal protection beyond the ordinary protections afforded regular trademarks.... Some national authorities have published lists of the marks considered famous and well-known in their jurisdictions; others leave it to their courts to decide on a case by case basis. Despite several years of work by an international panel convened by WIPO, however, there remains no agreed definition of what constitutes a *globally* famous or well-known mark, so WIPO proposed to set up a tribunal to rule on applications for this status. Marks found sufficiently famous would be entitled to additional protection against having domain names with the same or similar character strings registered in the domain name system by anyone but the famous mark holder. (18; Emphasis in the original)

By then, the Internet Corporation for Assigned Names and Numbers (ICANN) had come into being: In 1997, President Clinton had asked the secretary of commerce to "privatize the management of the domain name system (DNS) in a manner that increases competition and facilitates international participation in its management" (ICANN and U.S. Department of Commerce 1998). In 1998, ICANN, a nonprofit organization, won the contract. In the fall of 2000, ICANN took charge of the domain dispute by specifying seven new gTLDs: .aero, .biz, .coop, .info, .museum, .name, and .pro. It also developed a dispute resolution policy for conflicts over rights to domain names, to which registries had to commit. According to Kleiman, director of the Internet Governance Project at the Association for Computing Machinery, this policy favored trademark holders (Kleiman 2003, 9).

In sum, corporations did not prevent the creation of seven new top-level domains; but their desire for protection had profound influence on the rules by which domains were assigned. This shows that the years between 1998 and 2000 were crucial for defining who had a right to domain names and creating the institutions by which disputes would be resolved. During those two years those who sought to advance flexible accumulation were present and participated vocally in the process of defining Internet governance. Actors from Third World economies, which lack famous marks and are therefore likely to favor less stringent protection for them, were not present.

Summary: New Rules Enter the IT Regime

Thus, the Internet was governed by a number of distinct coalitions: In the 1970s there was the defense coalition, and it included ARPA. In the 1980s, it was supplanted by the research coalition, which received funding from the National Science Foundation. In those years, corporate users of computing technologies recognized the Internet's potential for supporting their quest to become both flexible and mobile, and they sought access to the network. In the 1990s, the research coalition was therefore replaced by the corporate coalition, which consisted of the Department of Commerce and American corporations. In Europe, this coalition was mirrored by an alliance between the European Commission and Europe's corporate sector.

The 1990s were a highly political decade for those who involved themselves in creating norms for the Internet. Participating in the creation of the many necessary ground rules proved especially influential because future decision processes would be based on them. A strategic vision for the network needed to be developed, which painted a future world society and put the Internet in its service. Frameworks for governance had to be put in place.

The norms that were created in those years became part of the global IT regime, and thus entered global social structure. There are, of course, some qualitative differences between the rules for telecom and those that emerged for the Internet. While telecom norms were based on intergovernmental consensus, Internet rules were largely forged by nongovernmental organizations, mostly from the private sector. Authors use different terms to capture this phenomenon. Froomkin (1999) calls it "semi-private rule-making." Kleinwächter (2001) speaks of the formation of a "rough consensus." Krechmer (2000) refers to "market-driven standardization."

Starting in the early 1990s, corporations became heavily involved in all three aspects of the rule-making processes: technical standardization, strategic vision, and Internet governance. Citizens of the core economies who favored a noncommercial agenda for the Internet had very limited venues for making their voices heard. Citizens from Third World economies were in an even worse position. While their counterparts in the core economies had physical access to some of the organizations that participated in Internet governance and could, if need be, protest in front of their gates, peripheral citizens had no such opportunities, because organizations that could have offered access points to them were excluded from the crucial decision processes. Because of the skewed ways of deriving norms for online communication worldwide, the Internet quickly became a means for deepening flexible accumulation.

PART II

The Rules of the Game are Enforced

CHAPTER 4

Bringing Poor Economies in Line

O n May 19, 1990, my parents, my brother, and I sat in front of the
television set at our home in Waldshut, Germany. We were watch-
ing *The March*, a BBC production that the German television station ARD had picked up. What we saw was eerie.

The drama originated in Sudan, a poor country in the north of Africa.
Impoverished village dwellers had reached the conclusion that their home-
land offered them neither food nor a future. Issa Al-Mahdi, a charismatic
leader, convinced them that the solution to their problem lay in Europe and
that they should go there to claim their share of the continent's wealth. The
villagers packed their belongings and embarked on a march. Their destination was the rich countries in the north.

It was not long until the media became aware of the procession and
started to trail the marchers. Interviewed by a reporter, Al-Mahdi explained
the migrants' position: "We are poor because you are rich." They passed
through the countries of North Africa, where more and more paupers joined
them, swelling the ranks of the procession until it comprised tens of thousands of starving travelers. At the southern shore of the Mediterranean, they
boarded a run-down fleet of boats and crossed over to the other side. When
they disembarked on the Spanish coast, officials of Fortress Europe awaited
them. Instead of rolling out the red carpet, they had mobilized their armed
forces.

The last scene depicts thousands of migrants facing off with European
soldiers who are prepared to shoot the intruders. The European high commissioner for refugees stands at the sidelines. Apologetically, she tells herself,
"We are just not ready for you yet" (Wheatley 1990).

The March has stuck with me ever since. This was partly because of its provocative content. But what made the movie even more memorable was the unusual commentary that the TV announcer delivered afterward. Compelled to calm the audience, he assured us, "This is a fictional account. The wretched of the earth are not going to overrun Germany. The Mediterranean is safe."

The film captured an important aspect of core-periphery relations, of which the shapers of globalization are aware. While the citizens of the periphery are too insignificant to be included into the negotiations that result in the global rules of the game, they nevertheless have some influence over the way the economic contest plays out; and if they decide to boycott global commerce, they may well jeopardize wealth creation in the core nations.

In *The March*, for example, Africans had begun to question the dominant economic paradigm, its geographic divisions, its property right definitions, and the allocation of wealth and property that it produced. Instead of accepting that a person could only make demands on a state that had accepted him or her as a national, the fictional Sudanese left their positions in the periphery and insisted that European governments take care of their needs.

In the film, the European Commission nipped the threat of disruption in the bud by forcing the offenders back onto their ships. In practice, however, poverty migration is not dealt with so easily. From 1991 to 1992, fifty thousand Albanians crossed over the Adriatic Sea into Italy. By 1996 their number had swollen to two hundred thousand, straining the ability and the willingness of the Italian government to provide support.

A Fragile System

The world economy is a complex and fragile system. It depends on the participation of all. Yet it is also true that only a small circle of powerful actors helped shape it. Quite likely, the system's institutions do constitute the first best choice for those without access to the formative negotiations. Therefore, the excluded have a reason for opting out of the system altogether or demanding that its rules be changed.

Why does it happen so rarely that the marginalized reject a game that they find unjust? How do the rules of the game discipline excluded actors into playing their parts? This is what this chapter is about. It serves as the entry point into the Egyptian case study, which will trace how the IT revolution disciplines actors from the periphery by altering the character of the Third World state.

The model that Berger and Luckmann developed in *The Social Construction of Reality*[1] can be used to explore not only the creation of rules and regimes, but also their enforcement. This is especially true when it is used in conjunction with concepts that are central to critical realism, a philosophy of science that is at home in Great Britain and largely unknown in the United States. Taken together, these components help explain how inequality of access to global decision processes yields a global social system that is governed by organizations with only a limited degree of accountability to human beings.

This chapter will discuss how these theoretical components, applied in combination, yield a framework with which researchers can paint a holistic picture of globalization. Understanding how regimes generate roles for social actors—specifically the peripheral state—and how those organizations that support the regimes help bring about role compliance will require a detailed discussion of Berger and Luckmann's idea of the enforcement mechanism and the critical realist ideas of causal powers, causal liabilities, and causal mechanisms.

In a nutshell, organizations that support the global IT regime in one way or other have specific causal powers. For example, they have the power to withhold development assistance, or the power to offer training to state bureaucrats. At the same time, the peripheral state has causal liabilities, which largely stem from indebtedness and financial vulnerability. When the causal powers of organizations that support the IT regime interlock with the causal liabilities of the Third World state, they generate what critical realists call a "causal mechanism," or what Berger and Luckmann name an "enforcement mechanism." Altogether, the numerous enforcement mechanisms that act on the peripheral state combine to push it toward role compliance.

Even though the subsequent chapters will focus on the workings of enforcement mechanisms on the Egyptian state, their goal is not simply to analyze the Egyptian political economy and the impact of the IT regime on it specifically. Rather, Egypt serves as a case study. Peripheral societies may differ in climate, geographic position, and resources endowments. Their dominant religious and ethnic groups may vary. But as we will see, the enforcement mechanisms that bear down on these societies are in important respects similar for, say, Egypt, Zambia, and Nicaragua. Consequently, if we study the enforcement mechanisms that were associated with the IT regime and that acted on the Egyptian state, we can learn a good deal about the exclusions suffered both by Egyptians and by the inhabitants of these other peripheral societies.

Together, the theoretical framework and the case study of the following chapters will help make a simple, yet powerful, argument. The decision processes of the global economic system may have deprived many citizens of the core economies of their autonomy, because they had limited capacity to influence those organizations that negotiated the rules of the game. Compared to their counterparts from the core, however, citizens of the periphery were in a far worse position. First, while numerous core citizens had limited access to global decision processes, peripheral citizens had none, because organizations to which they could have had access were not included in the negotiations that shaped the regime.

Second, peripheral citizens experienced injury when enforcement mechanisms that were tied to global social structure pushed the peripheral state into role compliance. This argument makes sense given the most basic tenets of democratic theory that we learned in civics class. Democracy literally means "government by the people," and it is a desirable form of government, because if it is done right, it respects the autonomy of the people. The American Declaration of Independence supports this idea when it states:

> We hold these truths to be self-evident, that all men are created equal, that they are endowed by their Creator with certain unalienable Rights, that among these are Life, Liberty and the pursuit of Happiness.—That to secure these rights, Governments are instituted among Men, deriving their just powers from the consent of the governed.

The Egyptian case study demonstrates that indeed, enforcement mechanisms push the peripheral state to comply with the role that global social structure has created for it. When the state is forced to bow to these mechanisms and shape its economic policies to please core organizations, it no longer responds to the desires of its people, who may have different policies in mind for their economy. The enforcement mechanisms are thus inherently undemocratic. While the IT revolution may have disrespected the autonomy of many core citizens once, it deprived human beings who resided at the margins of the global economy twice.

The IT Regime: Fuzzy at the Fringes

The previous chapters explained how the institutions that governed IT came into being and resulted in a new regime at the global level. The regulations were made by organizations from the core economies, and their intent was to facilitate the transition to flexible accumulation.

The new rules for telecom encouraged the privatization of the telecom monopolist, introduction of competition into the sector, and the creation of an independent regulator. In the 1990s an entirely new set of rules for the Internet was put into place, because the previously existing regulatory framework was rudimentary and did not address the concerns of the corporate private sector.[2] The new body of institutions was expansive, covering not only questions of protocol or Internet governance, but also customs, taxation, electronic payments, privacy, and security—all pivotal issue areas for creating a global information infrastructure that supported trade in knowledge-intensive services.[3] Together, the rules for telecom and the Internet formed a nascent "IT regime," which molded the ways in which individuals and organizations used information technology, encouraging some behaviors while discouraging others. Most importantly, they encouraged online trade.

Chapters two and three showed that the IT revolution buttressed the transition to flexible accumulation. In this chapter, we will see that its institutions were closely aligned with non-IT rules that had been forged in the 1980s and the 1990s.

An important area in which an alignment between the IT revolution and other aspects of globalization occurred was intellectual property rights (IPR). Prior to the 1980s individual societies were largely at liberty to define intellectual property in ways that reflected their own historically grown understandings of right and duty, public and private. Beginning in the 1980s this changed. In those years American corporations—especially those in the film and pharmaceutical industries—pushed for an IPR regime that was global in scope and linked intellectual property to trade. In 1984, the U.S. Congress picked up their battle and legislated trade sanctions against economies that violated American IPR interests. Peter Drahos (1998) of the Australian National University explains:

> In 1984, the U.S.A. amended its Trade Act of 1974 to include intellectual property in the "section 301" trade process. The 1984 amendment had a sequel in the form of the Omnibus Trade and Competitiveness Act of 1988. This latter Act strengthened the 301 process by adding more processes called "Regular 301," "Special 301" and "Super 301." Essentially these provisions required the Office of the United States Trade Representative to identify problem countries, assess the level of abuse of US intellectual property interests and to enter into negotiations with those countries to remedy the problems. Ultimately, if this proved futile, the U.S.A. could impose trade sanctions. (10)

When the Uruguay round of trade negotiations concluded in 1994, it established the World Trade Organization (WTO). It also created a globalized IPR regime, which was enshrined in the Agreement on Trade-Related Aspects of Intellectual Property Rights (TRIPS). TRIPS bound all WTO members without exception. It defined knowledge and information as commodities in which private ownership was possible, and it established standards that states had to incorporate into their national laws to protect this kind of ownership. According to IPR expert Christopher May (2004), this new, globalized conception of knowledge strongly privileged the interests of enterprises in the wealthy, industrialized economies.

The TRIPS agreement shaped the way electronic commerce evolved, because defined information as a commodity that could be owned and traded. At the same time TRIPS influenced numerous industries—for example, the pharmaceutical sector—that had little to do with telecom, the

Internet, or online trade. TRIPS was therefore not a component of the IT regime, but it makes sense to treat TRIPS and the IT regime as ideologically aligned with one another.

The point that this example seeks to make is that the IT regime was not a crisply bounded set of rules. Rather, it was fuzzy at the fringes, overlapping with other regimes that had been created to ease the transition to flexible accumulation. As a regime it was part of a global social structure that emphasized free trade to an ever-increasing degree.

Rules Give Rise to Roles

Social structure is the web of institutions that govern social interaction. Regimes are subsets of institutions that cover specific issue areas. Berger and Luckmann explain that social structure—and hence regimes—creates roles, that is, sets of performance expectations that apply to types of actors. For example, a type might be "girl." The set of performance expectations associated with girls might be "Girls should not whistle," "Girls should be accommodating and friendly," and so on.

How does this idea apply to the global social structure that was associated with the IT revolution? In this case most types of actors were in place by the 1980s, when the first elements of the IT regime began to take shape. The world already consisted of incorporated companies, individuals, creditor states, debtor states, developed (i.e., core) and developing (i.e., peripheral) economies, to name only a few. Consequently, the IT regime did not generate many new types. Instead it accomplished something more subtle. Together with other aligned regulatory frameworks, it *redefined* the expectations that were associated with the various existing types. That is, it changed their roles.

For example, under Fordism it was expected that states would act as buffers to shield the domestic from the global economy. By contrast, the IT regime, which advanced flexible accumulation, institutionalized the expectation that states ease the integration of their domestic economies into the world market.

The Peripheral State

Under Fordism Third World states in particular had been expected to pursue Keynesian policies and a strategy of industrialization through import substitution. How did globalization and the IT revolution affect their roles?

There are two methods for discerning the new behavioral expectations that were tied to the type of "state that presides over a developing economy."

Either one queries the body of rules that helped define this role, or one inquires into the expectations that the makers and supporters of flexible accumulation had for the peripheral state. Following the second route leads to profound insights.

In 1990 John Williamson, who served as senior fellow at the Washington-based Institute for International Economics, wrote an essay titled "What Washington Means by Policy Reform." (1990). In it, Williamson explained that Congress, senior members of the administration, the international financial institutions, the treasury department, the Federal Reserve Board, and the prominent Washington think tanks had reached a "Washington Consensus," which urged economic policies on Third World economies that "may be summarized as prudent macroeconomic policies, outward orientation, and free-market capitalism." The policies Williamson identified included fiscal discipline achieved through a decrease in public expenditure, a significant reduction in subsidies, the creation of an exchange rate that encouraged export growth, an overall emphasis on export growth rather than import substitution, import liberalization, an encouragement of foreign direct investment, the privatization of state assets, economic deregulation, the definition of property as privately owned, and the enforcement of such private property rights.

Specialized policy papers of the U.S. government, the European Commission, and the World Bank reveal that all three organizations put telecom and Internet policy in the service of the Washington Consensus, thus helping redefine the roles of the peripheral states. For example, the *Framework for Global Electronic Commerce*, which President Clinton and Vice President Gore put out in 1997, stated that

> Commerce on the Internet could total tens of billions of dollars by the turn of the century. For this potential to be realized fully, governments will need to adopt a nonregulatory, market-oriented approach to electronic commerce, one that facilitates the emergence of a transparent and predictable legal environment *to support global business and commerce.* (Emphasis added)

Although this statement targeted states in general, it was soon translated into policy advice for Third World countries. In October 1998, Vice President Gore launched the administration's Internet for Economic Development Initiative, which aimed to demonstrate successful models for development using the Internet. The U.S. Agency for International Development (USAID) was charged with implementing the initiative. One of the chosen sites was Morocco. As part of the Moroccan demonstration project, USAID wrote an assessment study, which copied the quoted passage of the *Framework for Global Electronic Commerce* word for word. The intent behind this was to outline the policy goals for Morocco in particular and "developing economies" in general (USAID n.d.a.).

The European Commission had similar ideas of how Third World states should leverage IT. In 1997 it issued its *Communication of 15 July 1997 on the Information Society and Development: The Role of the European Union* (European Commission 1997b). The document began with the idea of a global information society in which all the countries of the world would be integrated. For that purpose it quoted the chair's conclusions of the conference on the information society, held by the G-7 in 1995:

> Our action must contribute to the integration of all countries into a global effort. Countries in transition and developing countries must be provided with the chance to fully participate in this process as it will open opportunities for them to leapfrog stages of technology development and to stimulate social and economic development.

The communication assumed that the information society had a heavy trade component and that free international trade was desirable. Economies that refused to participate in this trade were bound to suffer: "Countries that shut themselves off from these changes [i.e., global integration], isolating themselves from international trade networks and investment flows and from networks of scientific and cultural creativity and their spread, would risk being marginalized." The document urged peripheral states to adopt the WTO Basic Telecom Agreement, liberalize the monopolistic telecom sector, and invite foreign investors to build out their telecom infrastructure.

The World Bank, whose board of governors was dominated by core states, also played an important part in formulating the role expectations for peripheral states. Reflecting the Washington Consensus, it demanded that states undergoing structural adjustment privatize enterprises that they owned and follow a strategy of private sector-led, export-led growth (Lehman 1993). In 2000, its Global Information and Communication Technologies Department wrote the study, *The Networking Revolution: Opportunities and Challenges for Developing Countries* (World Bank, GICT 2000). It captures the Bank's approach to the IT revolution. Its argument is summarized here.

The World Bank's overarching goal for peripheral economies was aggregate economic growth. Other potentially conflicting policy goals that Third World societies might have valued, such as state control over national assets or the preservation of cultural integrity, were subordinated to this primary objective. Economic growth was to be achieved through integration into the global economy and development of the telecom infrastructure.

The World Bank argued that the networking revolution rang in a new era, with a "new economy." This new economy featured rapid growth in e-business and thus had a large impact on information-intensive industries (1). It was marked by tight economic integration among economies, with the Internet serving as the platform for a global marketplace (6). To bring the new economy about, peripheral states needed to reform their telecom sectors, that is, they had to privatize the monopolist, introduce competition, and establish an independent regulator. Moreover, they needed to adopt the rules necessary to enabling electronic commerce:

> A modern information infrastructure is the first building block of the "new economy." In this context, a proper telecommunications regulatory environment is fundamental. In order, however, to fully engage in the networking revolution, countries have to go beyond traditional regulatory reform, addressing the challenges of convergence and setting the rules needed for the expansion of e-commerce. (21)

By creating a pro-competitive environment and attracting investments in the IT infrastructure, peripheral economies could catapult themselves past stages of network development. This would create vast new opportunities in the global value-chain, ranging from linking into global supply chains to exporting new services. The Bank went on to explain that "the new business environment created by the Internet offered the chance for countries to 'leapfrog' to high-skill, high-wage industries" (9).

In order to bring home the spoils of the networking revolution, Third World states were to take several steps. First, they needed to reform investment policies and eliminate trade controls to attract investment in the IT infrastructure. Second, they needed to improve their financial systems, put in place a regulatory framework that encouraged e-commerce, and upgrade supporting services such as their postal systems. Third, they had to introduce competition throughout the economy. Fourth, they needed to adopt the telecom consensus that the core states had negotiated among each other and then carried into the WTO.

Taken together, the policy documents of the U.S. government, the European Commission, and the World Bank paint a clear picture of the expectations that these powerful organizations associated with the role of "Third World state." The state had to desert its Keynesian policy of old. Instead of acting as a buffer that shielded the domestic from the global economy, it was to facilitate the economy's integration into the world market.

It was expected to pursue a policy of private-sector led, export-led growth. Adopting the tenets of the IT regime was part of this process. The IT regime thus helped redefine the role of "Third World state."

How Enforcement Mechanisms Impose Roles

But how are the states prodded into role compliance? How are the rules from which the roles stem enforced?

Berger and Luckmann tell us that social structure hails actors to become role compliant. This happens through the simple presence of societal norms that, as norms, possess compelling character. A government—the state's command center—may evaluate a new norm, find that "this is how a modern state does things," and hence adopt it. In addition, there are concrete enforcement mechanisms that strengthen the call to role compliance.

The following chapters will identify concrete enforcement mechanisms at work and argue that they pushed the Egyptian state to comply with its new role under flexible accumulation. But doing so requires an understanding of what kind of theoretical beast an enforcement mechanism is. For that, we will need to spend a few paragraphs discussing critical realism, the philosophy of science position that guides this study's inquiry, and the things it has to say about enforcement mechanisms (Saleh 2009; Sayer 1994).

There are numerous ways in which critical realism differs from positivism, the philosophy of science position that dominates political science in the United States. One of the more fundamental distinctions is that while positivism has an atomistic perception of the objects that populate the world and does not inquire into their internal structure (Patomäki 2002), critical realists are keenly interested in the inner make-up of objects, or their internal structure, for they believe that this structure provides the object with the ability to impact the world around it in numerous, very specific ways. This potential to impact the world is called "generative" or "causal" power (Collier 1994, 62; Sayer 1994, 5 and 104f). Each object usually has several different generative powers. It also has "causal liabilities," that is, the vulnerability to be impacted by the world in various ways (Sayer 1994, 104f). Because these powers and liabilities emerge from the object's structure, they are an intrinsic aspect of the object's being.

Critical realists also embrace the notion of "causal" or "generative" mechanisms. A causal mechanism is the interlocking of one object's exercised causal power with the target object's causal liability.

This begs the question of what is meant by an object's exercised power. Critical realists distinguish between the exercise of power and its actualization. An object that possesses a causal power may do so without ever exercising it, that is, without ever directing it toward a target or, to use a different expression, setting the corresponding causal mechanism in motion. For example, Jenn has the causal power to submit her extra credit assignment to her professor, who in turn has the causal liability of receiving and grading the assignment. But a riveting television show may keep Jenn from submitting her assignment.[4]

Once something (it may be a reason, or an influence external to the object) stimulates the object to exercise its power and triggers the causal mechanism that connects it with the target object, this power may nevertheless remain unactualized; that is, it may fail to have the impact it could have had, had the object's mechanism worked unimpeded. For example, once the television show is over, Jenn attaches her assignment to an email message, addresses the message to her professor and hits the "send" button. Against her expectation, this action does not result in credit from her professor, because her causal power to deliver the assignment is not actualized: her professor's e-mail server stopped functioning and discarded Jenn's message instead of forwarding it into the professor's "inbox."

Once a power is actualized, it produces an event. For example, if Jenn had hand-delivered the assignment to her professor, she would have triggered his causal liability of receiving the assignment. The corresponding phenomenon would have been the assignment changing hands.

An enforcement mechanism can be viewed as a specific kind of causal mechanism. Here, the objects with causal powers are those actors that support social structure. In the IT case, they include the organizations that have forged the Washington Consensus, but also other organizations with stakes in the persistence of the new rules of the game that have entered social structure. Examples are the European Commission and the Global Information Infrastructure Commission. The causally liable object, in this case, is the Third World state. Enforcement mechanisms come into being when the causal powers of those actors that support the new regime interlock with the causal liabilities of the peripheral state, and when the state is prodded toward role compliance.

There are numerous ways in which such interlocking may happen. Here is only one. A specific international organization has the causal power of offering peripheral states training to inform them of new international norms (Finnemore 1996). The peripheral state Pyranao has the causal liability of requiring training in order to understand its new legal environment. The causal mechanism is that the international organization in fact trains the state. The phenomenon consists of four Pyranaoan bureaucrats sitting at the international organization and listening intently to an instructor.

Enforcement mechanisms are a function of the causal ability of organizations that support the new social structure to withhold loans, train bureaucrats, or mete out trade sanctions. What may be less obvious is that these mechanisms are also a function of the economic vulnerability of the Third World state. Economic vulnerability renders the state causally liable to require a loan or to depend on training offers from outside sources. When these causal powers and liabilities interlock, a causal mechanism emerges. The case study of Egypt will uncover several causal mechanisms. Because they are all tied to social structure and geared toward the enforcement of its norms, they constitute enforcement mechanisms in the sense of Berger and Luckmann. The economic weakness of the peripheral state thus gives rise to causal liabilities that make the state vulnerable to enforcement efforts on the part of the shapers of the IT regime.

These causal liabilities may indeed be part of the answer to the question posed at the beginning of this chapter: "Why do actors who were not involved in making the rules of the game so rarely reject the game in its entirety?" Clearly, if an actor is economically weak, he has a rationale for rejecting the rules of the game, because he did not participate in their making. At the same time, however, he may be too vulnerable to resist the causal powers of those who seek to perpetuate those rules. This reasoning applies to organizational actors just as it does to human beings, and it may explain why scenes such as that depicted in *The March* are rare occurrences.

Ideology

There is, however, a second part to the answer, and that is ideology. Ideology is a set of narratives that the shapers of institutions create to generate voluntary compliance on the part of those actors who had no say in creating the institutions. In the present case ideology comes in the form of the leapfrogging promise, which chapter one discussed and which played itself out in the communications of both of the European Commission and of the World Bank. Because it helped generate role compliance, the idea deserves to be explored in greater detail.

The notion of leapfrogging was based on the assumption, held in the 1980s, that Third World economies possessed scant communication infrastructure at a time when the core economies had vast analog networks. Since the technological state of the art advanced fast, moving from traditional analog telephony to digital telephony that could either be wired or wireless, it became feasible for poor economies to move from a state of no telecom infrastructure at all to one of digital networks. They were thus thought to bypass the analog stage through which the core economies had gone, thereby "leapfrogging technological development."

The idea of technological leapfrogging was problematic, because it assumed that Third World economies received intensive infrastructure upgrades while core economies stood still, thus closing the technological gap. In reality, the core economies experienced continuous infrastructure upgrades, so that the networks in the wealthy societies continued to outperform those in the poor societies.

Numerous analysts in the world of development policy carried the idea of leapfrogging from the technological realm into that of economic development, where its merits were feeble at best. The understanding was that technological leapfrogging would accelerate a poor country's rate of economic growth vis-à-vis the wealthy countries, thus allowing it to leapfrog economically and catch up with the wealthy core economies. In other words, technological leapfrogging would lead to economic leapfrogging, and this in turn would allow peripheral societies and their states to join their wealthy counterparts as players of equal status in the fierce politics of culture, economics, and diplomacy.

An example of an analysis that made unsubstantiated promises about leapfrogging was the World Bank's 2000 study on *The Networking Revolution*, which spoke of leapfrogging development and leapfrogging into high-value niches in the global economy. Two years later the Bank acknowledged that the leapfrogging promise was flawed. It did so, however, without admitting its own part in overselling the concept:

> The oft-cited opportunity for the developing world is to harness the power of information and communication technologies to leapfrog ahead economically by developing its capacity to compete in the global knowledge economy. The stark reality is that access to the tools for knowledge and wealth creation is still highly inequitable. In many cases, developing countries lack the legal and policy frameworks [information infrastructure], and [information and communication technology] applications that have enabled Organization for Economic Cooperation and Development (OECD) countries to exploit emerging technologies. (World Bank 2002, 5)

How does all this relate to social roles of peripheral states? The answer is that a role is a coercive construct, because it constrains an actor's behavioral freedom. When the role for "developing state" changed from favoring import substitution to demanding export-led growth, states that were pushed into role compliance by enforcement mechanisms faced the unpleasant task of discarding an economic strategy from which several domestic constituencies derived benefit. The state thus ran the risk of incurring the wrath of the population that it governed. The leapfrogging idea made this task easier, because it promised that any hardship a society encountered in becoming role-compliant would be worthwhile, as growth and wealth awaited the economy in the long run. The leapfrogging promise thus had an ideological function that supported the causal mechanisms in engendering role compliance.

An Intricate Division of Labor

Thus far, we have encountered many different organizations that eased the world's transition to flexible accumulation. They did not engage in a conspiracy—no central planning committee existed that hatched a scheme for the future of world trade and then controlled all other actors to bring the scheme about. But if the organizations did not conspire, how can the rather orderly outcome we have thus far observed be explained?

This study suggests that the entities that helped shape globalization were bound together by a decentralized yet hierarchical division of labor. Specifically, one can identify five different categories of organizations, each of which captures one specific function in making globalization happen. First, there were what we might call the *original drivers* of flexible accumulation. This group includes states of the core economies, acting in particular through high-level agencies tasked with formulating trade policy. Examples are the U.S. Department of Commerce, the European Commission (acting in particular through its trade-related directorates), and the EU Council of Ministers. They were joined by corporate actors such as Electronic Data Systems, the insurance industry, and multinational service companies. Chapter two showed that once telecom monopolists were exposed to domestic competition, they also became part of this group. While members of this category rivaled with one another either for international power or for market share, they agreed on the rough layout of the terrain on which they wanted their rivalry to unfold.

Although these original drivers perceived a need to integrate world trade, they did not have the expertise to conceive of appropriate IT rules or the stamina to pursue their institutionalization. For this reason, they launched *specialized business associations* with a mission of observing and influencing the trade and IT regimes. Examples of such associations are the Coalition of Service Industries, the Global Business Dialogue on Electronic Commerce, and the Internet Law and Policy Forum.

Other organizations served as *negotiating fora*. Instances include the GATT (and later the WTO) through its ministerial meetings and the International

Telecommunication Union, which, as discussed in chapter two, experienced pressure to become more inclusive of private sector actors. Once core states had reached a narrow coalition for, say, treating the cross-border provision of services as a trade issue that should be regulated by GATT norms, these fora enabled them to reach out to additional states and thus widen the coalition.

Once the IT regime was formulated, it was left up to *disciplinarians* to ensure that actors adhered to its strictures. Examples of disciplinarians are the WTO through its dispute resolution process; the U.S. Trade Representative through its 301 process, the Internet Corporation for Assigned Names and Numbers (ICANN) through its dispute resolution policy for domain names; and the World Bank, which after 1995 made lending in the telecom sector contingent on sector reform.[5] What united the disciplinarians was that they were either created by the original drivers of flexible accumulation, as in the case of ICANN, or that original drivers dominated their board of governors, as in the case of the World Bank. Consequently, the disciplinarians were beholden to the economic vision of the drivers.

Next in line were the *sellers* (or ideologues), those organizations that interacted with peripheral societies and explained why the rules of the game that had been forged without their full input were in their best interest. Like the disciplinarians, the sellers were obliged to the original drivers, for one of three reasons. Either they were directly created by the drivers, as in the case of the United States Agency for International Development (USAID), a lower-level agency of the U.S. government. Or they were funded by the drivers, as was the case for infoDev, a small subsidiary of the World Bank dedicated to encouraging the use of IT in poor countries.[6] Or their board of governors was dominated by the drivers, as for the World Bank.

In one way or other, all these organizational categories had stakes in the enforcement of the IT regime, and all partook in it in somehow, as the following chapters will reveal. An upshot of the upcoming discussion is the insight that development policy—which is administered by organizations such as the World Bank or USAID—is a disciplinary tool in the hands of the original drivers of flexible accumulation and not a selfless effort to help poor societies chart their own chosen political course.

Why Role Compliance is Rarely Complete

With so many powerful organizations vested in globalization, the pressure on the peripheral state to comply with its new role prescription is great. But even though rejecting the game of flexible accumulation is rarely an option for peripheral states, compliance with roles is seldom complete as well. Why is this? Three explanations present themselves. First off, even though the number of peripheral states is large, they vary greatly among each other. This has implications for causal powers and liabilities, and therefore for enforcement mechanisms that act on them. For example, not all states are equally poor or indebted. Therefore, their degree of exclusion from the formative negotiations varies, and they are also not equally vulnerable. While many states are thus in the periphery, their degree of "peripherality" varies. Therefore, their causal liability to being pressured also varies, which means that not all enforcement mechanisms work for all states. For example, if a state is not sufficiently indebted to require a structural adjustment loan, it cannot be threatened with the withholding of a loan.

Second, the causal powers of international organizations may be confined to certain geographic regions or specific issue areas. If a peripheral state is not located in the region, it will not be exposed to the causal power of an organization. For example, the European Commission had the causal power to pressure those states that were members of the Euro-Mediterranean Partnership into trade liberalization (see chapter six). This enforcement mechanism worked only for states that were located in the southern Mediterranean. It did not work for Bolivia, which is located in an entirely different world region.

Third, a state's resistance to enforcement mechanisms will depend on the extent of countervailing pressure it faces from domestic constituencies. What a state ends up doing is a compromise between these conflicting commitments.

How Does One Study Role Compliance?

Because the IT regime is aligned with a number of other, non-IT, regimes that support globalization, it is neither possible nor desirable to study the enforcement of rules for IT in isolation from the enforcement of more generic rules for globalization. Here is why.

Both sets of rules—from the IT regime and aligned non-IT regimes—worked in tandem as they defined roles for economic actors. It is therefore likely that their enforcement mechanisms complemented one another as well. This is especially plausible as several organizations that supported the IT regime also supported other, aligned regimes, and thus ensured that the impacts of these rules complemented and magnified one another. For example, the World Bank prodded governments to open their economies to foreign investment and in so doing, implement the Agreement on Trade-Related Investment Measures that had been negotiated at the WTO. At the same time, it urged them to invite foreign consortia to invest in their telecom sectors.

A study of the ways in which the IT revolution helps push actors into compliance with their new role expectations should therefore pay close attention to IT rules. But at the same time it should examine the enforcement of aligned rules that are not a part of the IT regime.

Discerning the enforcement mechanism as it applied to the case of Egypt requires two steps. The first involves searching for linkages and interactions of two kinds.

(a) *Linkages or interactions between the Egyptian state and other states or international organizations that had stakes in the enforcement of the IT regime or aligned regimes.* For example, we know by now that the European Commission sought to open foreign markets to European exports and that it viewed telecom reform in third countries as part of this process. The next question is whether the Commission and the Egyptian state had any interactions that had to do with the opening of the Egyptian market or with the reform of the Egyptian telecom sector. In fact, as subsequent chapters will explore, they did. Egypt and the EU negotiated an association agreement that promised to open Egypt's economy to European industrial exports. One of its articles provided for technical assistance and cooperation on matters related to telecom.

(b) *Linkages or interactions between organizations that operated inside the Egyptian economy and the Egyptian state, on the one hand, and international actors that supported the new regimes, on the other.* Take Egypt's International Forum, an association of prominent Egyptian entrepreneurs. The organization cultivated ties with global corporations and states, and it shared their desire that the IT regime's norms be implemented in Egypt. At the same time, it maintained close connections to the Egyptian government. As will be explained further on, this organization drew on political resources from corporations and core states and leveraged these as it lobbied the Egyptian state to obtain IT reform.

The second step in this investigation will be to glean the causal powers and liabilities of the actors that were involved in these interactions, using transcendental questions such as the following: "What was it about the European Commission that enabled it to make Egypt promise to open its markets to European exports?" As we will see, the Commission's causal power lay in the EU's very limited dependence on the Egyptian economy. Egypt accounted for only a small share of the EU's trade volume, which enabled the EU to threaten market closure if the Egyptian state failed to cooperate. Meanwhile, the causal liability of the Egyptian state lay in Egypt's dependence on the economy of the EU, which was much larger than the Egyptian economy and absorbed a large share of Egyptian exports. The enforcement mechanism then reads as follows: The European Commission made the Egyptian state sign an association agreement that opened the Egyptian market to European industrial exports.

Egypt experienced a number of enforcement mechanisms. They pushed the indebted Egyptian state to open its economy to the world market. They also pressured it to implement the tenets of the IT regime and aligned norms. In 1999 the combined workings of the enforcement mechanisms bore fruit. The Egyptian state created a ministry for IT that maintained close ties to global corporations and that supported the strategy of integrating Egypt into the world economy.

Investigating One Case but Learning about Many

Once the enforcement mechanisms for the Egyptian case are uncovered, the following question arises: How can findings from the Egyptian case be generalized to other, unexamined, cases? In other words, does what happened in Egypt really reveal what happened during the IT revolution throughout the Third World? As Berger and Luckmann explain, social structure creates roles not for individual actors, but for types of actors ("girl," "woman," "Third World economy"). Therefore, social structure addresses actors as members of a type, rather than as beings that are completely unique. Through its enforcement mechanisms it then demands that the actors fulfill the roles that are associated with their type. Turning this logic around can yield revealing generalizations. The procedure for doing so consists of the following prescriptions:

First, study one single actor and glean the enforcement mechanisms that are at work. How this is done was introduced earlier. Second, ask yourself "As a member of what *type* is the enforcement mechanism addressing the actor?" For example, in negotiating its association agreement with the Egyptian state, the European Commission addressed the state as a member of the type "Southern Mediterranean partner of the EU."[7]

Third, ask yourself "What other members does the identified type contain?" For example, the type "Southern Mediterranean partner of the EU" contains Algeria, Tunisia, Morocco, and about seven more member states. In fact, all of these states signed association agreements with the EU that closely resembled the Egyptian agreement.

Fourth, draw the inference that the specific enforcement mechanism gleaned from the one case you studied will apply to the other social actors whom you have identified as members of the same type. For example, it is very likely that the enforcement mechanism identified for Egypt—"the

Commission made the state sign an association agreement that opened the national market to European industrial exports"—applies to the other Southern Mediterranean partners as well.

In sum, studying one member of a type reveals a great deal about all other members.[8] This is what the next chapters will do.

CHAPTER 5

Egypt in the World Economy

E gyptians like to tell guests that their country is the mother of the world. Indeed, it is an old country, which over the millennia belonged to a variety of cultural regions. Located in the Sahara and bordering on the Mediterranean Sea, it forms a junction between Europe and Africa. Sharing borders with Israel and access to the Red Sea with Saudi Arabia, it is also an integral part of the Middle East. Its society of about eighty million furnishes an armed force of over four hundred thousand (Harb 2003). Thanks to Egypt's entertainment industry, which supplies the Arab Middle East with motion pictures, the local dialect is understood throughout the Arab world.

Ninety percent of Egyptians are Sunni Muslims. About ten percent are Christians. Dating as far back as the fourth century AD, their churches are among the oldest in the world. While most of these ancient houses of worship are located in smaller towns across the countryside, a good number can be found in the old parts of Cairo. Perched between residences of a much later era, they remind visitors of the time when Egypt was part of the Byzantine Empire.

In the days of the Pharaohs, when Europeans scrambled to reach the Bronze Age, Egypt was at the core of the world economy. At different times in their history, ancient Egyptians set up trade routes into the Mediterranean to acquire luxury items from Greece, Cyprus, and Crete. Under the New Kingdom, which lasted from the sixteenth to the eleventh century BC, the state annexed parts of what is today Sudan and large swaths of the region that we now know as the Middle East. Conquest of new territories frequently involved enslavement of the vanquished peoples.

More than a millennium of military and economic dominance ended with Egypt's empire in 343 BC, when the Persians invaded from the east, relegating the country to the status of a peripheral economy. It became a subject of Rome, then Byzantium, and later the Ottoman Empire. When the nineteenth century turned, the European states had long surpassed Egypt and its Ottoman rulers in technological development. They used their advances in weaponry, transportation, and communication to subjugate the African continent and extend their influence into the Middle East. This wave of imperialism engulfed Egypt as well. In 1882 Britain invaded and made the country its de facto colony. Since then, Egyptians—like other societies in the Middle East and in Africa—have struggled with the fact that the rules of the game in which they participate are made in Europe or the United States.

Between World Wars I and II, anti-imperialism swept the Arab world. In Egypt it expressed itself either as secular nationalism or Islamism. By 1952 resistance against the presence of the British and their alliance with Egypt's Albanian puppet monarch had grown to the point of revolution. In October a group of Egyptian officers, with the tacit support of the Islamist Muslim Brotherhood, staged a coup d'état. They took over the reigns of government and ensured that, for the first time in more than two thousand years, the country was governed by its native children. The Young Officers quickly abolished the monarchy and established a republic.

Since then, Egypt has had four presidents—Muhammad Naguib (1953–54), Gamal Abdel Nasser (1954–70), Anwar Sadat (1970–81), and Hosni Mubarak (1981–the present). They presided over an authoritarian state, which depended on the military for stability.

When Egypt's Free Officers seized the reigns of government, they quickly found themselves wedged in between the international and the domestic economy and forced to negotiate the demands of both. The international realm was populated by states with far greater resources than Egypt, who sought to either maintain or improve their ranking in the hierarchy of states. They fell into two camps—the Eastern Bloc and the West. At the center of each alliance were the USSR and the United States, two superpowers that competed for new clients such as Egypt.

In this context, the Egyptian state tried to enhance its own standing in the international pecking order by pursuing three strategies. It worked to increase its capabilities by extracting financial and military assets from the superpowers, which it played off against each other. It positioned itself as a broker of Arab politics, rallied the populations of the Middle East behind it, and thereby increased the political capabilities that it brought to the international bargaining table. It created a third camp of nonaligned nations and positioned itself as their leader.

The domestic terrain that it faced consisted of a large population whose members varied in their access to the means of production, their ideological allegiances, and the extent to which they were affiliated with organizations, which in turn differed in their interests, internal structure and cohesion. In dealing with this rather complex set of actors, the state secured its domestic monopoly over the use of coercive power by inviting some Egyptian organizations into alliances, stifling the activities of others, managing the demands of citizens with both carrot and stick, and crushing its main challengers, the Islamist opposition groups.

The political drama to which this chapter is dedicated played out between 1952, when the postimperial Egyptian state came into being, and 1991, when the Soviet Union collapsed. During those years, the Western part of the world economy was Fordist. Core economies were marked by a tripartite coalition of states, labor unions, and corporations (Cox 1987). In the 1980s the transition to flexible accumulation began; but its impact on the Egyptian economy remained limited, because the new consensus on how the global economy was to be run had not yet matured, and the Eastern Bloc continued to counterbalance the reach of the West.

Examining the years from 1952 to 1991 is necessary because this allows us to situate the state in relation to those actors that in the 1990s created the IT regime and wished to see it enforced, as well as the domestic citizenry who should be the source of all government. This in turn provides a perspective from which to evaluate whether or not Egyptians were deprived of their autonomy when social structure hailed the state into the new role that flexible accumulation had assigned to it.

The state under Nasser tried to overcome the legacy of imperialism. In mediating between the domestic and the international arena, it pursued two separate strategies. At home, it practiced economic nationalism. At first it based this strategy on a Fordist tripartite coalition with domestic capitalists and their companies on one side, the labor unions on the other, and the state in between. When this failed, the state disowned the capitalists and took over their companies. By transforming industry into low-level state organs that produced commodities, the state increased tremendously in size and became the economy's largest employer. With the capitalists out of the picture, it forged a bipartite alliance with the labor unions.

Internationally, the state engaged in a strategy of Arab nationalism, attempting to lead the Arabic-speaking societies and more generally, the nonaligned movement of Third World nations.

These two strategies proved too expensive for Egypt to maintain. To protect its resources, Sadat's state withdrew from Arab nationalism, but it could not renege on its alliance with the labor unions. In 1981, Mubarak became president. He pushed Sadat's retrenchment further.

By the early 1990s the state was heavily in debt and entangled in a web of dependencies on the core states. They could now prod Egypt to embrace a global trade system that emphasized free trade, instantaneous communication, and corporate mobility.

The State under Nasser

In the Middle East, the period after World War I was one of great turmoil. The Ottoman sultan, who had ruled over the region for centuries, had lost the war and looked on as Britain and France dismantled his empire. Control of Syria and Lebanon fell to France. Palestine became a British mandate. Even though Britain discouraged immigration into the Promised Land, Zionist Jews from Europe arrived in droves. In confrontations that frequently turned violent, they competed with the resident Arabs for territory.

In that period, Egypt was governed as a monarchy. Its Albanian king Farouq possessed little splendor. Officially the head of state, he was in fact a puppet of Britain. British troops occupied strategic sites in Egypt, most importantly perhaps the Suez Canal, which separated mainland Egypt from the Sinai Peninsula. Because the canal connected England with India, it was a critical linkage for the British Empire. The agents of King George guarded it jealously.

Egyptians chafed under this foreign rule. During World War II the economy was drained to support the British Empire in its stand-off with the Axis powers, impoverishing the country's middle class. Determined to rid themselves of their Christian overlords, Egyptians by the thousands joined the Muslim Brotherhood, an organization that advocated resistance to the occupation. By the time World War II ended, the organization had chapters all over the country.

In 1948 Egyptians saw an opportunity to reclaim a measure of collective pride. A year earlier, the British government had come to the conclusion that the political cost of controlling the Arab and Jewish insurrections in Palestine outweighed the benefits, and it announced that it would withdraw its troops by mid-1948. Sensing that statehood was imminent, Zionist guerilla organizations intensified their insurgence and expanded their territorial reach. In May 1948, when the last British troops left Haifa, guerilla leader David Ben Gurion proclaimed the state of Israel. Reacting to what they viewed as yet another European intrusion into Muslim land, the governments of Egypt, Transjordan, Lebanon, Syria, Iraq, and Saudi Arabia mounted an attack that aimed to eradicate the nascent state and resurrect the trampled glory of Islam. Things did not go as planned, however. Although the Arab armies outnumbered their Israeli adversaries, they lost the battles, and the war ended with a permanent armistice. Egyptians were distraught. Instead of restoring their pride as Muslims and Egyptians, the war against Israel had added insult to injury.

King Farouq was unable to free Egypt of its foreign yoke, and so a group of disenchanted young army officers decided to oust the monarch. In July 1952 the Free Officers staged their coup. It succeeded without much bloodshed, largely because the Muslim Brotherhood, which at the time was the largest nongovernmental organization in the country, had quietly supported the takeover.

Immediately after the coup, the Free Officers invited the Brotherhood to join the revolutionary cabinet and become part of the Egyptian state. The Brotherhood refused, because it feared compromising its moral purity. Sensing that the popular organization might threaten the existence of their government, the Free Officers decided to crush the Brotherhood, declared it illegal, and jailed many of its members. The occasion for this move was an assassination attempt on Gamal Abdel Nasser, which the government blamed on the Muslim Brotherhood. It is not certain whether the Brotherhood in fact committed this act or whether the government had staged the scene to legitimize subsequent mass arrests (Carré 1984, 12). But from then on the Brotherhood became an illegal opposition force. Throughout the following decades the state sought either to co-opt or suppress the organization, which constituted the most potent challenge to its own legitimacy.

In 1954 Gamal Abdel Nasser, one of the Free Officers, seized control of the state and declared himself Egypt's president. His nationalist ambitions manifested themselves in the two strategies mentioned earlier. The first was economic nationalism. It was directed at the domestic economy and aimed at strengthening Egyptian industry. Its result was a set of norms that embodied a social contract between workers and the state. To enforce these norms, the state created the Egyptian Trade Union Federation (ETUF).

The second strategy, Arab nationalism, was directed at the international economy. It sought to establish Egypt as a regional leader that spearheaded the fight against Israel and resisted the dictates of the superpowers. In order to implement the two strategies, the state manipulated the growing conflict between the Soviet Union and the United States and sapped its own resources.

The Strategy of Economic Nationalism

The Egyptian government based its nationalist economic strategy on the assumption that citizens did productive work not because they were narrowly self-interested, but because they wanted to improve the situation of the Egyptian nation. At first, the government sought to realize its strategy in cooperation with Egyptian capitalists. Nasser's plan was a guided nationalist capitalism. It was based on the idea that class cooperation—between peasants, employed labor, and capitalists—would lead to rapid economic development. To diminish their potential for mobilizing society, Nasser crushed organizations that refused to be won over. The Muslim Brotherhood and communist groups bore the brunt of this crackdown.

Meanwhile, the government cautiously engaged those organizations that did not question its leadership, such as the unions. Under the monarchy there had been a measure of corporatism. That is, a number of guilds had existed, each counting all performers of a particular trade as its members. Each guild had exclusive authority to regulate its sector and communicate its concerns to the government. Between 1952 and 1961 the state expanded this corporatism until it permeated most of the economy (Bianchi 1989). This had political benefits. While parties offered citizens holistic visions for the society that stood in competition with that of the government, corporatism divided the working citizenry into small segments with a narrow range of concerns they could legally raise. In contrast to parties, corporatist organizations would allow the state to segment, channel, and control its relations with the country's workforce.

The corporatization of the economy occurred in stages. In 1953 party competition was abolished. In 1956 the National Union was founded, a single party that would screen access to the newly established National Assembly by selecting nominees. In 1961 the National Union was replaced by the similar Arab Socialist Union; and the labor movement was consolidated with the creation of fifty-nine unions, which in turn were incorporated in a national confederation, the Egyptian Trade Union Federation (ETUF) (Pripstein Posusney 1997, 64–67). The peasants were not integrated into this corporatist hierarchy but maintained their cooperative structure. However, it was so weak that it could not effectively aggregate political demands (Bianchi 1989).

Soon after the revolution, the capitalists thwarted the government's expectations by failing to invest. The state responded by pushing them aside. It sequestered their property and that of rural landlords, and it took over strategic industries, confining private investment to small-scale manufacturing (Ajami 1982). Now the state would drive the nationalist economic project forward and bring about industrialization in cooperation with employed labor. With the socialist decrees of 1961, it obliged the workers to do their best. In return it agreed to provide them with social security. This included guaranteed employment, health benefits, free education, and food subsidies.

Marsha Pripstein Posusney (1997), a professor of political science at Bryant University, describes the social contract between labor and state as follows:

> In what came to be known as "the socialist decrees" of July 1961 'Abd al-Nasir greatly expanded the sphere of the state in the economy, and the protections it afforded to labor. Explicitly suggesting that these measures obligated workers to dedicate their efforts to expanding the national economy, Nasir formally endorsed the idea of a social contract...
>
> A large number of manufacturing and commercial concerns were wholly or partly nationalized by the socialist decrees, greatly expanding the size of the public sector. Concomitantly, a series of laws were issued which aimed at material improvements in workers' living standards. Law 133 of 1961 limited the work week in industrial establishments to 42 hours...A compulsory social insurance scheme was introduced in the 1961 laws and modified in 1962, increasing the employer's contribution from 7 to 17 percent of salary. Further, in an effort to reduce unemployment, the government committed itself to provide administrative jobs to all university graduates and manual employment to all graduates of secondary schools...
>
> In addition, the government obligated itself to guarantee the compliance of private capitalists with minimum wage standards and other laws protecting workers. The Nasir regime also took on more of a distributive function by extending the previously existing system of price subsidies to include many essential food items, as well as energy. This was coupled with a wide-ranging system of price controls. (69f)

The idea behind the socialist decrees was that they would motivate workers to be productive and that this in turn would boost economic growth rates. The unions, meanwhile, were to inculcate the workers with the government's doctrinal views (41). But this plan was a double-edged sword. By passing the decrees and establishing unions to support them, the government had created a set of norms that bound not only the workers, but also the state. The unions turned out to be an organizational stronghold that defended the entitlements of their constituents and prevented the state from pulling out of the social contract in the 1970s, when it realized that the expected economic growth had not set in.

The Strategy of Arab Nationalism

In parallel to his economic nationalism, Nasser attempted to secure a regional leadership role for Egypt. The ideology of Arab nationalism, which held that the Arabic-speaking peoples of the Middle East constituted a nation that should be united, served as his vehicle. By presenting himself as a man of the people who was eager to put Israel in its place and refused to be cowed by the great powers, he antagonized the conservative Saudi government but obtained broad popular approval across the Middle East.

What contributed greatly to Nasser's reputation was the Suez War of 1956, during which Egypt stood up to France, Britain, and Israel without being crushed. As a step toward realizing the idea of Arab unity, Egypt and Syria entered a union in 1958. The endeavor did not amount to much—the Syrian government left the union in 1961 when it began to fear Egyptian domination. From September 1962 to December 1967, the Egyptian army was engaged in the civil war in Yemen.

Financing the Whole Endeavor

The strategies of economic and Arab nationalism needed to be financed. The armed forces required supplies, and the domestic labor force demanded salaries and fringe benefits. In the short run, until the expected economic growth would set in, expenditures for development projects and armament would have to be funded by foreign loans. This was feasible, since the Soviet Union and the United States were competing vigorously for regional clients. The United States had committed itself to protecting the young Israeli state and thus antagonized Arab governments. The Soviet Union, by turning its back on Israel and funding Arab militarization, succeeded after 1958 in orienting the trade relations of Egypt, Syria, Yemen, and Iraq toward the Eastern Bloc.

The story of the Aswan Dam illustrates how easy it was to extract concessions from the rival superpowers. In the early 1950s, Nasser's government decided to build a high dam by the town of Aswan and harness the flow of the Nile for electricity to energize Egypt's industrialization schemes. To build the dam, the government set about negotiating a financing scheme with Britain, the United States, and the World Bank. Since the negotiations were drawn out, Nasser tried to extract better concessions from the United States by citing Soviet willingness to finance the project. Initially this tactic was successful. Seeking to prevent the Soviet Union from gaining a foothold in the region, the United States leaned toward accepting the financing request. However, when Nasser purchased weapons against Israel from the Soviet Union, the U.S. government reneged on the loan offer, and Britain and the World Bank followed suit (Wheelock 1960, 186–204).

Eager to demonstrate that Egypt would not be blackmailed by a foreign power, the government nationalized the British and French-owned Suez Canal Company. This launched the Suez War, which U.S. mediation ended before Egypt could be defeated. Nasser now turned to the Soviet Union for assistance, and it readily agreed. The U.S. government was dismayed. Like President Tito of Yugoslavia or President Nehru of India, Nasser refused to commit himself either to the Eastern Bloc or to the Western camp (Wheelock 1960, 195).

In the end, however, Nasser failed to achieve his political goals. Economic growth did not set in as envisaged. Thanks to the social contract, the state was responsible for providing for a growing workforce without earning the means with which to fulfill that responsibility. At the same time it was over-extending itself regionally by pursuing costly military campaigns for which it did not have the funds.

In the June War of 1967, Israel dealt Egypt a crushing defeat, in the course of which fifteen thousand Egyptian soldiers lost their lives. The war had devastating economic consequences: Egypt lost the Sinai oil fields. The Suez Canal was closed, which meant that the state lost the fees it charged tankers for passing through. Tourism declined steeply. Altogether, the war caused heavy losses in foreign exchange, and the country began to experience balance of payments difficulties.

The government considered approaching the International Monetary Fund (IMF) for a loan but then decided against it (Pripstein Posusney 1997, 82). Instead, it entered a phase of retrenchment, criticizing the public sector for inefficiency, reducing the financial allocations for public housing, and making concessions to the more affluent strata, by, for instance, allowing an increase in the number of private cars that could be imported (Ajami 1982, 476 f).

With its costly strategy of Arab nationalism, the state incurred a rising burden of foreign debt. Its economic nationalism heightened the financial squeeze by creating high welfare expectations among white and blue collar employees. Opting out of the bargain it had struck with labor was impossible, because the unions demanded that the state fulfill its contractual obligations even though it was increasingly unable to do so.

Sadat's Reign: Egypt is Isolated and Indebted

In September 1970 Gamal Abdel Nasser died of a heart attack. Anwar Sadat, his vice president and a fellow Free Officer, took the reigns of office. He inherited a troublesome situation. Nasser's expensive foreign policies constituted a mortgage for the economy in general and the state in particular. Compounding the problem, the Egyptian population was growing at a rapid pace, straining the state's capacity to provide employment, housing, and schooling. The government had the option of either drastically cutting expenditures and pulling out of the social contract or reducing its foreign policy obligations and locating new external sources of funding.

The president tried to withdraw from the nationalist economic project, but countervailing pressure from domestic organizations was strong. The unions resisted privatization of state-owned enterprises, and a structural adjustment agreement that Sadat negotiated with the IMF led to riots. Even though the state sought backing from the private sector and verbally attacked the public sector, it had to live up to its commitment to guaranteed employment, health benefits, and food subsidies for a growing population, whose ability to feed itself was declining. The effort to withdraw from the nationalist economic project was unsuccessful and resulted in a standoff between a small segment of newly rich and old rich private sector operators, on the one hand, and the employed workforce with union support, on the other. The state found itself unable to satisfy either side.

To ease the financial pressure, it gave up on its strategy of Arab nationalism, which was to a large degree based on anti-Zionism. By achieving rapprochement with Israel the state could hope to gain back the Sinai and stop sinking money into a war that it was unable to win. By making peace with its former enemy and aligning itself firmly with the United States, the state gained access to new loans and could continue to honor its obligations under the social contract, even if not to the satisfaction of the contract partners. The details of the decline of economic nationalism and Arab nationalism, laid out here, reveal the factors that led to Egypt's failure to advance into the core of the global economy.

Economic Nationalism under Attack

Under Sadat the state carried on with Nasser's efforts at domestic retrenchment. Trying to counterbalance the unions, which were opposed to any economic retreat of the state, it encouraged the creation of business associations. By inviting the private sector's most prominent members into policy workshops with high-level government officials, it also granted that sector preferential access to the state (Ajami 1982).

In June 1974 Sadat secured passage of Law 43, launching his famed open door policy (*infitah*). The law opened the economy to numerous Western imports that had previously been prohibited. It provided generous incentives to Western investors (Pripstein Posusney 1997, 173). Law 188 of 1975 expanded on these policies. It ended the public sector monopoly over foreign trade and allowed the private sector to import most goods on its own. To attract investors, he supported very limited political liberalization—so limited, in fact, that Ninette Fahmy of the American University in Cairo finds it more appropriate to speak of political diversification. Specifically, Sadat supported the creation of three "platforms" within the Arab Socialist Union: A center platform, which represented the government, one to the left, and one to the right. Both left and right functioned as "loyal opposition." Since the government platform had privileged access to logistical and communication facilities, says Fahmy (2002, 62–64), it easily won a majority in the 1976 parliamentary election. Because of this favorable outcome, Sadat agreed to the transformation of the three platforms into political parties. The center government platform became the National Democratic Party.

The economic laws of 1974 and 1975 notwithstanding, domestic manufacturers continued to be protected by high tariff barriers. Still, many more foreign goods were imported than had been in the past, and this made it difficult for state-owned enterprises to sell their output (Dessouki 1991, 262).

The *infitah* was controversial because it assaulted the tradition of import substitution and the nationalist rationale that had motivated it. To generate support within Egyptian society, the state cautiously mobilized the middle class of white collar employees. For that purpose it created a new syndicate of commercial employees whose 160,000 members supported the open door policy. To gain the acquiescence of the older professional syndicates, the state encouraged them to go into business with the private sector (Bianchi 1989, 85). Sadat hoped that if he allowed them to profit, they would come aboard the *infitah* and persuade the rank and file of the syndicates to do the same. In 1978, the Egyptian Businessmen's Association was founded. Its goal was to free market forces, abolish bureaucratic and fiscal hurdles to private sector activities, and provide resources for businesses (Awad 1991, 29).

With the organizational landscape thus remolded, the government launched its attack on the "socialist gains" of Nasserism in the realm of discourse. It allowed ministries and civil society to criticize the public sector. Professor Ali Eddin Hilal Dessouki of Cairo University explains that starting in 1974, the weaknesses of the public sector became a constant topic for public discussion (Dessouki 1991, 262). By making the rights, obligations, and performance of the public sector a matter of debate, the state began to erode the notion that the social contract was an immutable fact. In addition, the *infitah* made possible the staggered privatization of the public sector through joint ventures (Pripstein Posusney 1997, 186).

However, Sadat's policy of state retreat ran into problems. First, foreign investors remained reluctant to move their operations to Egypt. Early in 1976 it was announced that only 17 of 144 approved foreign investment projects had actually been implemented (EB 1977, 304). Second, those social groups who were put on the defensive—unionized employees of the parastatals[1]—refused to be muted. The unions successfully fought efforts at outright privatization of public sector enterprises (Pripstein Posusney 1997, 177f). They also contested increased private sector participation in parastatals through joint ventures (178).

The *infitah* thus did not radically alter state-society relations, nor did it lead to anything resembling a liberal market economy. Instead, a private sector grew stronger beside a much larger and dominant public sector. While allowing the private sector to grow, the government was unable to curtail the rights of the public sector effectively. In addition, it needed to dole out select privileges to various segments of civil society in order to win their support in the face of mounting budget problems. As a result, the domestic economy began to fragment into different enclaves, a process that would gain momentum under Mubarak (Bianchi 1989, 37; Springborg 1989).

Far from solving the country's economic difficulties, the *infitah* exacerbated inflationary pressures. With the expanding possibilities for consumption of foreign products and the liberalization of the exchange rate, purchasing hard currency became more expensive. In 1976, the rate of inflation was 30 percent per year (EB 1977, 305). The standard of living of the middle and lower classes, whose income was fixed, deteriorated as a result. Many state employees had to take on additional jobs to complement their small government salaries.

The End of Arab Nationalism

The state's domestic strategy did little to relieve its financial burden. Its international strategy, however, fared better. Soon after Sadat came to power, he departed from the foreign alliances that his predecessor had forged. In 1972 he expelled the Soviet advisers from the country. At the same time he entered into secret negotiations with the United States, seeking an accommodation with Israel that would restore the Sinai peninsula to Egypt and end the war of attrition that had been underway since the 1967 defeat.

Preoccupied with the Vietnam War, the U.S. government failed to respond to Egyptian overtures. To attract its attention, Sadat, in 1973, launched a limited attack against Israel, which raised the specter of a direct superpower confrontation. In support of the offensive, the oil exporting Arab countries boycotted economies that entertained friendly relations with Israel. This 1973 oil embargo led to a surge in world oil prices, quickening the transition to flexible accumulation in the United States and Western Europe. The war made it clear that Egypt was pivotal not only to regional stability, but to the economic security of the industrialized world.

Finally, the U.S. government paid attention. The January 1974 separation of forces accord between Egypt and Israel induced the United States to commit $8.5 million for an initial program to help clear the Suez Canal of war debris and to begin the reconstruction of the canal cities (Weinbaum 1986, 42). In 1974, Secretary of State Henry Kissinger engaged in shuttle diplomacy between Egypt and Israel, facilitating a rapprochement. After asking Congress for $250 million in aid for Egypt, President Richard Nixon paid a visit to Cairo (EB 1975, 264f). The U.S. government sought to ensure that its aid had a positive impact on the economy, so that the Soviet Union would not regain influence over Egypt (Weinbaum 1986, 33). In 1975 the U.S. Agency for International Development (USAID) opened its field office in Cairo. By 1977 U.S. aid to Egypt stood at about $900 million per year (EB 1978 352). It was USAID's task to funnel the money into development projects that fulfilled the aspirations of both the U.S. Congress and the Egyptian government.

In 1978 President Sadat embarked on an historic trip to Jerusalem. In the following year he and Israel's prime minister Menachem Begin signed the Camp David Accords, which restored the Sinai to Egypt and institutionalized a peace between the two countries. With this peace treaty, Sadat formally rejected Nasser's nationalist foreign policy, of which anti-Zionism had been an integral aspect. The Arab states reacted with anger, excluding Egypt from the Arab League and terminating development aid. The core states, however, rewarded Sadat's action with new loans (Weinbaum 1986, 38). The United States alone paid handsomely: By 1983 U.S. military and economic assistance exceeded two billion dollars (table 5.1).

Table 5.1 U.S. assistance to Egypt, 1980–2000

Year	Military assistance in million $	Economic assistance in million $	Year	Military assistance in million $	Economic assistance in million $
1981	551	829	1991	1,302	783
1982	902	771	1992	1,302	893
1983	1,327	750	1993	1,302	748
1984	1,367	853	1994	1,301	606
1985	1,177	1,065	1995	1,301	976
1986	1,246	1,069	1996	1,301	824
1987	1,302	820	1997	1,301	811
1988	1,302	718	1998	1,301	828
1989	1,302	817	1999	1,301	860
1990	1,296	901	2000	1,301	741

Source: U.S. Census Bureau.

Nevertheless, in the 1970s the Egyptian state maneuvered itself into an increasing bind. At the time of Nasser's death in 1970, Egypt's total public civilian external debt had been at $1.7 billion (Amin 1995, 7). Under Sadat this debt grew dramatically. In the first half of the 1970s, the state imported an increased amount of capital goods (11). Because agricultural self-sufficiency had decreased, it had to purchase more staples on the world market, and it frequently did so with high-interest loans. In the mid-1970s Sadat was forced to enter a structural adjustment agreement. As a condition for the loan, the state had to cut back subsidies for basic food items. Sadat implemented this condition, triggering riots that almost toppled him and forced him to withdraw the measure. By 1981 total civilian external public debt, both long and medium term, had risen to $14.3 billion (12).

Mubarak until 1991: No More Bold Strategies

By the end of the decade, President Sadat was isolated. In response to the brutal suppression that Islamist groups experienced at the government's hands, the Islamist movement radicalized. Syndicates and other factions of civil society resented the state's rapprochement with Israel, because it failed to resolve the Palestinian problem. Large segments of the population were angry at their declining living standard. Increasingly insecure, the president in 1981 ordered the arrest of fifteen hundred individuals whose views spanned the political spectrum (Heikal 1983). By that year the radical Islamist *Jihad* organization had managed to infiltrate the Egyptian armed forces. In October 1981 three of its members participated in the parade commemorating the 1973 October War. They approached the stand where President Sadat and Vice President Hosni Mubarak were sitting. Then, they opened fire and killed Sadat.

A bomber pilot by training and vice president since 1975, Hosni Mubarak suddenly rose to the helm of the state. Sadat had inherited an uncomfortable legacy from Nasser, and Mubarak's position was equally difficult. By 1982, the state had become the world's tenth largest debtor (EB 1983, 338). Inflation was soaring; the annual rate was between 25 and 30 percent (EB 1982, 241). The economy was fragmented. Labor was still formally privileged. But those who were employed by the state saw their standard of living erode and protested further incursions into their privileges—either through their organizations or through wildcat strikes. Capitalists had returned to the political landscape and become more vocal. Radical Islamist groups engaged in regular confrontations with the state. Although the Islamists were far too weak to overthrow the government, they could make Egypt unattractive as a destination for tourism and investment.

President Mubarak was lucky in one regard: Sadat had signed the peace treaty with Israel and come under fire for it. Mubarak could therefore reap its rewards without having to shoulder the blame.

An End to Economic Strategy?

According to Middle-East expert Robert Bianchi, Mubarak's state moved from consumptive to productive *infitah*:

> The Mubarak government has tried to strengthen the Egyptian element in the private sector equation even more by redefining the major role of foreign participation as the contribution of advanced technology instead of the mere provision of capital. By carving out a protected market for domestic producers in light industry, the architects of the "productive *infitah*" are hoping to direct toward manufacturing some of the local profits acquired during the earlier period of liberal importing. This amounts to a new division of labor in which foreign capital is being assigned the task of long-term industrial deepening while native capital is invited to turn toward lucrative import substitution. The result has been a clear "re-Egyptianization" of many consumer goods. (Bianchi 1989, 51)

However, while Bianchi discerns a shift in economic strategy, Robert Springborg, director of the American Research Center in Egypt, doubts that the president had a political vision at all. In Springborg's presentation (1989), Mubarak treated domestic politics as a series of isolated issues, not as the staging ground for a coherent political strategy (40). He protected himself against criticism by "not becoming personally identified with controversial policy initiatives, allowing and probably encouraging them to be pressed not even by the Prime Minister, to whom he is too close, but by cabinet ministers, from whom he is insulated" (62).

The state continued to cultivate the private sector. The Ministry of Social Affairs, in charge of licensing voluntary organizations, helped in this process. It readily granted licenses to business associations. Other organizations had to struggle for the permission to operate legally. In addition, capitalists enjoyed privileged access to the formal electoral process. In fact the parties, which had become more numerous under Mubarak, represented solely the bourgeoisie, because peasants and workers were too dependent on the state to support opposition parties openly. Furthermore, in a political system where the parliament was weak and could be suspended at the whim of the president, winning a seat in the National Assembly primarily served the purpose of obtaining patronage resources. Influencing the nation's policies was of secondary importance. For this reason the parties' leaders did not see the need for appealing to non-bourgeois groups (Springborg 1989, 164 and 187).

Despite the fact that the National Assembly was weak, the state took care to ensure that it remained docile. Its method consisted of doing whatever was necessary to secure electoral victories for the president's party: It placed obstacles to party formation through the licensing process; it altered the electoral system in between elections; it resorted to intimidation during the elections and at times engaged in ballot forgery. Once elections were over, parliamentarians who had won against candidates of the National Democratic Party frequently joined it.

The state carried on with its efforts to pull out of the social contract. Drawing its lesson from the 1977 bread riots, it treaded with care. When it had to cut subsidies for bread, it instructed its bakeries not to raise the price per loaf; instead, they were to reduce the size of the loaves. Rather than reneging on the employment guarantee, the state increased the job search period for university graduates before they could apply for entitlement under the guaranteed employment scheme. By the mid-1980s Mubarak abandoned the time-honored practice of appointing the president of the Egyptian Trade Union Federation to his cabinet. The state's efforts were only moderately successful, however. Rather than declining in size, the public sector continued to grow (Dessouki 1991, 263; Pripstein Posusney 1997, 16 and 113).

Inflation remained high. From 1980 to 1987 the consumer price index tripled. Those hardest hit by inflation were civil servants and white-collar employees in public enterprises. This forced more and more civil servants to engage in moonlighting (Zaytoun 1991).

The unions were sufficiently entrenched to forestall an open assault on the social contract. Cairo University's Ali Eddin Hillal Dessouki (1991, 266–267) points out that until 1989 Mubarak refused to consider proposals for the sale of the public sector seriously, in order to avoid a direct confrontation with the labor unions. Why this was the case becomes clear when looking at the size of the ETUF. By 1991, the ETUF served as the umbrella organization for 22 unions, established along industrial lines. Its membership amounted to 4.5 million workers from both the public and the private sector, endowing the organization with political clout (Awad 1991, 278).

In its relationship with the Islamist movement, the state pursued an ambivalent strategy. The Muslim Brotherhood, which represented the Islamist mainstream, remained officially banned, as it had been since 1954. This alone prevented the organization from entering parliament as a political party. While the state tried to control the Brotherhood, it was well aware of the strong support the organization enjoyed among an increasingly conservative population and of the radicalization of the Islamist movement. In its effort to co-opt the moderate factions of the movement, the state allowed individual Brothers to enter parliament in 1987. The intention was to broaden the political consensus so that it would cover the Islamist mainstream. The Brotherhood, however, was not going to be co-opted with cosmetic concessions. Presented with obstacles in the electoral process, it sought alternative venues through which it tried to influence state policy. The economy's corporatist structure provided venues for doing so, and after 1985 Islamists won elections to the boards of various syndicates.

The radicalized factions of the Islamist movement remained excluded from the formal political process. Their strategy was one of head-on confrontation with the state, and the state responded in kind: In 1983 alone, 176 radical Islamists were put on trial, accused of plotting to overthrow the government (EB 1984, 338).

All in all, the political climate became more polarized. Confrontations between workers and the state increased in number. The same was true for clashes between radical Islamists and the state and between radical Islamists and Coptic Christians. The president reacted to Sadat's assassination by obtaining parliament's approval to rule under emergency laws. These approvals have been renewed to the present day. Among others, the laws restrict the right to assembly and allow detention without trial.

These domestic troubles gave new stature to the armed forces. Relegated to a minor foreign policy role by the Camp David accords, the military could now play a new political role as guarantor of internal security. Mubarak courted the military. He provided the officers with salary increases and a wide range of new benefits. He also allowed the military to expand into civilian production and encouraged them to enter into joint ventures with the private sector (Springborg 1989, 103, 117). This led Springborg to conclude that during the 1980s the bourgeoisie and the armed forces were the two social groups whose star was ascending.

Creditors Close In

While Egypt's government tried to steer the course between a growing private sector and the unions, it experienced an international environment that was gradually changing. Under Ronald Reagan the United States had bled the USSR in Afghanistan, and it was becoming clear that the Soviet Union was economically less powerful than intelligence analysts had assumed. In 1985 Mikhail Gorbachev became secretary general of the Communist Party. He began charting a new course of economic reconstruction in the Soviet Union and sought détente with the states of the West. The bipolar world order slowly moved toward unipolarity, leaving the United States as the sole remaining superpower. In 1986, one year after Gorbachev's election, the Uruguay round of trade negotiations began in Punta del Este. In 1994 this round would produce the World Trade Organization, a new entity that supported the dismantling of barriers to trade more effectively than the old GATT secretariat had done. With the Soviet Union weakened, smaller states had fewer opportunities for playing the superpowers off against one another and extracting financial concessions. Moreover, a new economic consensus took shape among the core states into which peripheral economies would have to be integrated.

Meanwhile, Egypt was submerged under a mountain of debt: "Egyptian foreign external debt stock increased to over US$ 40 billion in 1989... Egypt was placed among the most heavily indebted countries in the world in terms of the absolute size of external debt and amongst the five countries with the highest debt to GDP ratio" (Nassar et al. 1992).

Consequently Mubarak's approach to regional politics was subdued. By letting the peace with Israel turn cold, the government was able to lead Egypt back into the fold of those states that had objected to the peace initiative. In 1984, Mubarak worked on improving relations with the USSR, while remaining firmly aligned with the United States (EB 1985, 486). This rapprochement enabled him later to negotiate a rescheduling of debt with the Soviet Union. At the same time Egypt drew on large U.S. loans (table 5.1).

In 1986 Egypt was hit by the Middle East oil price slump. As a medium-sized oil exporter, the state experienced this decline in oil prices as decrease in revenues from oil exports and as decline in worker remittances. Compounding Egypt's already precarious financial position this crisis caused Egypt "deep trouble" with its creditors from the core (EB 1987, 449f).

The government therefore entered negotiations for an IMF loan. In May 1987 the IMF approved an eighteen-month standby credit program (EB 1988, 409). As a major condition, the Egyptian state was to reduce its budget deficit by means of spending restraint: subsidies to basic consumer goods were to be cut, energy subsidies had to be eliminated, public investment was to be curtailed, and the Egyptian pound had to be devalued. In addition, the state was to expand its revenue base by improving its tax collection procedures (Awad 1991, 281; EB 1989, 408). In response to this agreement, the Paris Club of creditor states decided to reschedule civilian and military debt-servicing payments in the amount twelve billion dollars over ten years, including a grace period of five years (EB 1988, 409). Thirty years earlier the Egyptian state had defied foreign domination by engaging the greater powers and their clients in confrontations. Now these foreign actors returned to

Egypt, this time not as colonizers, but as economic advisors and creditors. And with them they brought globalization.

Fearful of social unrest, the cornered Egyptian state stalled at several conditions contained in the loan agreement. Mubarak sought a longer timetable than the one required by the IMF. To that end he lobbied Western leaders bilaterally, hoping they would pressure the IMF into approving his slower reform program (EB 1989, 408). In 1989, Egypt and the IMF negotiated another standby credit agreement. It would allow the country to negotiate a fresh rescheduling of debt payments with the Paris Club, covering eight billion–ten billion dollars in debt service payments due between June 1988 and December 1990 (EB 1990, 427).

In 1991, when Saddam Hussein invaded Kuwait and Egypt proved to be a loyal ally to the U.S.-led coalition, creditors granted the state a respite. But pressures from the global economy grew stronger. Eventually the unions would have to give way.

CHAPTER 6

Creditors Close In

By the late 1980s, all anticolonialist bravado had vanished. Egypt's state had painted itself into a corner: chafing under a heavy debt burden, it found itself entangled in a web of dependencies that seemed to permanently shackle it to the creditor states of the global economic core. All it could offer the creditors in return for their generosity was continued peace with Israel, the promise not to let the nation fall into the hands of Islamists, and the agreement not to align itself with the Soviet Union.

Domestically, the state faced contradictory demands. The unions continued to insist on the entitlements of the social contract, and they balked at suggestions that state-owned enterprises might be sold to reduce the public debt burden. Private sector companies had gained some political ground, but they had to compete with state-owned competitors and faced a regulatory framework that contained much red tape and little transparency. The Islamist movement, which had once consisted exclusively of the Muslim Brotherhood, was now fragmented. The moderate Brotherhood continued to enjoy widespread support among the population. Although the government perceived it as a threat to its legitimacy, it could not afford to crush it and so pursued a strategy that oscillated between co-optation and exclusion from the political system. While the Brotherhood tried to work with the state, using the political openings the government granted it, a number of small radicalized groups rejected the system in its entirety. They either founded their own counter-societies, or attempted to undermine the political system and assassinate its leaders.

The state was trapped by the necessity to ask core states for financial resources and its own inability to strip the unions of the benefits of the social contract. Importantly for this analysis, the economy over which it presided looked very different from the model economy that the Washington Consensus envisioned. If, as sociologists Peter Berger and Thomas Luckmann suggest, social structure had disciplinary effects, these effects should have made themselves felt in the 1990s. In the form of specific enforcement mechanisms, they should have pushed the state to fall in line with the requirements of flexible accumulation.

The First Three Enforcement Mechanisms Summarized

Using the procedure outlined in chapter four, this chapter uncovers three such mechanisms. In all three cases, the causal power of core actors was based on their financial strength. The causal liability of the Egyptian state, in turn, was based on its financial weakness.

Mechanism One

In the early 1990s, the Egyptian state entered a structural adjustment program, which the World Bank administered and the International Monetary Fund (IMF) reviewed. The program took years to implement. It entailed, among others, the dismantling of barriers to trade, the privatization of state-owned enterprises, and the floating of the exchange rate.

What was it about the state and its creditors that brought the program about? The causal powers and liabilities that emerge from this transcendental question are based on the financial strength of the Paris Club and the financial weakness of the Egyptian state. Specifically, in its relation with the indebted Egyptian state, the financially strong World Bank, the IMF, and the Paris Club of creditor states had the causal power to *demand* that the state implement a structural adjustment program. Meanwhile, in its relationship with the financially strong World Bank, the IMF, and the Paris Club of creditor states, the indebted Egyptian state had the liability of having to *accept* a structural adjustment program.

These powers and liabilities produced the first enforcement mechanism, as follows:

> **Enforcement Mechanism One:** The World Bank, in cooperation with the Paris Club of creditor states and the IMF, *imposed* a structural adjustment program on the Egyptian state.

Mechanism Two

In 1995, the European Commission and the states of the Southern Mediterranean established the Euro-Mediterranean Partnership that was aimed at strengthening the economic and cultural integration of the Southern Mediterranean economies with the European Union (EU). In the context of this partnership, the Commission negotiated a bilateral association agreement. It stipulated that Egypt, over a period of up to fifteen years, would dismantle its tariffs on industrial imports coming from the EU. In return, the EU offered Egypt improved concessions for agricultural products. These were, however, subject to regular renegotiation. The agreement therefore improved the bilateral trading conditions for the EU permanently and to a greater extent than it did for Egypt.

What was it about the Egyptian state and the Commission that led them to sign an association agreement that favored the EU? The causal powers and liabilities that emerge from this question are due to the fact that the EU possessed a large market while Egypt had a small one. This gave the EU the authority to threaten Egypt with ending its preferential access to the European market, should it fail to comply with European demands.[1] The threat—even if not openly expressed—was credible, because exports to Egypt constituted only a small percentage of Europe's gross domestic product (GDP). The loss that the EU would have incurred by ending its preferential trade relations with Egypt would therefore have been negligible. Egypt, on the other hand, possessed only a small market, and preferential trade with Europe formed a large percentage of its GDP. If the EU had denied Egypt its preferential market access, the Egyptian economy would have shrunk considerably, and the state would have had to face the wrath of Egyptians who lost their livelihood. Consequently, in its relationship with the Egyptian state, the European Commission had the causal power to *demand* that Egypt sign an agreement that opened Egypt to European industrial exports. Meanwhile, in its relationship with the European Commission, the Egyptian state had the causal liability of having to *accept* an agreement that opened Egypt to European industrial exports.

These causal powers and liabilities produced the second enforcement mechanism, as follows:

Enforcement Mechanism Two: The European Commission *made* the Egyptian state *sign* an association agreement that opened the Egyptian market to European industrial exports.

Mechanism Three

This mechanism operated in a more complex fashion than the previous two, for here the interaction involved not only the Egyptian state on the one hand and actors from the core on the other. Instead, it involved a third party—Egypt's globalization elite—that mediated between the other two. Here is how. During the 1990s, development organizations such as the World Bank and the U.S. Agency for International Development (USAID) implemented programs to improve the situation of Egypt's private sector. These efforts fostered Egypt's "globalization elite," a set of English-speaking wealthy entrepreneurs with close connections to companies in the core economies. By fostering the globalization elite, USAID and the World Bank helped create an Egyptian constituency for globalization, and they enabled it to lobby the state on behalf of flexible accumulation. Hence, in its relationship with the Egyptian state, USAID and the World Bank had the causal power to support the globalization elite with financial and political resources, thereby *increasing this elite's causal power to demand* an export- and trade-friendly policy from the state. The state meanwhile, in its relationship with the globalization elite, had the causal liability of *having to give the demands* of the globalization elite *a hearing* and possibly act on them.

These causal powers and liabilities produced the third enforcement mechanism, as follows:

Enforcement Mechanism Three: The World Bank and USAID *raised the causal power of the globalization elite to authoritatively demand* flexibility and IT connectivity from the state.

The Collapse of the USSR as Background Factor

All these mechanisms worked on the background of the collapse of the Soviet Union, which occurred between 1989 and 1991. The implosion altered the power relations between the Egyptian state and the core actors, by weakening the former and strengthening the latter in two ways. First, the Soviet collapse eliminated a source of Cold War rent for Egypt. As chapter five showed, the Egyptian state had benefited from Soviet-American competition for allies in the Middle East. As a result, it had been able to collect more generous loans than it could have in the absence of superpower rivalry. When the Soviet Union ceased to be, the United States could be more selective in funding peripheral allies. The U.S. Congress recognized this fact, and in the early 1990s it moved to reduce assistance to foreign countries. Instead of providing aid, it wanted to strengthen trade ties with those economies and open their markets to U.S. exports (USAID, Center for Development Information and Evaluation 1994, v). This decision impacted Egypt directly. In 1998 the U.S. government decided to lower economic assistance to Egypt by 5 percent per year, so that by 2008 the nonmilitary aid volume would have shrunk by 50 percent (American Chamber of Commerce in Egypt 2003). In light of this, the Egyptian government needed to come up with ways to strengthen its economy and extract the assistance streams that remained accessible.

Second, resistance to a paradigm is only as good as the alternative vision that drives it. The collapse of the USSR discredited both socialism and state capitalism as economic paradigms. In 1989, Johns Hopkins University's Francis Fukuyama famously announced the end of history and the universalization of Western liberal democracy as "the final form of human government." This statement, which fired the imagination of America's educated public, shows what an ideological effect the Soviet implosion had. Free market capitalism no longer appeared as one of many ideological constructs, but as a natural state of being.

Peripheral economies lacked alternative metanarratives that could have guided resistance to flexible accumulation. By forestalling alternative trajectories, the Soviet collapse increased the ideological dependency of peripheral states on their counterparts from the core. The following analysis will paint this picture in richer detail.

Egypt Undergoes Structural Adjustment (Mechanism One)

By early 1990 the Egyptian state choked on decades worth of debt, and all signals were set towards structural adjustment. But then Iraq's leader Saddam Hussein invaded Kuwait, and President Mubarak did something that earned him the gratitude of core governments: He supported the U.S.-led coalition that formed to repel the invasion. By furnishing thirty thousand troops to the coalition, President Mubarak helped the United States make quick tactical progress and showed the world that America acted in agreement with Arab governments.

In response to this gesture, the U.S. government announced in October 1990 that it would forgive $7.1 billion of military debt that Egypt had accumulated. A month later the Paris Club of creditor nations followed suit. It announced that it would cut Egypt's $20 billion debt burden by half (Weiss and Wurzel 1998, 24 and 44). By May 1991 the Club decided on the exact modalities by which this debt relief would happen. Egypt was to undergo a structural adjustment program. The Paris Club would provide its debt relief in three stages. The first stage would happen in July 1991, and 15 percent would be cancelled. Then, Egypt would implement the structural adjustment program, and the IMF would review its progress. If the IMF was satisfied with the country's performance, the state would receive another 15 percent of debt relief in January 1993. It would continue with structural adjustment and undergo another performance review. If the review was positive, the Paris Club would forgive another 20 percent of the debt in July 1994. The remaining $10.1 billion would be rescheduled over twenty-five years (EB 1992, 379). The World Bank supported this plan with an adjustment loan and a detailed strategy for adjustment.[2]

This procedure gave the IMF and the World Bank leverage over the Egyptian government, as they could withhold performance reviews. It also motivated the government to swallow the bitter pill of economic reform. At first, Egypt fulfilled its adjustment commitments reluctantly and incurred the ill will of the IMF. As a result, the IMF delayed the second tranche of debt relief by one year. The third installment materialized not in July 1994, but in October 1996 (Weiss and Wurzel 1998, 65–66). As a result of this reform pressure, the state modified its tariffs, privatized several companies, reformed the banking system, created a stock market, reduced the budget deficit, and passed a land reform law.

In 1991, the government took the first step and unified the exchange rate. In 1992, it eliminated all export taxes. A tariff reduction from a maximum of 120 percent in 1991 to 70 percent in 1994, followed (EB 1992, 379; Handy et al. 1998, 60 and 65).

The state also laid the foundations for privatization of state assets. In 1991 it passed a law removing public sector companies from their line ministries and bringing them under the supervision of holding companies, whose task was to privatize the parastatals. Beginning in 1992, public sector companies no longer received explicit subsidies from the state budget (Handy et al. 1998, 48–50; Khattab 1999). Mokhtar Khattab, an undersecretary of Egypt's Ministry of Public Enterprise, explains:

> Privatization in Egypt went through two distinct stages. The achievements of the first stage, which lasted from 1991 to 1996, were modest. The government sold only three companies to strategic investors using direct negotiations: Coca Cola, Pepsi, and Al Nasr Boilers. It floated majority shares, ranging from 5 to 20 percent, of 16 companies in the stock market and it sold a majority stake in 10 companies to their employees. (Khattab 1999, 96)

The capital market also changed. First, the government reformed the banking sector by raising private sector participation: In the 1970s it had allowed the private sector into the banking system through the establishment of joint venture banks, in which state banks held part of the shares; in late 1993 the government began to sell public bank equity in these banks.

Second, in 1992 the state created a stock market by having the National Assembly pass a new capital market law. This law established the Capital Market Authority and authorized it to supervise stock trades. It also created rules by which investment and brokerage companies were to operate; and by eradicating taxes on stock and bond income, it encouraged investors to invest in stock. In addition, the state allowed foreign investors into the market, strengthened the rules for financial disclosure, and established a system for dispute resolution (Handy et al. 1998, 59–60; Khattab 1999, 102).

Furthermore, the state made stop-and-go efforts to reduce the budget deficit. For this purpose it expanded tax collection and eliminated subsidies. In May 1991 it increased the price for gasoline, cooking gas, and public transportation. Three days later it introduced a new sales tax that covered most goods and services. However, to prevent criticism from public sector employees, the government reduced the impact of these measures on many ordinary Egyptians: In July 1991 it raised public sector wages by 15 percent (EB 1992, 379).

Thus, Egypt's financial weakness forced the state to bow to the demands of its creditors and move its economy toward compliance with the model of the Washington Consensus. The state clearly took the reform steps because its creditors made debt relief contingent on implementing the reform program. The structural adjustment program therefore constitutes an enforcement mechanism.

The European Union Seeks An Association Agreement (Mechanism Two)

While Egypt stepped into its structural adjustment program, EU member states worried about their periphery in the Southern Mediterranean. They were specifically troubled by Muslim fundamentalism and potential poverty migration to the north. To secure stability and prosperity within its borders, the EU needed to forestall any political experiments that might call into question its normative underpinnings, threaten its borders, or disrupt its supply and trade flows. The EU therefore sought to bind the periphery closer to the center (Saleh 2007).

For that purpose the Commission devised regional cooperation schemes that projected its vision of trade and governance into its periphery. In the Southern Mediterranean, where Egypt was located, this drive manifested itself in the Euro-Mediterranean Partnership.

In 1995 the Commission convinced the European Council that a Euro-Mediterranean Partnership would create a stable environment surrounding the EU. Stability was to be achieved by integrating the Mediterranean countries into the world economy in general and deepening their economic ties to the EU in particular (European Commission, Directorate General 1B External Relations 1998).

Formally established in Barcelona in November 1995, the Partnership involved ten states: Algeria, Egypt, Israel, Jordan, Lebanon, Morocco, the Palestinian Authority, Syria, Tunisia, and Turkey. It had three aspects: political and security, economic and financial, and social and cultural. These aspects were to be realized through two tracks. The multilateral track juxtaposed the EU with the collectivity of partner states. On this track two ministerial meetings and five meetings at expert level were to be held each half-year. The Commission supervised the day-to-day work of the multilateral track. It also administered the EU's funding package for the Partnership.

In addition, the Partnership had a bilateral track, which juxtaposed the EU and each individual partner state. In the past, reaching back to the 1970s, the European Community had concluded cooperation agreements with the Southern Mediterranean states that granted them free access to the Common Market for most industrial products. In addition the agreements contained limited mutual concessions for agricultural imports, which were renegotiated on a regular basis, and they had multiyear financial protocols attached. With these the Community committed itself to providing financial support for its southern neighbors, which were much weaker economically. In fact, they were so weak that Community concessions for industrial products from the south posed little actual threat for European manufacturers. Meanwhile, the agricultural concessions that the European Community granted remained limited in order to safeguard European farmers.

Now, under the bilateral track of the Partnership, these old agreements were to be replaced by new ones that aimed at creating a free trade area between the EU and each individual partner economy. The demands that these treaties made on the economies of the Southern Mediterranean reached farther than those of their predecessor agreements. Specifically, the new association agreements required each Mediterranean economy to reciprocate the preferential treatment that it had previously received from the EU. It was to dismantle all industrial duties over a period of twelve–fifteen years, enabling competitive European companies to import their products into North African and Middle Eastern markets.

Table 6.1 contains trade data from 1994 for all Southern Mediterranean partners of the EU, except the Palestinian Authority, whose trade relations were controlled by Israel, and Turkey, which enjoyed a special status as it sought to become an EU member and entered a customs union with the EU in 1996. The table shows that for all countries, with the exception perhaps of Jordan and Lebanon, export to the EU constituted a very sizable proportion of the GDP. Consequently, producers in the country would have suffered considerably had the EU let the old trade agreements run out without

Table 6.1 Trade flows between the EU and eight Southern Mediterranean countries in 1994

Country	Country's exports to the EU in million $	EU exports to country in million $	EU exports to country as percent of EU gross domestic product	Country's exports to the EU as percent of country's gross domestic product
Algeria	6900.5	4930.4	0.07	16.22
Egypt	3336.5	4930.4	0.07	6.43
Israel	5163.6	13147.7	0.18	6.92
Jordan	110.2	1643.5	0.02	1.77
Lebanon	108.9	3286.9	0.05	1.13
Morocco	4428.1	4930.4	0.07	14.59
Syria	1914.2	1643.5	0.02	18.91
Tunisia	3754.8	4930.4	0.07	24.02

Sources: Petri (1997), World Development Indicators Database.

replacing them with new ones. The table also demonstrates that export to each Southern Mediterranean country constituted only a minor proportion of the EU's GDP.[3] Therefore, if an old trade agreement had run out without being replaced, the EU economy would have suffered hardly any repercussions.

Each Southern Mediterranean country thus depended more on access to the European market (mostly for its agricultural products) than the EU depended on access to any individual market in the Southern Mediterranean. This gave the Commission leverage, enabling it to draw up one single template agreement for all bilateral partnerships, then fine-tune it to the needs of each partner (ERCIM 1995; Villani 2002). Using a template meant that the content of each agreement was largely determined by the Commission, leaving the partners only limited room to make adjustments.

The association agreements had the long-run effect of permanently opening the southern economies to European imports, while resulting in modest agricultural concessions on the part of the EU, which were subject to periodic renegotiation.

The EU began renegotiating its bilateral agreements with the Northern African states in 1995. Egypt signed its new agreement in 2001. By signing its association agreement, the Mubarak government moved Egypt closer to the ideal of the Washington Consensus, because it opened the economy to foreign imports, if only those from the EU. For this reason, the signing of the association agreement constitutes an enforcement mechanism.

The Globalization Elite Gains Influence (Mechanism Three)

As this discussion shows, pressure from the global economy on the Egyptian state intensified in the 1990s, pushing it to remold the Egyptian economy on the image of the Washington Consensus. In implementing the reforms to which it had committed itself, the government affected the distributive entitlements of social groups, and this was bound to cause resistance.

If it wanted to obey creditor demands without incurring domestic protests, the state had to reposition itself at the intersection of international and domestic society. It had to restructure civil society, weaken those organizations that worked to protect the social contract, and strengthen those domestic actors who supported globalization. As it shouldered its economic reform mandate, the government therefore cultivated the private sector, particularly larger companies that owned a considerable amount of capital.

Core organizations also worked hard to increase the political impact of the wealthy private sector: They launched research that investigated private sector needs. They helped create a political network among larger businesses by funding the operations of their civil society organizations, and they promoted their access to ministries.

For example, the U.S. government provided financial and political support for the Egyptian Center for Economic Studies (ECES). Founded in 1992 by a group of Egyptian business leaders, the Center served as a policy research and advocacy organization for Egypt's globalization-oriented private sector. ECES assisted policymakers and the business community with a neoliberal approach to policy reform, which was compatible with the ideological outlook of the U.S. government. In 1993, therefore, USAID signed a cooperative agreement with the organization, promising to provide funding from 1993 through 1998. In that five-year period, 90 percent of the Center's funds came from USAID. Only 10 percent came from one-time financial contributions by members of the board (SRI International 1998).

Another example of core support for wealthy companies was the conference titled "Private Sector Development in Egypt: Investing in the Future." The Egyptian government, in partnership with the largest local business associations, held this event on October 9–10, 1994. Funding came from the World Bank, USAID, and the United Nations. In preparation, the World Bank issued a report on private sector development in Egypt (World Bank 1994). The conference turned out to be an important political networking opportunity. It "brought together national and international expertise, private agents and civil servants, producers, traders and financiers, official donors and nongovernmental organizations, the public in general, and the media" (Giugale and Mobarak 1996, i).

The conference induced the government to create the Private Sector Development Steering Committee. Its purpose was to direct the process of private sector development. Cochaired by the ministers of public enterprises, justice, and international cooperation, it comprised the chairmen of Egypt's five largest business associations, the Egyptian Trade Union Federation (ETUF), and the Banking Federation (World Bank 1995a).

These examples show that those international actors with stakes in the enforcement of social structure lent strong backing to the private sector. Importantly, though, they did not assist all private sector members equally. Small to micro enterprises received little systematic help. Wealthy, English-speaking owners of large companies, especially those who favored globalization, could count on a good deal of assistance. By supporting this globalization elite, the actors from the core increased their causal power to make demands on the state. The members of the elite used their ability for just that purpose. Support for this group of local entrepreneurs therefore constitutes an enforcement mechanism.

A Globalization Elite Emerges

In the second half of the 1990s, the Egyptian state cultivated the globalization elite by facilitating the foundation of civil society organizations that aggregated elite demands. As a consequence, a variety of new groups emerged. The four most influential groups were ECES, the U.S.- Egypt's Presidents' Council, Egypt's International Economic Forum, and the Future Generation Foundation.[4] These organizations formed the organizational underpinnings of a close network between export-led Egyptian companies and the state leadership, and between export-led local companies and transnational corporations. They lobbied for trade liberalization and IT connectivity. The following section shows how they wielded their influence.

The Egyptian Center for Economic Studies, 1992
Founded in 1992, ECES maintained strong ties to organizations from the core economies that supported flexible accumulation. A glance at the Center's leadership, its location, and the list of invited speakers makes this clear. In 1996, Ahmed Galal, a former staff member of the World Bank, became the head of ECES, which until 2003 was fittingly located in Cairo's World Trade Center. For research the Center drew on prominent scholars, among them economic "shock therapy" expert Jeffrey Sachs and Stanford

University's Anne Krueger, who later became the deputy managing director of the IMF.

In terms of methodology and presentation, the Center's analyses were highly professional. Between 1996 and 1998, ECES produced four major projects, each resulting in research papers. These covered the EU-Egypt association agreement, the possibility of a free trade agreement with the United States, reform of the financial sector, and, importantly, telecom privatization and liberalization. Most research papers were authored in English. This is understandable, as they were written by non-Arab experts. What is remarkable is that they were not available in Arabic translation. As a result they remained inaccessible to the majority of Egyptians, who were not bilingual. Also, at least through 2003, the Center's website was in English only. Both aspects are indicative of the elitist character of the Center and its ideological orientation toward the global, English-speaking economy.

ECES had excellent access to the government. Cooperation between the Center, the new business elite, international experts, and the government worked through roundtable discussions, which brought together ministers, prominent members of the private sector, and the media. According to the USAID consultancy SRI International, it was the quality of its output that gained ECES the ear of government officials (SRI International 1998). However, support by the globalization elite played a part as well. So did ideological proximity: ECES offered to make globalization work in Egypt's favor.

As will be discussed in chapter seven, the Center actively supported telecom reform. In 1997 it held a roundtable discussion on reform of the telecom sector. Several members of the Cabinet attended the event, and Björn Wellenius, who had drafted the World Bank's telecom strategy for the 1990s, gave a presentation on telecom privatization.

The U.S.-Egypt's Presidents' Council, 1994

The U.S.-Egypt's Presidents' Council represented a second venue for the globalization elite, which it shared with the American corporate sector. The Council was a component of the Gore-Mubarak Partnership, an initiative that the U.S. government had designed to advance trade liberalization in Egypt (Momani 2003).[5] The Council consisted of fifteen Egyptian and fifteen U.S. business leaders. Its mission was to advise the two governments—in practice mostly Egypt—on methods for enabling a private sector driven, globalization-oriented national economy.

To fill the Egyptian delegation, President Mubarak appointed prominent members of Egypt's private sector on an annual basis. Gamal Mubarak, the president's son, chaired the delegation. The Council became an important policymaking forum on economic issues:

> Public impression of the Council was that it had become the prime source for policy ideas, and in effect the new "shadow cabinet" in Egypt. This was, however, denied by members of the Council itself. The Egyptian Co-chair of the Presidents' Council remarked, "The Council has a purely consultative role and has no executive authority of any kind." A United States Information Service (USIS) spokesperson suggested that, despite the Egyptian Council's attempts to keep a low profile, it is widely regarded as an elite club. (Momani 2003)

That the Egyptian delegation had thrown its weight behind the strategy of export-led growth and globalization becomes clear from a brochure that the Council issued on the occasion of the MENA (short for: Middle East and North Africa) conference that took place in Cairo in late 1996. In it, the Council outlined its policy recommendations to the Egyptian government. They covered banking sector reform, a free economic zone law, a free trade agreement with the United States, build-operate-transfer projects, government procurement policies, and privatization:

> The Council maintains a dialogue with the President and senior Government officials on the importance of privatization, and encourages proposals for the Government to give greater attention to explaining the importance and urgency of privatization to the workers as well as the public. The Council has also stressed the need to continue the accelerated pace of privatization. (Egypt-U.S. Presidents' Council 1996, 11)

The Presidents' Council played an active role in advancing the cause of telecom liberalization. The brochure stated,

> Telecommunications is a key element to successful economic development in today's information age. A national economy must be supported by a modern, widely accessible communications network if it is to be competitive in the global marketplace... Competition in this sector, accompanied by effective regulation, is one of the fastest, most efficient ways to ensure availability, growth and cost-competitiveness for consumers, as well as increased revenue for the Government of Egypt. The Council has proposed possible options to open up the telecommunications sector, and hopes that the Government will move forward with consideration of these in order to spur the sectoral growth needed to address the

needs of business, education, and the health care sector, among others. The Council urges the Government of Egypt to continue its efforts to improve the country's communication capabilities, particularly as low-cost wireless applications become more available. (12)

Egypt's International Economic Forum, 1998

The third major civil society organization that represented the globalization elite was Egypt's International Economic Forum (EIEF), whose resemblance in name with the World Economic Forum was probably intended. Fifteen business leaders founded the organization in 1998. Its mission statement indicates that it was oriented toward realizing economic integration into the global economy:

The Forum (1999), a nongovernmental, nonprofit organization, has the following objectives:

- to host general and specialized business and economic events in Egypt and abroad;
- to develop and maintain strategic business contacts on a global and national basis;
- to organize and support business trade missions;
- to develop and maintain a database of studies, business opportunities, and general economic information on Egypt; and
- to maintain a dialogue with government bodies and agencies, business organizations and associations, research institutes, and think tanks on a national and global basis. (2)

The forum had the full support of the government. In September 1998, Foreign Minister Amre Moussa acted as keynote speaker at an EIEF conference in New York City. In October the Forum hosted a dinner meeting with the secretary general of the International Chamber of Commerce in Cairo. Several Egyptian ministers attended, as well as members of the Egyptian private sector and foreign diplomats. In November, the director of the World Economic Forum visited EIEF to discuss his organization's Middle East Business Initiative. In January 1999, EIEF attracted illustrious guests:

On the 12th of January [1999] the Forum proudly held its inaugural event with H.E. Amre Moussa, Minister of Foreign Affairs as guest of honor and keynote speaker. The fete was attended by over 250 guests comprising: ministers, high-level government officials, foreign ambassadors, heads of Egyptian business and economic organizations, members of the Egyptian private sector as well as representatives of the media, academia and international organizations. H.E. Minister Amre Mousa's speech discussed the "Economic Dimensions of Egyptian Diplomacy" and offered a sweeping review of Egypt's activities in the global economy. (EIEF 1999, 7)

By December 2003 the forum had 108 member companies. Another 59 individuals registered as professionals, even though it is likely that some of these chaired companies. In September 2003, the EIEF hosted the "Third Conference on Information Technology and Telecommunications in the Arab World," with a successor conference in September 2004. The events indicate that the organization considered the IT revolution an important aspect of a private sector led, globalization-oriented national economy.

The Future Generation Foundation, 1998
Founded in 1998 under the chairmanship of Hosni Mubarak's son Gamal, the Future Generation Foundation ostensibly aimed at improving management capabilities in Egypt so that the private sector could compete in the global economy. In addition to the chairman, the 2003 board of the Foundation had six members. According to the website, the organization sought to promote a workforce culture that was more responsive to a liberalized economy and competitive marketplace. This in turn "will require reorientation of organizations' culture and operating environment, reengineering of systems and processes, and adopting new technologies to produce the high-quality, low-cost products and services desired in today's global markets."

That this small and exclusive organization had the ability to realize these goals is doubtful at best. In fact, while social change was the official purpose of the Future Generation Foundation, its real function may have been to provide a political platform for Gamal Mubarak, presenting the president's son as being supportive of globalization and flexible accumulation. This in turn would help him obtain the support of the U.S. government when it came to determining presidential succession.

The New Inner Circle
Formally, these four organizations were separate entities, but in practice their leadership overlapped markedly. For example, seven members of the fifteen-person strong 1999 executive board of the EIEF also served on the U.S.-Egypt's Presidents' Council. This demonstrates that the globalization elite had an inner circle, which was a tight-knit, exclusive group with excellent access to the president's family. Table 6.2 provides a comparison among memberships of the Egypt-U.S. Presidents' Council, the executive board of

Table 6.2 Members of Egypt's globalization elite

Person's name and organizational affiliation	Was the person a member of the Presidents' Council in 1996?	Was the person a member of the Presidents' Council in 1999?	Was the person a board member of EIEF in 1999?	Was the person a board member of the FGF in 2003?	Was the person a member of ECES in 2003?	Was the person a member of the NDP in 2003?
Muataz Adel Al Alfi, Kuwait Food	Yes	No data available	No	Yes	Yes	No data available
Ahmed Bahgat, Bahgat Group	No	Yes	Yes	No	Yes	No data available
Ahmed Ezz, Ezz Group	No	Yes	Yes	No	Yes	Yes
Shafik Gabr, Artoc Group	Yes	Yes	Yes	No	Yes	Yes
Taher Helmy, Baker & McKenzie	Yes	Yes	Yes	No	Yes	No data available
Rachid M. Rachid, Unilever Egypt	No	Yes	Yes	Yes	Yes	No data available
Galal El Zorba, Nile Clothing	Yes	Yes	Yes	Yes	Yes	Yes

ECES: Egyptian Center for Economic Studies; EIEF: Egypt's International Economic Forum; FGF: Future Generation Foundation; NDP: National Democratic Party.

EIEF, and the membership of ECES. It suggests that about seven businessmen belonged to the globalization-oriented inner circle.

One member of the elite's inner circle deserves particular attention: Shafik Gabr, chair of the ARTOC Group. ARTOC was a holding company with interests in everything from newspaper publishing to real estate, automotive imports, manufacturing of specialized vehicles, steel production, and import of sporting equipment. ARTOC was headquartered in Egypt but had branches in the United States and Eastern Europe. As a former Egyptian diplomat told me in 2002, Shafik Gabr was the "regime's front man."

In September 1998 Gabr gave a presentation in which he called for increasing Egypt's global competitiveness by bringing the IT revolution to Egypt:

A second [worldwide] development [that has impacted the Arab Middle East] has been the revolution in telecommunications and information technologies. Technological advances now enable new linkages, permit greater transparency, and are transforming the way we do business and accelerating economic activity. This development has forced some Arab economies, business, financial institutions, capital markets and stock exchanges to re-engineer their capabilities and enhance their technological in-house resources. Such technological change is necessary to strengthen their competitive edge and prepare for the global economy that is impacting the Arab world whether we like it or not.

This shows that the members of Egypt's globalization elite had aligned themselves ideologically with those organizations from the core that had created the IT regime and now sought its implementation.

By helping to raise the profile of the globalization elite and increasing their causal power to make demands on the state, the core actors contributed to the enforcement of social structure. This fact makes their support for the globalization elite an enforcement mechanism.

And Autonomy?

The reform process increased the ability of the globalization elite to make demands on the state. This had negative consequences for the autonomy of many Egyptians. Living in an authoritarian system where the state habitually engaged in human rights violations, Egyptian citizens had little autonomy to begin with. They were used to being shut out of decision processes that yielded societal rules. That the government pursued economic policies in consultation with foreign actors such as the World Bank or the creditor states but failed to involve its own citizenry was therefore not surprising. Remarkably, however, the repression of citizens intensified when the state moved toward role compliance. This shows that both global social structure and globalization had qualities that were deeply disempowering.

Cultivating the Private Sector, Weakening the Unions, 1991–95

In 1991, President Mubarak and his cabinet decided to comply with creditor demands and divest its state-owned enterprises. It was clear that the unions would resist if the government did not prevent them from doing so.

Marsha Pripstein Posusney, an expert on Egyptian labor relations, explains that the state employed a number of tactics to forestall union resistance.[6] First, it split the hierarchical cohesion of the unions. For this it manipulated labor union elections so that leadership positions would be filled with government loyalists. By co-opting the union leadership, it passed resistance to privatization down to the level of the federations, which were in better touch with the base but had less access to the government. By splitting the leadership of the Egyptian Trade Union Federation from the Ministry of Labor, the state encouraged a power struggle that, for several months, diverted the attention of the union leadership from the privatization drive. In addition, it treated established workers differently from temporary workers. Temporary workers did not have access to severance packages, whereas established workers did. On the part of established workers, access to severance pay hinged on their cooperation. If they volunteered to be made redundant, they could expect lucrative severance packages. If they resisted and went on strike, they faced police force and lost their entitlements. This raised the opportunity cost of noncompliance for established workers.

Second, the state leadership withdrew from the social contract in stages. In 1991, when Law 203 was passed, the state promised employees that only loss-making parastatals would be sold. In early 1992 it became clear that profitable enterprises would also be put up for sale. Now the state modified its promise and said it would not sell out workers' rights. In 1992, the Ministry of Labor rescinded the employment guarantee piecemeal, telling people who worked in the private sector that they were being taken off the waiting list for public sector employment. Only in 1995 did the government begin to admit that privatization might bring about job losses (Pripstein Posusney 1997, 220–243).

In addition to weakening the unions, the state upheld its efforts to control the formal venues for aggregating citizen demands. In 1994, for instance, the National Assembly passed a law abolishing local elections. Village mayors were now appointed by the central government (EB 1995, 402).

The stand-off between radical Islamists and the state continued. The severely repressed militant Islamists had attempted to assassinate political figures. Beginning in 1992 they resorted to a new resistance strategy. By attacking foreigners they aimed at driving away tourists, thus depriving the state of an important source of foreign currency. The first such attack occurred in October 1992, when Islamists ambushed a tourist bus in Upper Egypt, killing a British woman and wounding two men. Between March 1992 and October 1994, 460 persons died from clashes between radical Islamists and the state, and 800 were injured (EB 1993, 382; 1995, 402).[7]

After 1995: Harsh Times for Peasants, Islamists, and Regime Critics

After 1995, the state implemented creditor demands more willingly. At the same time, the state apparatus became more repressive. Beneficiaries of Nasser's social contract—especially the tenant farmers—saw their old privileges erode. The state cracked down on Islamists, sought to bring the mosques under control, and passed a new law for nongovernmental organizations. All in all, state-society relations began to resemble what political scientists call exclusionary authoritarianism.[8]

Unrest in the Countryside
Thanks to tenancy contracts that dated back to the days of Nasser, leases on the countryside had been perpetual, and their price had been kept low. In 1992 the National Assembly passed a new law that deregulated rents on rural land. The law terminated the Nasserist tenancy contracts effective September 1997, freeing landowners to negotiate higher rents or reclaim the plots. Tenant farmers who could not afford the higher rents lost their subsistence and faced the prospect of being thrown deeper into poverty.

Laurence Roudart, an agricultural engineer and researcher at the National Institute of Agronomy in Paris, explains that the state took a number of measures to limit resistance to the law's implementation. First, it offered tenant farmers who could no longer afford their rents the option of relocating to plots in the Sinai that had been reclaimed from the desert. Tenants who were eligible for this offer had to leave their families behind, as the living conditions on the new land were harsh and profits were not expected to materialize in the first few years of cultivation. Second, the state commanded that provincial governors set up mediation committees in the villages. These committees were usually staffed by village notables who were landlords themselves. As such they did not mediate, but persuaded the tenants to accept their new contracts. Third, the government furnished a loan program for tenants who wished to buy the land that they had cultivated. However, the amount of funding was only sufficient for buying 1 percent of the cultivated land kept under tenancy contracts. Finally, the state resorted to force, arresting the leaders of resisting farmers (Roudart 2001).

All in all, Roudart estimates, 900,000 farmers and their families were affected by the law. Nevertheless, when the law went into effect in September 1997, the *Economist Intelligence Unit*, a publication that tracks political developments for foreign investors, did not foresee widespread rural insurgence severe enough to threaten regime stability: "It is highly unlikely that this rural discontent will escalate into anything that might affect political stability, as the only organizations inclined to mobilize the tenant farmers are the opposition parties which are well aware of the savage government crackdown they would provoke" (EIU 1997/3, 6). Similarly, Roudart conjectures that the law had only been passed because the farmers had no lobby or political leverage. This description coincides with the analysis of Egypt expert Robert Bianchi. He explains the cooperative structure on the countryside had been weak since the days of Nasser and could not serve to provide organizational support for coordinated protest. In the absence of an organizational support network, the rural tenants could engage in locally dispersed confrontations with land owners and the police, but not in serious rebellion (Bianchi 1989). Violence related to the law caused the deaths of 25 people and the injury of 210 persons in the month after the law went into effect. Between early 1998 and late 1999, 107 individuals were killed and 586 injured in violence related to the law (EIU 1997/4, 14; Land Center for Human Rights 1999).

Crackdown on Islamists
In the second half of the 1990s the government adopted a harsher approach towards the Islamist movement, cracking down not only on the radical factions, but also on its mainstream, the Muslim Brotherhood. This harsher approach may have been prompted by an attempt on the president's life when he visited the Ethiopian capital Addis Abeba in June 1995.

In November 1995, shortly before elections to the National Assembly, the state clamped down on the Muslim Brotherhood, thus preventing their effective participation in the election. In 1996 the government departed from its policy of confining arrests to the Brotherhood's grassroots activists and began to arrest prominent members of the organization. This strategy was persistent. In 1999, the Egyptian Organization for Human Rights reported that the arrest wave against members of the Brotherhood had continued throughout 1998 and that the crackdown had been overwhelming (EB 1996, 400; EIU 1996/2, 14; 1999/1, 14).

Severe government repression was capable of quelling most protest and weakening the Muslim Brotherhood. Radical Islamists, however, resorted to new tactics. With hard targets out of reach, they attacked tourists with increased brutality. The progressively more violent stand-off between the state and Islamists resulted in a high death toll. Between 1992 and early 1996, around one thousand people died as a result of clashes between the radical Islamists and the state. On November 17, 1997, Islamists opened gunfire on tourists visiting a pharaonic site in Luxor. Four Egyptians and fifty-eight foreign tourists were killed. The assault achieved its goal. The incident caused a five hundred million dollar decline in tourism revenue (EIU 1996/2, 12; 1998/3, 20).

The state's quest to crush the Islamist movement extended to the professional syndicates. In 1996, after the Muslim Brotherhood won the elections to the board of Egypt's Bar Association, the association was put under judicial control until 2001. In the same year, Sadat's idea of reigning in the mosques received new attention. In December the National Assembly declared it illegal to preach in a mosque without a license from the Ministry for Religious Endowments. After that the government worked to bring the country's thirty thousand private mosques under state control (El-Nahhas 2003; EIU 1997/1, 15).

> By late 2003 the number of independent mosques was drastically reduced: Following a 1996 law, the Egyptian government has been assuming control of mosques at a rate of some 6,000 per year, according to the Deputy Minister of Awqaf Muhammad Zidan. On 7 August [2003] Zidan told the Cairo Times the task was nearly complete. "Within a year or two we will control all the mosques," the bearded and imma-clad Zidan said from his spacious office inside the ministry, a neo-Islamic building in downtown Cairo. (Levinson 2003)

Other Opposition Groups
The state's efforts at domination were not limited to the Islamists, but extended to organized public opinion in general. In 1998 the government moved to bring the country's nongovernmental organizations, especially advocacy and human rights groups, under its tutelage (EIU 1998/3, 6). For that purpose the National Assembly passed a new NGO law in 1999. The *Cairo Times* (1999) explains:

> The new law gives the government extensive and elastic powers to intervene in the administrative and financial affairs of the country's 14,000 non-governmental associations (NGOs). It can dismiss members of boards of directors of NGOs and replace them with hand-picked government representatives. It can close groups that it deems do not accomplish their stated purpose. It requires all NGOs who receive foreign funding to obtain prior permission from the government. In effect, a nongovernmental organization—despite the name—becomes an agency completely under the governmental thumb.

Criticism of the law was widespread, both in Egypt and abroad. In 2000 the Supreme Court ruled the law unconstitutional. In 2002 a similar law succeeded it.

Conclusion

As this chapter has demonstrated, three enforcement mechanisms bore down on the Egyptian state, pushing it to comply with its role under flexible accumulation: A structural adjustment program, a bilateral association agreement with the EU, and a globalization elite that was increasingly outspoken. These mechanisms operated against the backdrop of the collapse of the USSR, which had the dual effect of weakening the state in relation to its creditors and emboldening core actors to push the agenda of flexible accumulation.

The state implemented the economic reforms and cultivated the globalization elite, which in turn demanded that Egypt embrace the tenets of the IT regime. While members of this newly empowered elite reveled in their improved access to the Mubarak administration, most Egyptians saw their autonomy dwindle. In the past they had had to endure a government that excluded them from most of its decisions. The additional repression they suffered now was a direct consequence of the state's determination to please its creditors. This clearly demonstrates that social structure can be repressive.

CHAPTER 7

The Telecom Monopolist

Globalization rests on the removal of trade barriers but also on a communication network that spans the countries of the globe. The new international consensus on telecom administration reflected this fact. As chapters two and four emphasized, the consensus favored sector liberalization in three steps:

1. Separating the operator and the regulator to ensure that the state-owned monopolist did not set its own rules.
2. Privatizing the operator, to ensure infrastructure investment and prevent the state from discriminating in the operator's favor.
3. Opening the telecom sector to competition to create impetus for innovation.

Like most peripheral economies in the mid-1990s, Egypt was far removed from this best practice. The country's telecom sector was state-owned and monopolistic, there was no independent regulator, and service quality was poor. As the sector's service provider and governing authority, the state was therefore far from role compliant.

On that background, two enforcement mechanisms emanated from social structure and helped push the Egyptian state toward the new administrative best practice. The first was tied to the U.S. Agency for International Development (USAID). Among the development agencies of the core economies, it had the largest presence in Egypt. As Egypt's reward for signing a peace treaty with Israel in 1979 and becoming America's largest ally in the Middle East, USAID paid the Egyptian government more than seven hundred million dollars a year, channeling these funds into mutually agreed development projects. Importantly, the money had to be programmed every year, which meant that the agency could not withhold funding from the Egyptian state if it wanted to do so. Its causal power vis-à-vis the Egyptian state did therefore not rest on simple financial coercion. Instead, it grew out of three more concrete interrelated causal powers:

1. The power to *fund* network upgrades that the government found increasingly important.
2. The power to *provide advice* on the new telecom consensus that was emerging at the global level and that the Egyptian state took increasingly seriously
3. The power to *discern fragmentations* inside the state and especially the monopolist.

The Egyptian state had three causal liabilities that paralleled the causal powers of USAID:

1. The liability to *require funds* for network upgrades.
2. The liability to *need information* on the new telecom consensus.
3. The liability to *exhibit internal fragmentation* into organizational units that operated at cross-purpose and sought to align themselves with outside actors such as USAID.

Since they all had the same thrust, these powers and liabilities can be summarized as a single enforcement mechanism, as follows:

Enforcement Mechanism Four: USAID *prodded* the state step by step toward telecom sector reform.

The second enforcement mechanism was tied to the European Commission and the Euro-Mediterranean Partnership. The Commission had the following causal powers:

1. The power to *demand* that the government of Egypt sign an association agreement that was sensitive to the new telecom consensus.
2. The power to *emphasize* the new telecom consensus during the multilateral partnership activities.

The Egyptian state, meanwhile, had parallel causal liabilities:

1. The liability to *have to accept* the demand for an association agreement that was sensitive to the new telecom consensus.

2. The liability to *have to realize* that the new telecom consensus received emphasis during the multilateral partnership activities.

These causal powers and liabilities also can be summed up as a single enforcement mechanism, as follows:

Enforcement Mechanism Five: The European Commission *prodded* the state to consider sector reform.

A detailed look at the way in which Egypt's telecom sector was organized in the early 1980s will help elucidate how these mechanisms worked themselves out.

Egypt's Telecom Sector: A Model of Mismanagement

In 1981, when Hosni Mubarak became the president of Egypt, Egypt's telecom system was Fordist. There was only one carrier that provided public-switched telephony. Its lengthy name was "Arab Republic of Egypt National Telecommunication Organization," but citizens referred to it simply as ARENTO.[1] The Ministry of Transport and Communication housed and managed ARENTO, in addition to being responsible for postal services and road infrastructure. The ministry was a product of the Egyptian revolution, and it embodied the belief that engineering talent, put in the service of the nation, could help modernize the country and rid it of its colonial memory. Here is an excerpt from a 1960 promotional booklet that captures this fact:

> In the battle to combat disease, illiteracy and poverty we work incessantly with the one objective—that of doubling the nation's GNP in ten years. Insuring a better transport system is no less vital in this battle than anything worth mentioning. The seven-year period since 1952 makes a panorama of great achievements; they reveal the strong will to implement a policy aimed at the overall modernization of the transport system—railway, road and water transports. The postal services and telecommunications have their shares too.
>
> This book has a modest aim—that of giving the reader a clear idea about the status quo in transport and communications at the end of 1959 in the Egyptian Region of the United Arab Republic. For it goes without saying that what has been achieved in seven years equals the achievements in the previous forty years to the great Revolution. Reconstruction is the symbol of the [United Arab Republic of Egypt] which is determined, under the

leadership of President Gamal Abdel Nasser, to make the future as great as the past. (United Arab Republic, Ministry of Communications 1960)

This passage reveals a number of things. First, the ministry perceived infrastructure improvement as an administrative engineering problem, where the state, rather than market forces, decided what the nation needed. Second, infrastructure projects had a symbolic function, namely to demonstrate to the world that Nasserism worked. Third, the ministry gave priority to the construction of physical transport by means of rail, road, and water. Post and telecom were assigned a back seat.

In 1980 Soliman Metwally became the new minister, and his tenure lasted until 2000. Metwally was a government bureaucrat without private sector experience. He had been born in 1927. In 1949 he graduated from Cairo University with a bachelor's degree in civil engineering, then worked his way up through the ranks of the Egyptian bureaucracy.

When Metwally was appointed minister of transport and communication, he inherited a poorly developed telecom network. Budget problems had caused the state to pull the brake on network build-out; and rapid population growth had caused demand for telephone hookups to increase from 15,500 in 1968 to over 373,500 by 1978. As a consequence, telephone availability, the percentage of direct exchange lines to expressed demand, had deteriorated from 96.9 percent in 1968 to only 49.4 percent in 1978 (World Bank 1981).[2]

In local exchanges, low availability of telephone mainlines exacerbated network congestion. Because so few telephones were available, existing mainlines were used by a large number of persons. They kept lines busy for long intervals. This in turn caused people who wanted to call a telephone and received a busy signal to try again and again, which clogged up the network without leading to actual conversations. In some areas, call failures topped 75 percent (ibid.).

Long distance communication was also riddled with problems. Because many exchanges in Egypt employed the old rotary technology, users could not call one another directly. Instead, they relied on operators in the switches to connect them. In 1981, the World Bank reported that calling Cairo from villages in the Minufiyya province took at least four hours (ibid.).

International telecommunications was cumbersome. Traffic to any country that did not share borders with Egypt was routed through Italy or Lebanon. Alternatively, it was passed through the Intelsat system of geostationary satellites, and due to the long distance the signal had to travel this led to unpleasant delays in communication. In 1981 the World Bank reported a piece of anecdotal evidence that it thought captured the state of affairs: A businessman from the Nile Delta tried to call a businessman in Montreal. For a month he was unable to establish a connection, and finally he sent his message via telex (ibid.).

Metwally himself did not treat telecom as a priority sector; and as several Egyptians interviewed for this book pointed out, he was unsupportive of ARENTO's efforts to expand network coverage. Instead, he used ARENTO as a cash cow, which generated funds that were then funneled into uses that were unrelated to telecom. This attitude was feasible as long as the Fordist framework prevailed in the core economies. However, once core actors' demand for high-quality communication services matured into an international consensus, Metwally's approach came under criticism.

USAID Calls for Reform (Mechanism Four)

In its possession of a poor network, Egypt was typical of a large number of peripheral countries. Strapped for cash and unable to keep track of their investments and debts, Third World states did not treat telephony as a national priority. Because of this, low call completion rates, long waiting lists, and poor signal quality were the norm rather than the exception.

Three Development Paradigms

Development organizations from the core economies tried to improve the state of telephony in the Third World. Three paradigms governed their strategy over the decades. The first, which shaped policy into the mid-1970s, held that development agencies should assist the state-owned monopolist in upgrading its infrastructure by financing the necessary equipment. Because aid was frequently tied, a recipient government had to spend money it received from Germany on German infrastructure components, while money from the United States and from France would be spent on American and French equipment, respectively. The result was a patchwork of network elements that were not designed to be combined and that were frequently incompatible.

In the late 1970s development organizations moved into the second paradigm. They became convinced that public utilities—be they for electricity, telecom, water, or other services—did not fail simply because their mass of equipment fell short, but also because they lacked the managerial acumen necessary for proper service provision. Lending agencies therefore began to concentrate on strengthening the utility's decision-making structures.

This approach dominated policy for about ten years. Around 1990 development organizations transitioned into the third paradigm. Adopting the telecom consensus while it formed at the global level, they began to call for sector reform. The intention was to separate the regulator from the operator, privatize the monopolist, and expose it to competition (World Bank, Operations Evaluation Department 1993).

The First Two Paradigms in Egypt

In Egypt of the 1970s, the World Bank was the main sponsor of telecom development projects. By 1978 World Bank loans amounting to eighty-five million dollars had kept the network from collapsing. In keeping with the first development paradigm, which simply aimed to pour money into infrastructure, these loans had not been predicated on reforms of any kind.

USAID was the first development agency to implement the second development paradigm, which sought institutional strengthening. In 1976, before sinking funds into Egypt's telecom infrastructure, USAID asked Continental Telephone International for a sector study, which was completed in 1978. The World Bank then provided in-depth comments and recommended ways in which the development program should be implemented (World Bank 1981 and 1989).

The report outlined several objectives that development assistance was to accomplish. The quality of existing services was to be improved, telephone waiting lists were to be eliminated, ARENTO was to be transformed into an efficient and effective organization, and a sound financial and institutional basis for ARENTO was to be created so that it would be able to grow sustainably. To turn ARENTO into an efficient organization, the study suggested that ARENTO's internal organization be restructured. In addition, a planning and project control system was to be created, the financial management system was to be strengthened, and commercial operations and personnel training were to be improved (World Bank 1981).

USAID's efforts to strengthen ARENTO had little success. The most tangible result was Law 153/1980, passed by the Egyptian National Assembly in July 1980. It was meant to provide the organization with a modicum of autonomy from the Ministry of Transport and stipulated that ARENTO could set tariffs subject to approval by the ministry. The law exempted the organization from the government policy of prescribing compulsory hiring quotas, which had grown out of the Nasserist social contract with labor. ARENTO was given the right to retain surplus funds for its investments, to set its own wage scale, and to implement a commercial accounting and billing system. ARENTO's telephone rates were to be regulated by the ministry, with input from the cabinet.

On paper, this constituted substantial reform. To USAID's dismay, however, the law was not properly implemented. Instead of being able to reinvest all its surplus funds, ARENTO had to pay to the government an annual sum of one hundred million Egyptian pounds. Only the remaining balance could be used for rehabilitation or network expansion (USAID Egypt 1992). The government also ignored ARENTO's exemption from the compulsory hiring mandate and forced the monopolist to hire more college graduates than it needed. By May 1982 the total ARENTO staff had declined from the previous peak of fifty thousand to forty-eight thousand employees. But then the payroll increased again and reached over fifty-four thousand in 1991. Clearly, ARENTO was unable to set limits on the size of its work force (USAID 1993).

In practice ARENTO remained semi-autonomous and depended on the ministry for all major decisions involving finances, tariffs, and employment. The ministry continued to funnel substantial telecom revenues into other projects within its purview.

Over the sixteen-year period between 1976 and 1992, USAID invested a total of $282 million in Egypt's telecom operator. These funds did not lead to progress toward making ARENTO an efficient organization, but they helped expand the network infrastructure. With the help of this money and supplier credits from a European consortium, ARENTO managed to improve the density of telephone service from a very low level of 1.2 mainlines per one hundred residents in 1981 to 3.9 in 1990 (USAID Egypt 1992).

The following indicators give an overview of the state of Egypt's telephone network in the early 1990s. Between 1981 and 1990, the number of local communities connected to the direct dial network increased from 7 to 189, the number of international circuits increased from 820 to 5,560 channels, the number of telephone lines increased from 510,000 to 2.15 million, and the telephone density increased from 1.2 to 3.9 lines per 100 people. Waiting lists continued to be long. By 1992, 1.2 million potential subscribers were on the waiting list. They expected to receive a phone line five–ten years later (USAID Egypt 1992).

The network was patchy. At the end of 1991, large parts still used analog technology—only 19 percent of the total switching capacity in Egypt was digital. Because ARENTO had drawn for so long on different aid programs and supplier credits, the telecom grid was a collage of switching equipment from eight different suppliers, all of which used different transmission standards. Consequently, switches from different manufacturers did not properly communicate with each other (USAID Egypt 1992).

By 1990, corporations in the core economies had become adamant about their need for a sophisticated telecom infrastructure. ARENTO, however, was in no position to meet these demands, because it lacked the capacity to set organizational goals and implement them. K&M Engineering and Consulting Corporation, a firm that USAID asked to diagnose ARENTO, identified two main problems. First, ARENTO's internal decision-making structures were at once highly centralized and disjointed. ARENTO was centralized in that the utility had a few vice chairmen who were in charge of a large number of departments. As was customary for Egyptian state agencies, an organizational culture of paternalism prevailed, where superiors expected to be in charge and subordinates expected to make no important decisions on their own. This left the leaders of the organization in charge of routine matters and distracted their attention from strategic decisions. Only rarely were such decisions made at all (K&M 1994).[3]

In addition, ARENTO's operations were disjointed. Departments were organized by region, rather than by function. This required supervisors to have a high level of cross-functional expertise and prevented specialization of employees. In addition, some functions that were crucial to organizational strength or even survival did not have a place in the organizational structure at all. The financing function is a case in point. In order to plan its future, an organization needs an overview of the inflow and outflow of resources. At ARENTO, financial matters were distributed across the organization, and no central accounting department existed. In the rare instances when ARENTO's management did make strategic decisions, these were based on poor information (USAID, Inspector General 1986, exhibit 1).

Second, ARENTO suffered from interference from other state entities, which either made claims on its resources or on its decision-making prerogatives. The Ministry of Administrative Development sought to dictate the hiring quota, and the Ministry of Finance interfered in the wage scale that the monopolist used to reimburse personnel. Consequently, ARENTO engineers made two–four times less than their counterparts at the Suez Canal Authority, and attrition was high. Furthermore, several government agencies did not pay their telephone bills. Despite Law 153/1980, which granted ARENTO the right to reinvest its surplus funds, the Ministry of Finance subtracted one hundred million Egyptian pounds annually from ARENTO's earnings (K&M 1994; USAID Egypt 1992).

ARENTO also did not have the means to procure equipment from foreign suppliers. Since the Egyptian pound was not convertible, ARENTO depended on its foreign exchange earnings from international settlements to procure infrastructure equipment. However, with the government suffering from permanent balance of payment problems, the Ministry of Planning had to approve the level of foreign exchange funds that could be used for these procurements, and more often than not other government procurement needs had priority over telecom equipment purchases (USAID Egypt 1992). For its infrastructure expansion ARENTO therefore depended heavily on foreign aid. Where funds were given—for instance, by USAID—the Ministry of International Cooperation signed an agreement with the donor agency and then provided the sum to ARENTO as a high-interest loan. Asked for the reasons that motivated such complicated and seemingly irrational behavior, former ARENTO chairman Osman Loutfi (2002) explained that USAID was willing to fund telecom projects but not projects in other areas that the government considered important. By treating the funds as a loan, the state could funnel USAID funds into other uses that the American agency would not have financed.

To summarize, ARENTO was weak internally, with a decision-making structure that made it difficult to arrive at policy decisions. Externally, it received cash injections from donor agencies, but at the same time various ministries raided its budgets and interfered in its operations. To draw an analogy, the monopolist resembled a patient who received dialysis while donating blood.

The Third Paradigm: Sector Reform in the 1990s

By the end of the 1980s the American idea that telecom was an economically strategic sector found its way into the development agencies of the core economies. Consequently, development agencies transitioned from the second development paradigm to the third: sector reform.

USAID reflected this trend. Congress and the executive branch wanted to use agency funds to advance U.S. commercial interests more aggressively, "without jeopardizing the international development objectives of the foreign aid program" (USAID, Center for Development Information and Evaluation 1994, v). America's political leadership demanded that economic development be pursued in the context of deepening flexible accumulation, and telecom investments were to support this agenda. USAID's Egyptian field office therefore assigned the telecom sector a new strategic role, which it explained in a 1992 statement:

> If the Egyptian economy is to expand, Egyptian financial institutions need access to up-to-the-instant information transmitted through global electronic networks in order to expand operations into new services and markets. The development of the private sector will depend on reliable

telecommunications that will link the Egyptian industry to world markets. If Egypt is to emerge as a gateway for trade between Africa and the developed world, instant access to international financial data banks and electronically driven exchanges are increasingly essential. (USAID Egypt 1992, 5–6)

In pushing for sector liberalization, USAID had to tread carefully. The money that it funneled into Egypt on behalf of the U.S. government was a payment for the peace treaty that Egypt had signed with Israel in 1979. It could not be withheld but had to be programmed in one way or other. Consequently, USAID did not have direct policy leverage over the Egyptian government (U.S. General Accounting Office 1985). For this reason USAID did not apply coercion. Instead, it improved the odds of desirable policy outcomes by promoting these options with the cabinet and the ministry, and the management of the operator. In parallel, it supported Egypt's globalization elite and their desire for a better communication infrastructure.

In 1992, ARENTO approached USAID to obtain funding for network upgrades. The project on which the two organizations agreed was a compromise. ARENTO would receive funding for capital improvements, in exchange USAID obtained a guarantee of sector reform. The project was planned as a six-year, two-hundred-million-dollar program that would finance capital improvements, training, and technical assistance. USAID would finance the project in tranches that would be authorized periodically following the state's compliance with specific reform targets. The understanding was that some reforms would be implemented by the operator, others by the Ministry of Transport and by the government of Egypt. If the reforms were not implemented, USAID would reserve the right to program the funds for other uses not related to telecom (USAID 1993; USAID Egypt 1992).

In 1992 the exact nature of the reform program was not yet clear. USAID Egypt made no references to privatizing the monopolist or opening the sector to competition. Rather, it spoke of putting ARENTO on a commercial footing, so that it would function like a private sector corporation (USAID Egypt 1992).

The lack of specificity at this early stage may have been due to lack of expertise. While the agency itself possessed some knowledge of the new directions in telecom, its understanding was limited, and so it drew on outside expertise for its reform endeavor. USAID commissioned a sector study from K&M Engineering and Consulting Corporation, which was headquartered only four blocks from the White House in Washington. The report was delivered in 1994. At the outset of the document, K&M

noted that its study team had evaluated all proposed changes against the common objective functions that would be associated with a "World Class Telecommunications Provider." These were stipulated as:

1. A state-of-the-art infrastructure [i.e., one that could satisfy the need of high-end customers for value-added services]
2. Market oriented service offerings from state-of-the-art technology
3. An investment grade financial position
4. The ability to attract, retain and develop world class personnel
5. High value services at competitive prices
6. An environment conducive to innovation and change in a global economy. (K&M 1994, 1.2)

All in all, the document presumed that Egypt would be a full participant in a global economy based on free trade and that ARENTO, as a "world class telecom provider," would cater to the needs of global corporations. In K&M's calculus it was only a matter of time until Egypt's infrastructure monopoly would fall. The following excerpt makes this clear: "ARENTO's authority in areas of pricing, service standards and market entry should be taken from the hands of other ministries and vested in a regulatory body *until these characteristics are eliminated through competition*" (1–6; emphasis added). USAID and K&M were clearly ahead of the Egyptian government, which had not voiced the desire to introduce competition. In its report, K&M established a set of benchmarks. They formed the so-called policy matrix and were to be implemented in three phases, each of which would last one–two years. The benchmarks were detailed prescriptions for five distinct issue areas: organizational framework, regulatory and legal framework, planning and management, employee staffing and development, profitability and self-financing assessment (K&M 1994).

Most of these areas dealt with ARENTO's internal operations. They were thus reminiscent of the second development paradigm which had dominated the 1980s and focused on institutional strengthening. However, the area of "regulatory and legal framework" had a much broader focus. It addressed the structure of the entire telecom sector, and while it did not directly demand competition, it referred to it as a distinct possibility. The benchmarks for this issue area called for a National Telecommunication Policy, to be issued by the government. ARENTO was to be turned into a government-owned corporation that would issue stock and declare dividends. A regulatory entity would be established by ministerial decree and chaired by the minister for transport and communication. The entity would supervise and regulate both ARENTO and other public and private sector firms active within the field of telecommunications.[4] The new international consensus on telecom administration obviously inspired these benchmarks.

Once K&M had devised the matrix, USAID asked two other contractors to supervise its implementation: first Booz-Allen & Hamilton, later GTE. Under the consultants' careful gaze ARENTO engaged in gradual reform. It improved the training offered to its engineers, conducted market research, redesigned its internal structure, decided on a strategy for computerizing operations, and undertook other improvements. Throughout this process the employment security of ARENTO employees was never put at risk, even though K&M's report had indicated that with fifty-six thousand employees the organization was overstaffed. In this case organizational efficiency took a back seat behind social peace, which neither the government nor USAID could afford to jeopardize by laying off unionized workers.

The contractors documented ARENTO's progress in annual reports to USAID. As the reform process went on, policy documents of Booz-Allen and GTE made increasing reference to a competitive telecom sector and utility privatization. This indicates that through its contractors, USAID broached the idea of competition to the government, demonstrating its viability and its usefulness for what creditors had decided would be Egypt's new economic strategy: export-led economic growth.

USAID at Work: Creating an Independent Regulator

According to the new wisdom at the commanding heights of the global economy, national telecom sectors were to be organized competitively. This had implications for the regulation of the sector. In order to ensure fair competition and interconnection among the operators, there needed to be a regulator that would act as an unbiased arbiter among the competitors and put the welfare of telecom customers before that of the carriers. The Federal Communications Commission of the United States served as the real-life model of this principle. In the undesirable case where the sector was not competitive, there at least had to be a regulator that was independent of the operator and could act as the customers' ombudsman.

In the early 1990s Egypt was far removed from this ideal. The sector was monopolistic, and the supervising ministry did not act as the telecom customers' ombudsman. Rather than maximizing the welfare of telecom consumers by lowering phone rates and building out the network, the ministry promoted the welfare of Cairo commuters by diverting ARENTO's resources into the construction of the city's metro.[5] By charging high accounting rates, the ministry promoted a high rate structure in international telecommunications. This filled the state treasury but was anathema to flexible accumulation and its emphasis on cheap cross-border communication.

USAID thus had its work cut out, and it seized the challenge. In its effort to push for an independent regulatory authority, the agency followed the strategy of keeping one step ahead of the government and prodding it little by little in the desired direction. This method had the benefit of minimizing resistance by the Ministry of Transport.

The policy matrix that K&M produced in 1994 therefore called not for an independent regulator, but more modestly for a regulatory board within the ministry. It was to be established by ministerial decree and chaired by the minister of transport. In May 1995, Minister Metwally responded with a decree that established a National Telecommunication Council. The minister would appoint five council members. He himself would serve as the chair. The council would manage the frequency spectrum, evaluate the operator's tariff structure, supervise technical standards, and ensure interoperability of all state-owned and private networks. Its stated goal was to encourage innovation and stimulate investment in the sector.

For 1996, the policy matrix required the state to pass a new national telecommunications policy. To help the state fulfill this obligation, Booz-Allen drafted the policy. It stated that the regulator would provide the institutional conditions to encourage telecommunication development in an open, pro-competitive, pro-private enterprise environment. Beyond that, it envisioned that the National Telecommunication Council would eventually be removed from the Ministry of Transport. Booz-Allen submitted the draft to the government, which signed off on it in order to receive the next funding tranche.

Why was ARENTO So Docile?

USAID's reform program called ARENTO's monopoly status into question. The example of AT&T in the United States and Deutsche Telekom and France Telecom in Europe would have suggested that the Egyptian monopolist would mount fierce opposition against encroachments onto its turf. But unlike its counterparts in the core economies, ARENTO offered little resistance to eliminating its monopoly status. Why was ARENTO so docile?

Several answers present themselves: First, as a utility with poor decision-making structures, ARENTO was incapable of deciding to oppose the dismantling of its monopoly status. Second, in light of the fact that ARENTO's managers found themselves in a less than supportive political environment, they may have welcomed the change. True, the program undermined the monopoly status of their utility; but at the same time it promised to repair the organization's weak internal structures and put it in a position where it could make decisions. It also protected the organization in its interaction with the rest of the state, including the supervising Ministry of Transport. Third, it was not obvious from the get-go that USAID and its consultants sought sector liberalization and privatization, even though in hindsight it is clear that the ideal of a competitive sector drove USAID's reform program.

The Euro-Mediterranean Partnership Offers Assistance (Mechanism Five)

While the U.S. government channeled its view on telecom policy in Egypt through USAID's field operations, the European Union used the Euro-Mediterranean Partnership as its vehicle. In 1995 the Commission organized the Barcelona Conference, which launched the partnership. The conference emphasized the need to modernize telecom in the Mediterranean. In May 1996, it organized a sectoral ministerial conference on the information society. The event stressed the need to separate telecom regulation from service provision (European Commission, Directorate General External Relations 1996).

In addition, the Commission negotiated bilateral agreements with the Southern Mediterranean states. For that purpose it drew up one template agreement and then modified it as it entered negotiations with each specific partner state. ERCIM, a consultancy hired by the European Commission, points out that the template contained specific provisions for IT:

Telecommunications and information technologies represent an integral part of the third generation agreements signed between the European Union and the [Southern Mediterranean countries], which provide for the creation of a wider Euro-Mediterranean free trade area within 10 to 12 years. In the section devoted to economic cooperation, article 56 specifies:
'Co-operative activities are particularly directed toward:
a. the general framework of telecommunications;
b. the standardization, compliance testing and certification of information and telecommunication technologies;
c. the introduction of new information technologies, particularly in terms of networking and network interconnections...;
d. the promotion of research and the elaboration of new communications and information technologies with the objective of developing the market of equipment, services, and applications linked to information technologies and to communications, services and installations.'
This is a standard article that is to be included in all future partnership agreements. (ERCIM 1995, 93–94)

Egypt signed its association agreement with the EU in 2001. In line with the Commission's standardized approach, this agreement contained an article that closely resembled the template.[6]

The State Commits Itself to Export-Led Growth

By 1995 the Egyptian government began to embrace the idea, promoted by the World Bank and the Paris Club of creditor states, that trade liberalization was necessary and that the country's economy would have to rely on export-led growth. As a result, the Mubarak administration began to open its mind to the need of having a "world class" telecom sector, which it knew was crucial for attracting investment.

In June 1996, it agreed to rename ARENTO into the more fashionable-sounding Telecom Egypt. In that same year, the government also determined that Egypt needed a cellular network. It was to be in place by November 1996, in time for the MENA (Middle East and North Africa) conference that would take place in Cairo.[7] The conference would be a good opportunity for showcasing Egypt's economy, and a modern cellular telephone network would demonstrate to potential investors that Egypt understood their demand for a high-quality communications infrastructure. Alcatel of France built the system, and ARENTO, or Telecom Egypt, administered it.

A year after the MENA conference, the government decided to admit private sector companies into the market for cellular telephony. Two motivations seem to have been at work when it made this decision. First, President Mubarak sought to "keep up with the Joneses" by emulating Malaysia, an economically successful country that had a well-working privatized cellular network. In early November 1997 Mubarak attended the G-15 summit in Kuala Lumpur. Here he learned about Malaysia's cellular system and saw how well it worked in support of the country's export-led economic strategy. Given that Egypt was embarking on an export-led strategy, he wanted a similar network. The *Cairo Times* commented:

> The seriousness of government intent [to issue a cellular license to a private sector player] is quite clear...Intent can...be measured by the lofty level at which the decision appears to have been made—namely, by President Mubarak himself. That Mubarak ordered it is likely, considering the speed with which the decision is being carried out and the fact that Telecom Egypt appears to have known little of the plan...The story goes that on Mubarak's return flight from Malaysia after the G-15 Summit three weeks ago, he made the decision that the government mobile network would be privatized. It seems Mubarak got a bit of a

wake-up call in Malaysia, where he saw how things work in a full-blown emerging economy. Perhaps he even felt a pang of distress that Malaysia's Mahathir Mohamed, who has been in power as long as he has, has presided over a hugely better rise in living standards for his people.

Catching up won't be easy, but since a modern, efficient communications system is a prerequisite for private sector-led growth, getting one is an obvious move to make. Plus, selling crown jewels impresses investors and international financial institutions. (Richmond 1997)

Second, President Mubarak felt compelled to appease the creditor community from the core and potential foreign investors. By proving that the state was willing to comply with the new telecom consensus and admit private sector providers into the telecom sector, he signaled that Egypt was firmly committed to globalization. The need to appease core actors arose on November 17, when radical Islamists assaulted Luxor, a pharaonic site and prominent tourist destination. An observer of the Egyptian economy described the nation as being in shock following the attack. The government asked the resident representative of the International Monetary Fund for advice on what to do, and he counseled that it should take a big step, to show the world that Egypt was still open for business. Two days after the assault, the government issued a tender for a mobile phone license in the *Al-Ahram* newspaper (Richmond 1997).

The circumstances surrounding the decision to issue a private cellular license indicate that globalization had entered the government's decision-making environment as a constraining factor. By adapting to the new telecom consensus, which called for competitive service provision, President Mubarak indicated that Egypt was willing to accept globalization as its new reality and submit to it.

The Globalization Elite Demands Liberalization (Mechanism Three Revisited)

The previous chapter showed that in the second half of the 1990s, an Egyptian globalization elite emerged with Gamal Mubarak, the president's son, at its center. Because it had stakes in a borderless world economy, the globalization elite threw its weight behind telecom liberalization.

Through its civil society organizations, especially the U.S.-Egypt's Presidents' Council and the Egyptian Center for Economic Studies (ECES), the globalization elite called for sector reform. In early 1997, ECES began studying ways of modernizing the sector. On November 13, 1997, it organized a pivotal seminar with the title "Telecom Egypt: The Road Ahead."

Approximately twenty individuals participated. Most of them were from the globalization elite, and several individuals belonged to the elite's inner circle. Also present were Atef Ebeid, minister of public enterprise; Youssef Boutros Ghali, minister of economy; President Mubarak's son Gamal; and Raouf Youssef from USAID. The minister of transport was conspicuously absent, and a lower-level bureaucrat represented the ministry. Two speakers were invited: John Cantwell, managing director of the New York-based investment banking firm Solomon Brothers, and Björn Wellenius, the World Bank's senior telecommunications advisor.

Cantwell explained to the round that he had come to ECES to represent the global carrier market. He then told the seminar participants how this market would react should the government choose one of the various options for modernizing the sector: floating a share of the operator on the stock market, bringing in a skilled Egyptian management team, selling a minority share to a strategic investor, selling the entire operation, and inviting foreign management expertise without transfer of ownership. Björn Wellenius spoke second. He discussed the efficiency gains that could be reached through sector liberalization and the regulatory implications of a competitive sector.

Within the round there was general agreement that the sector had to be modernized. Gamal Mubarak commented that telecom reform was crucial and necessary for attracting investment. Atef Ebeid summarized the government's dilemma: "Given the government's will, which is there: Where do we start?" The one dissenting voice came from the bureaucrat representing the Ministry of Transport. He pointed out that the powerful G-7 nations made the rules and that peripheral economies were forced to implement them.

Now It's Moving

The USAID policy matrix was being implemented; rebranded as Telecom Egypt, ARENTO was on its way toward becoming an efficient organization; the EU promoted awareness of the IT revolution; the globalization elite sought a better operator, and the government decided to admit a private cellular provider into the telecom sector.

Now things evolved fast. Early in 1997, Telecom Egypt invited bids from private companies for two licenses to install and operate public payphone systems using prepaid smart cards. These would complement Telecom Egypt's own sparse offering of about five thousand payphones. The payphone operators offered their service under license from the monopolist. This meant that the latter remained in charge but admitted new investors to step into its terrain (Arab Advisors 2002a; EIU 1997/1).

In the second quarter of 1997, the government announced its decision to turn Telecom Egypt into a corporation, separating it from the Ministry of Transport to give it both accountability and freedom, and to split the roles of operator and regulator (EIU 1997/2).

In late November 1997, the government declared that it would privatize the state-owned mobile phone network (EIU 1998/1). In January 1998, it announced that it would sell a stake of 10–20 percent of Telecom Egypt by mid-1998. In early February, it sold 30 percent of Telecom Egypt's cellular operations, the Egyptian Company for Mobile Communications (ECMS), on the stock market. At the same time, it tendered a five-year license for a second cellular network, which would operate in competition with ECMS.[8] This was a major stride toward USAID's goal of introducing competition into the telecom sector and privatizing the state's network assets.

In March 1998, the National Assembly passed a new telecom law.[9] It transformed Telecom Egypt from a public authority into a joint stock company with the ability to create fully or partly owned subsidiaries. The law made private equity in the monopolist possible. Specifically, Article 8 stated that the cabinet of ministers could offer company stock for sale through public subscription, provided that the state kept the majority share. Article 10 stated that until stocks were floated, the general assembly of the company would be made up of a council that comprised the company's board of directors and three experts to be selected by the minister of transport. The minister himself chaired this general assembly. According to Article 2, labor relations were to be governed by labor law 137/1981, which stipulated that employees who had passed the probation period could not be fired unless they had committed a grave mistake such as theft. Effectively this law gave the labor force of Telecom Egypt a high degree of employment security.

In March 1998, the government awarded licenses for payphone operations. One license went to the Menatel consortium. It consisted of France Telecom (44 percent), National Bank of Egypt (18 percent), the National Telecommunications Corporation (18 percent), Orascom (10 percent), and three institutional investors, each contributing 5 percent or less. The other consortium was Nile Telecom, which was composed of Landis and Gyr of Switzerland, in addition to several Egyptian investors. Each provider was to install and operate at least twenty thousand payphones nationwide (Arab Advisors 2002a).

In the same month, the government sold the license for the cellular network that was to compete with the cellular service of the Egyptian Company for Mobile Services (ECMS), which was managed by Telecom Egypt and 70 percent government-owned. The winning bidder was the Misrfone consortium (later called Vodafone): Vodafone of the United Kingdom, AirTouch of the United States and local partners, the Alkan Group, the investment house EFG-Hermes, Mobile Systems International, and Banque du Caire. Submitting a bid of $516 million, the consortium won against the MobiNil consortium, which consisted of France Telecom Mobiles International, Motorola, and local partners Orascom Technologies, the Al-Ahram Press Group, Motorola's agent in Egypt, Systel, and Alcatel agent Raouf Abdel Messih (EIU 1998/3).

Even though Misrfone won the contract, MobiNil did not accept defeat. Instead of withdrawing from the competition, it approached the government with the proposal of buying its share in ECMS. Dazzled by the high license fee it had obtained from Misrfone, the government decided to sell its share in ECMS to MobiNil for £E 249 million and to charge ECMS $516 million for a five-year license. From then on, the two cellular operators sold their services under the brand names of MobiNil and Click, later Vodafone, respectively (EIU 1998/3).[10] Table 7.1 depicts these ownership relations.

The state made a handsome profit. The license terms included the £E 1.77 billion royalty fee, a basic annual license fee of £E 20 million, in addition to annual fees for the use of microwave channels, frequencies, connection, the lease of Telecom Egypt facilities, and a fee for each subscriber set (EIU 1998/3).

Finally in April, President Mubarak issued a decree that established a Telecom Regulatory Authority (TRA) and attached it to the Ministry of Transport and Communications. It was to protect the interests of the state in terms of national security, make sure that the state's telecommunication plans would be applied, and guarantee optimal use of the radio frequencies spectrum. For that purpose the TRA would license companies that operated in the field of communications. It would monitor their performance and set rules to ensure legitimate competition. Last, the TRA was to make sure that tariffs for telecom services were appropriate.

Importantly, Article 9 of the decree stipulated that the TRA would have its own budget, made up of allocations from the general budget of the state, fees for services provided by the TRA, and grants and donations obtained by the regulator with the approval of the Council of Ministers. The board of directors that governed the TRA was chaired by the minister of transport. Besides the chair there were ten additional members, among them the director of the signal corps of the armed forces.

This overview shows that the state attempted to align its regulatory mechanisms with the ideal enshrined in the new global telecom consensus. The regulator had a measure of independence from the ministry. Unlike its predecessor, the TRA had been established by presidential, not ministerial, decree, a fact that endowed its work with greater authority. Moreover, vague

Table 7.1 The two Egyptian cellular operators from February to April 1998

Formal name of operator	Date	Managerial responsibility	Owners	Brand name
Egyptian Company for Mobile Services (ECMS)*	February 1998	Telecom Egypt	32% Egypt's four main state banks; 8% state pension funds; 28% Telecom Egypt; 2% Employees of Telecom Egypt; 30% Public flotation	None
	April 1998	MobiNil consortium	68% MobiNil consortium (France Telecom, Motorola, Orascom, Al-Ahram Press, Systel, Raouf Abdel Messih); 2% Employees of Telecom Egypt; 30% Public flotation	MobiNil
Misrfone	April 1998	Misrfone consortium	Vodafone of the UK, AirTouch of the U.S., and local partners (the Alkan Group, the investment house EFG-Hermes, Mobile Systems International and Banque du Caire)	Click (later Vodafone)

Note: *ECMS was created in 1996 as a state-owned subsidiary of Telecom Egypt. In February 1998, the state sold a 30% minority share by public flotation on the stock market, and in April it sold its remaining majority share of 68% to the private sector MobiNil consortium. To reflect these changes in ownership between February and April 1998, ECMS was assigned two rows in the table.

provisions for its budget had been made. Finally, it regulated an increasingly competitive sector.

In terms of service quality, the decision to license private sector companies for payphones and cellular services was a great success. In the payphone segment, which Telecom Egypt now shared with Menatel and Nile Telecom, the number of payphones more than tripled in a period of less than two years. By December 1999, Egypt had a total of 16,241 payphones.[11]

The same is true for the privatization of cellular services. For reference, Telecom Egypt had only managed to set up 83,000 cellular accounts one year after its service was launched. The two private sector operators performed much better: Click announced in April 1999 that its subscriber base had risen to over 110,000 customers five months after its launch on November 30, 1998. When it was launched, MobiNil took over Telecom Egypt's 83,000 accounts. Over the next five months it almost doubled their number to 157,000 (EIU 1999/2).

Pressure from transnational corporations, core states, development agencies, and the domestic globalization elite had considerably changed Egypt's telecom sector between 1981, the year in which president Mubarak came to office, and early 1999. Communication services had improved, preparing the country for foreign investors, should they choose to come.

CHAPTER 8

Egypt's IT Stakeholders

The previous chapters chronicled how pressures from the international economy bore down on the Egyptian state, pushing it to embrace globalization and the tenets of the IT regime. By the second half of the 1990s, the coalition between the World Bank, USAID, U.S. corporations, and the European Commission, on the one hand, and the Egyptian state and the globalization elite, on the other, tightened. Business conferences and events sponsored by those privileged civil society organizations that represented the globalization elite were the glue that held this coalition together.

There was yet another set of actors to help ready the economy for globalization. Peripheral societies of the 1990s contained individuals whose skills qualified them as technology experts. With the society-wide adoption of IT, their skills would become sought after, and their social and economic status would improve. Technology experts therefore had stakes in pushing the cause of technology to the top of the country's political agenda. This is why I will call them "IT stakeholders."

As long as the IT stakeholders were dispersed throughout society, their individual desires to promote the new communication technologies were bound to be ineffectual. This was true especially in the early stages of the IT revolution, when most peripheral governments did not recognize the transformative potential of the Internet. Those technology experts who managed to organize themselves, however, had chances to see their wishes fulfilled, for organizing allowed them to coordinate their activities, share information, and engage in joint lobbying efforts. It also enabled them to tap the wide range of funding opportunities that corporations, creditor governments, and development agencies provided in the 1990s for IT projects in poor countries.

Egypt's technology experts were masters at building coalitions and accessing funding sources. Consequently, they played an important part in advancing the cause of IT and flexible accumulation in Egypt. The individual that spearheaded their efforts was Hisham El Sherif, a skilled political entrepreneur who founded the Information and Decision Support Center for the Egyptian Cabinet (IDSC).

This chapter will trace the story of Hisham El Sherif and IDSC. El Sherif's interest in bringing IT to Egypt converged with the desire of core actors to fund IT projects that demonstrated the viability of flexible accumulation. He cultivated his contacts with these actors and extracted as many political and financial resources from them as he could. In the late 1990s, he saw that the globalization elite sought to increase Egypt's ties to the core economies and liberalize the telecom sector, and he formed a loose alliance with these businessmen. As a result, the coalition that sought to bring Egypt into compliance with its new role under flexible accumulation expanded. In addition to the World Bank, creditor governments, corporations, the Egyptian globalization elite, and the Egyptian state, it now included IDSC and its network of IT stakeholders.

Core actors played an important part in the political ascent of Egypt's IT stakeholders. They funded their projects, provided them with political resources, and offered them technical support. In doing so, they enabled the IT stakeholders to lobby the state and demand that it assign priority to IT policy. In its relationship with the Egyptian state, core actors thus had the causal power to *increase the IT stakeholders' causal power* to demand of the state that it move IT policy to the top of the political agenda. Conversely, in its relationship with the IT stakeholders, the state had the causal liability of *having to take* the demands of the IT stakeholders *into consideration* and possibly act on them.

These causal powers and liabilities produced another enforcement mechanism, as follows:

Enforcement Mechanism Six: Through their support for the IT stakeholders, core actors *helped prod the state* to move IT policy to the top of the political agenda.

Hisham El Sherif Visits the United States

Born in 1952, Hisham El Sherif was a hard worker with a rapid academic career. In 1978, he acquired a master's degree in computer science from Alexandria University and shortly thereafter a management diploma from the prestigious American University in Cairo. In 1979, the government sent him to the Massachusetts Institute of Technology (MIT) for his doctoral training. Here, he enrolled at the Sloan School of Management, majoring in engineering and management.

The education that El Sherif received at MIT left a lasting impression on him. The Sloan School was the hub for studying decision support systems, at that time the cutting-edge means for simplifying management decisions. A decision support system can be understood as a routinized procedure of identifying a manager's information needs, identifying the data source, collecting the data, writing a computer application to analyze the data, and conducting data analysis that yields information useful for fulfilling the decision maker's needs. Today, standard spreadsheet and database applications fulfill many of these functions. Before the advent of such user-friendly software, DSS allowed managers to ask "what if" questions, such as "What will the increase in revenue be if price is raised by one percent?" (Power 2003).

Titled *An Accelerated Development Strategy for Developing Countries: An Informatics, Decision Support Systems Approach*, El Sherif's dissertation applied the latest research on decision support systems to the Cairo transport authority. His goal was to demonstrate how management and IT expertise of U.S. organizations could be adapted to Egyptian organizations of a similar function, thus improving their efficiency. By adapting knowledge that U.S. organizations had acquired in a long process of trial and error, he sought to shorten the learning curve associated with IT deployment. El Sherif (1983) referred to the process of learning by adaptation as "accelerated development" (38–39).

The dissertation successfully showed how decision support systems could render individual organizations more efficient. But Hisham El Sherif pursued a far more ambitious objective. His goal was to "propose a strategy for the most effective use of informatics in accelerating the development of countries" (15).

The development approach that he laid out in his study would later inform his professional work in Egypt and constitute the basis for his claims that he had found a way of accelerating the country's development. It was seriously flawed.

El Sherif acknowledged that "development"—a term that he left undefined—was a phenomenon with several dimensions at the national level, in particular class structure, organization of the defense system, and political ideology. A careful reading of his study suggests that he understood development as a national process of productivity improvement and economic growth and that he adhered to a stage theory of the kind that Walt Rostow had put forth in his 1960 book *The Stages of Economic Growth: A Non-Communist Manifesto*. According to this model, poor countries were poor because they had not yet developed the economic differentiation and specialization that marked wealthy industrialized economies. To become wealthy, poor countries therefore needed to emulate mature economies, especially the United States.

For El-Sherif, who proposed that organizations in the developing economy should be rendered efficient by borrowing ideas from their U.S. counterparts, development thus became the process of transferring U.S. experience and information technology to the developing economy, organization by organization. With organizational performance thus improved, accelerated development for the entire economy would come about. In other words, by bridging the numerous individual gaps between developed and developing organizations, Egypt would ultimately bridge the economic gap that separated it from the countries of the core.

This approach to development was tenuous in several regards. To begin with, El Sherif assumed that organizations in the peripheral context had the same needs as those in the core context and access to the same resources to fulfill these needs. Second, he overlooked the fact that the institutional structure in which the organizations were embedded and that shaped their goals and identities differed from country to country. Third, he ignored several important works and schools of thought that by 1980 had gone a long way toward discrediting Rostow's stage theory.[1]

Altogether, El Sherif's dissertation combined a sophisticated method of deploying decision support systems with a crude view of development, which advocated imitation of the United States and the ideal of a competitive world economy in which the strong players did not bend the rules.

Back in Egypt

In 1983, with his newly earned PhD in hand, Hisham El Sherif returned from the high-tech hub of Cambridge, Massachusetts, to a country that had hardly any IT base. Egypt's networking environment was embryonic. The telecom grid was congested and dysfunctional; and with its disjointed and centralized internal structure, ARENTO was unable to track the latest communication trends and adapt them to the national context. The state of computing technology was poor, too. El Sherif reports that in 1980, Egypt had only 138 computers. Most of these were outdated. The more modern equipment consisted of 28 mainframe machines, 26 minis, and 4 micros. Altogether, Egypt's computers had a capacity of 10.3 megabytes (El Sherif 1983). Third, the country fell short on computing talent. There were more than 100,000 college graduates per year, but only 3,705 professionals populated the computer field. Of these, 1,205 held a bachelor's degree and only 100 had a PhD or a master's degree (ibid.). The Egyptian Society for Information Technology held the small community of post graduate computer scientists together. Unlike El Sherif, this society had little interest in export-led growth or the world market.

Hisham El Sherif had few peers in Egypt. Quite likely, he was the only computing expert at the time who harbored visions of a borderless world economy. When he tried to put the lessons he had learned abroad into practice, he faced a fight against the odds, but he accepted the challenge. In 1984 he approached Atef Ebeid, then minister of cabinet affairs and administrative development, with the idea of providing decision support to the Egyptian cabinet. Ebeid liked the suggestion and obtained approval from the prime minister (Khalil 2001).

Sherif Founds the Information and Decision Support Center

In 1985, El Sherif established the Cabinet Information and Decision Support Center or, as everybody called it, IDSC. Short of funds for basic supplies, he requested assistance from the United Nations Development Program (UNDP), which were duly granted.[2]

IDSC's official mission had three components. First, the organization was to develop decision support for the Egyptian cabinet and high-level decision makers. Second, it was to help the ministries use information resources efficiently by building them in-house decision support centers. Third, IDSC was to encourage and support informatics projects in Egypt's government agencies, so as to speed—or "accelerate"—their managerial and technological development (IDSC [1988]).

A charismatic leader, Hisham El Sherif managed to attract a remarkable pool of engineering and management talent. Of his agency's 156 staff members 21 held PhD, 9 had master's degrees, and 82 had bachelor's degrees (IDSC [1988]). The number of foreign-educated PhDs who worked at IDSC in the late 1980s and early 1990s was high. Table 8.1 lists only a fraction.

To fulfill Nasser's promise that every college graduate would find government employment, state agencies had to hire a prescribed contingent of university graduates each year. Only in exceptional circumstances could they lay off personnel. IDSC rejected the Nasserist employment guarantee from the outset, because it did not reward performance. Instead, it adopted the practice of issuing renewable employment contracts (Radwan 2002). This way it could let go of staff members who did not live up to expectations. Customary in the United States, this procedure was highly unusual in Egypt, especially within the state bureaucracy.

IDSC's reliance on renewable contracts made it the first government agency that did away with the Nasserist social contract. Not even El Sherif himself was a civil servant (Khalil 2001). Although he presided over IDSC, he was formally an advisor, namely the chairman of the Advisory Board for the Cabinet Information Systems Project. Similarly, his deputy Ahmed

Table 8.1 Select IDSC personnel with doctoral degrees and their educational affiliations

Name	Year in which PhD was awarded	University awarding PhD	University's location
Hisham El Sherif	1983	Massachusetts Institute of Technology	USA
Tarek Kamel	1992	Technical University of Munich	Germany
Sherif Kamel	1994	London School of Economics	United Kingdom
Ahmed Nazif	1983	McGill University	Canada
Sherif Hashem	1993	Purdue University	USA
Raafat Radwan	not known	Claremont University	USA

Nazif held the title of deputy chairman of the Advisory Board for the Cabinet Information Systems Project.[3]

To keep track of the productivity of its staff and ensure transparency in its operations, IDSC managed its projects using the concept of billable hours (El Sherif and El Sawy 1988). Staff appreciation events served the purpose of boosting morale. Altogether, the small agency offered unique opportunities to qualified individuals who longed to apply their engineering talents in an environment where individual initiative was appreciated. IDSC may therefore have had more in common with a U.S. company than with a typical Egyptian state agency that tended to be overstaffed and centralized its decision-making at the highest administrative level.

Building a Support Network

Personnel practices were not the only thing that set IDSC apart. As an agency that advocated the use of computers for problem solving, IDSC was something of a novelty in the state bureaucracy. In order to find acceptance from the rest of the state and, most importantly, the government, IDSC needed to prove itself. Aware of this fact, it set out to ease the lives of cabinet members by applying the ideas of MIT's Sloan School of Management.

In supporting the cabinet El Sherif attempted to stay true to his dissertation, where he had argued that problem solutions designed for the developed context should be transferred into the developing context. He and his colleagues tried to apply these concepts; however, they ran into difficulty:

> Initially, IDSC thought the answers were "out there somewhere" and sought comparative information from similar projects in other countries. While these inputs were very helpful, it became painfully obvious to IDSC that it would have to devise both the design and delivery process, as well as the organizational design, through its own contextual learning in the Egyptian Cabinet's strategic decision-making environment. (El Sherif and El Sawy 1988, 556)

In addition, IDSC found that in the peer group context of a cabinet the ministers did not frame their problems as semi-structured "what if" questions that would have lent themselves to simple decision support solutions. Instead, they framed their problems as issues, which evoked heated debate within the cabinet. Decision support therefore consisted, to a large extent, of structuring strategic issues. Besides developing computer programs as they had planned, representatives of IDSC had to engage in shuttle diplomacy, conflict resolution, and consensus-building. Putting dissertation ideas into practice turned out to require adjustment (El Sherif and El Sawy 1988).

The organization quickly adapted to the challenge. In addition to figuring out how to work within the cabinet environment, IDSC learned how to win the allegiance of other state agencies when it came to implementing its ideas of state computerization. Raafat Radwan, IDSC's director in 2002, explained that the agency's leaders started out with management concepts they had acquired in the United States, but then modified them to fit the Egyptian cultural context. For example, in the United States, professional interaction is highly goal-oriented, and little time is spent building personal relationships. In Egypt, on the other hand, good personal relationships are a prerequisite for a successful business partnership. Consequently, the leaders of IDSC took great care to establish a personal rapport with the insiders of ministries that they sought to computerize, among others by keeping track of important events—birthdays, holidays, weddings—that unfolded in the lives of these individuals (Radwan 2002).

Helping the State Understand its Debt

By early 1987, two years after the agency had come into existence, twenty-four projects were underway (El Sherif 1990). An important project for IDSC's standing with the cabinet was Egypt's debt database. The country's thirty-three-billion-dollar public debt was fragmented into five thousand different loans with a large number of creditor countries, banks, and international agencies. The government, which was in the process of rescheduling its debt obligations, lacked an overview of what it owed to whom (El Sherif and El Sawy 1988).

By 1988, after eighteen months of work, IDSC had built a computer-based centralized database at the Central Bank of Egypt. It contained information on the range of governmental loans—from the private sector, international agencies, foreign governments, and others—and allowed users to compile analytical reports that evaluated the impacts of different "what if" scenarios. Once again, UNDP provided funding, this time in conjunction with the United Nations Conference for Trade and Development (UNCTAD). The database made the government's rescheduling negotiations much easier (El Sherif and El Sawy 1988; IDSC and Central Bank of Egypt [1989]).

The project increased the prestige of IDSC with the government. By saving the state leadership potentially large sums of money, IDSC amortized its operating costs of two million dollars and legitimized its existence (El Sherif and El Sawy 1988).[4]

Giving the State Access to the Countryside

In late 1987, IDSC initiated another project that proved the agency's value to the cabinet. It was the governorate decision support project, which sought to install an information and decision support center in each of Egypt's twenty-seven provinces. With this project, IDSC departed from its previous practice of confining support activities to the Cairo-based ministries.

Appointed by the president, Egypt's provincial governors administered the provinces on behalf of the central government. Each governor presided over directorates that were the local extensions of central ministries. As such, they reported directly to Cairo. Each governor had a statistics unit that collected data from these directorates and summarized them for him. IDSC, through the governorates' decision support project, sought to improve these data analysis capabilities. Each governorate was to receive an information and decision support center that would comprise the existing statistics unit as well as a new computer resource unit, a new decision support unit, a new library unit, and a new publications unit. The center was to report directly to the governor. IDSC furnished each center with personal computers and databases that it had designed to cover the different sectors of the Egyptian economy. These databases were identical across the provinces, to enable the merging of data. If successful, they would provide the government with standardized economic information about Egypt's countryside (Nidumolu et al. 1996).

During the first two years, when El Sherif himself concentrated his attention on the informatization of the Cairo ministries, most governors treated the project with skepticism:

> Although the project was sponsored by Cabinet IDSC, whose chairman reported to the minister for Cabinet Affairs, the relatively low Cabinet priority given to the project in the first two years only served to make it difficult for social influence to be exerted on the governors. During this period, the Egyptian Cabinet and the Cabinet IDSC were more preoccupied with the computerization of the central ministries in Cairo. The general perception of the project during these years was that of an experimental, rather unglamorous effort by a small section of Cabinet IDSC with unknown benefits and opportunities. (208–209)

The governors' reservation was increased by the fact that they had to contribute financially: two hundred thousand Egyptian pounds to build the center and one hundred thousand Egyptian pounds in annual operational cost. In 1989–90, El Sherif devoted his personal attention to the project and pushed its implementation. Then he decided that IDSC should organize a governors' conference in Cairo (Nidumolu et al. 1996).

Held in February 1992, the conference turned out to be an excellent public relations tool for IDSC. The prime minister, who presided over the event, had each governor demonstrate how he used his information and decision support center. Impressed by the project, the central government made it a national priority and allocated ninety-two million Egyptian pounds for its expansion. Among other things, it decided to connect the centers with the Ministry for Local Administration by means of a wide area network. The governorates project greatly enhanced the government's data collection abilities and was therefore a practical success. Once again IDSC had proven its worth, and the cabinet took notice (ibid.).

CAPMAS, the "Big Black Hole"

While IDSC gained popularity with government officials who benefited from its projects, it encroached on the turf of a much older and larger state agency. The organization in question was CAPMAS, the Central Organization for Public Mobilization and Statistics.

CAPMAS had been established in the era of Nasserist planning. In the early 1980s, its responsibilities included mobilizing young men in case of a war and putting together statistics needed for national planning. It also monopolized the import of computing equipment. During 2002, well-connected observers in Cairo invariably described the organization as a large but inefficient agency. A British observer offered her evaluation, which was echoed by others. "CAPMAS is like a huge black hole, unwieldy, old-fashioned and statist. It is an organization of many people who do very little. At the beginning, when I wanted some statistics, I would go to CAPMAS, but I soon learned better."

IDSC's interest in computers and data collection meant that it was only a matter of time before it undermined CAPMAS's monopoly over the allocation of computing resources and the compilation of statistical reports. CAPMAS inevitably grew resentful. In 2002, a former professor from Cairo University and one of the early IT stakeholders explained:

> In the 1980s, information technology comprised mainly very large computers spread throughout the universities. No one could buy a computer without obtaining the approval of CAPMAS, and that impeded the spread of IT throughout the government and society. When IDSC concerned itself with information technology, CAPMAS was very unhappy about it.

However, despite the fact that the dinosaur held a grudge against IDSC, the rivalry never erupted into an open collision, because Atef Ebeid protected IDSC. Thanks to this patronage, CAPMAS did not prevent IDSC's informatization efforts, and it did not openly object when the young entity began to collect its own data at the level of the governorates.

Outreach to International Peers

By 1988, El Sherif had built a small organization with a committed and gifted staff. It had installed 110 personal computers at various ministries. With increased acceptance of the concept came more requests for similar services from state agencies. The amount of recognition IDSC enjoyed was reflected in the quality of office space assigned for its work. At first, it was given a small office space on Qasr El Aini Street in Cairo. Then it was allotted medium-sized old villa on Hassan Sabry Street, in the wealthy Cairo neighborhood of Zamalek. In 1990, it shifted its headquarters to the centrally located Maglis El-Shaab Street, where it moved into a brand-new seven-story building of sixty-four hundred square meters with state-of-the-art computing and conferencing facilities (El Sherif and El Sawy 1988; IDSC [1988] and [1990]).

That IDSC advanced in the state's bureaucratic hierarchy is no coincidence. Its leaders understood the value of marketing and publicity for garnering support. In addition, they established contacts with their counterparts from the core economies. With great skill for politicking, Hisham El Sherif employed two mutually reinforcing networking practices. When dealing with partners abroad, he built credibility by leveraging the governmental support his agency enjoyed in Egypt. In his dealings with Egyptians, on the other hand, he increased his stature by pointing to the interest that IDSC invoked among his partners abroad.

In his effort to make international contacts, El Sherif employed multiple strategies. He and his colleagues wrote academic papers about their operations, which they presented at international conferences for operations research before publishing them in specialized peer-reviewed journals. In addition, El Sherif entered his agency into international competitions in the management sciences. In 1987, it won the Third World Prize of the triennial conference of the International Federation of Operations Research Societies. In 1989, it won the Franz Edelman Award for management science achievement (El Sherif 1990; El Sherif and El Sawy 1988; IDSC [1990]; Kamel 1993).

IDSC also initiated an annual international prize competition for outstanding innovations, achievements, and applications of decision support system technology. The competition was to be offered annually by the Egyptian Institute of Management Sciences' College on Information Systems. In the first year, awards went to researchers and practitioners in government and *Fortune* "500" companies (IDSC [1990]).

The agency complemented these networking and outreach activities by publishing its own brochures in English. They featured IDSC's achievements by summarizing its most important projects and awards. In the 1990 brochure, for example, the organization claimed worldwide recognition for its efforts in the development, implementation, and institutionalization of information and decision support systems in Egypt (IDSC [1988] and [1990]).

Core Actors Support the IT Stakeholders (Causal Power Six)

IDSC's mission statement committed the agency to providing decision support for the state. However, El Sherif wanted more than that. He believed in the ideals of competition, individual reward, and export-led growth. Status-conscious and competitive, he measured his success by the degree to which he lived up to standards set by the Sloan School of Management, and he measured Egypt's success by the degree to which it managed to prosper in a world where the United States set the rules. As a patriot, he was determined to make his country succeed, accelerating its development and enabling it to compete on equal terms with the best in the world.

His goal was to turn Egypt into a software exporter that would supply the world market with affordable computer programs. Without much fanfare, he therefore expanded IDSC's mission and tasked it with serving as a reservoir and advocate for IT policy ideas. The agency began to call for a technology park that would export high-tech products and software. It then created a program that fostered awareness of high-technology as a potential export sector and put together an industry lobby. In 1992, it founded the Regional Information Technology and Software Engineering Center (RITSEC), a hybrid between an intergovernmental and a nongovernmental organization with close ties to the state. In taking these measures, IDSC kept a close eye on funding opportunities from the global economy.

These activities merit a closer look. The discussion that follows will show that actors from the core provided ample funding for IT projects, as well as political resources and contacts. These resources helped IDSC as it advanced its cause of pushing IT to the top of Egypt's political agenda.

The Pyramids Technology Valley Project

As early as 1987 or 1988, IDSC made plans for a Pyramids Technology Valley, a technology park in 6th of October City. In this scheme, export figured prominently:

> The Pyramids Technology Valley Project aims at creating a suitable environment for the development of Egypt's electronic and software industries; attracting new foreign investment in high-tech projects; assisting in the creation of new opportunities for small business enterprises; and exporting software to other countries. (IDSC [1988])

To generate support for its idea, IDSC organized the national Pyramids Technology Valley conference, which took place in Cairo from December 18 to 20, 1989. But the proposal for a technology park did not receive high-level backing; and although IDSC held on to the project, it would be another ten years before it materialized.[5]

IDSC continued to promote the cause of IT. In 1991, it contacted the U.S. Investment Promotion Office (USIPO) to obtain financial assistance. USIPO had been established by USAID as a nongovernmental organization. Its purpose was to assist potential investors in Egypt's export industry, thereby promoting Egypt's integration into the world market. IDSC wanted a marketing study on the Egyptian high-technology industry. Since this plan fit USIPO's mission, it agreed to provide funding. IDSC used the money to hire the Californian firm Dataquest and have it analyze the possibilities a high-tech electronics and computer industry might offer Egypt. IDSC hoped that this report would demonstrate the feasibility of its technology plans (Dataquest 1991).

Dataquest's results (1991) must have pleased El Sherif and his colleagues. The study recommended that Egypt focus on software. It cited the following reasons:

- Current average backlog in major U.S. corporations for software development is three years. This is because of lack of available personnel. Egypt, with its large work force of trained manpower, could target this area effectively.
- There will be a shortage of computer software personnel worldwide. MITI in Japan forecasts that there will be a shortage of 1,000,000 software personnel in Japan alone by the end of this decade. The number of students enrolling in the United States for computer software courses is far short of the projected demand. These worldwide shortages create opportunities for Egypt.
- Getting into the software business would be a low-cost strategy. As compared to hardware manufacturing, software production requires much less capital expenditure...
- Within the high-technology industry areas, software is the most developed in Egypt. This can be developed into a core competency of Egypt, very much like what India has done. India today has over 100,000 software personnel.
- Software development is a very high value-added activity. (2–49)

This recommendation confirmed what the leaders of IDSC had been thinking all along: The world market offered a niche for Egypt. The country's future lay in software exports.

Forays Into the Private Sector

To systematize its efforts at industrial policy, IDSC established its Technology Development Program, which was to work toward a high-tech industry in Egypt. The program proceeded along three tracks. It took over the Pyramids Technology Valley project; it worked to create a favorable business environment for technology development; and it sought to develop a human resource base that could support a high-tech industry (IDSC, TDP 1994).

Beginning in 1994, the Technology Development Program published catalogs that listed IT companies in Egypt. These volumes could serve as a means for creating a political network among IT stakeholders. Published in English, they enabled backers from abroad to become involved by entering into joint ventures with local companies or pursuing other forms of cooperation.

Besides the Technology Development Program, Hisham El Sherif also put in place the Hi-Tech Business Council, which he personally chaired (IDSC, TDP 1996). On good terms with government officials, IDSC now made forays into the globalization-oriented private sector.

RITSEC: IDSC's "International Arm"

In the late 1980s, another opportunity for strengthening Egypt's IT stakeholders presented itself, and El Sherif did not pass it up. Since the mid-1980s, the Arab Fund for Economic and Social Development (AFESD) and UNDP had been in consultation on an informatics strategy for the Middle East. In 1986, they decided to develop and support a regional project. In February 1987, they agreed to fund a regional software technology center in Kuwait.

By 1988, El Sherif must have gotten involved in the discussions, for it was then that the donors decided to establish two centers instead of one. The center in Kuwait would produce education and business-related software. Another center in Cairo would create software for decision support and database management. In 1989, the governments of Egypt and Kuwait, as well as UNDP and AFESD, signed an agreement establishing the Regional Software Technology Centers Project. The Egyptian government appointed Atef Ebeid, El Sherif's longtime patron, to represent it on the executive board of the Cairo center, which came to be known as the Regional Information Technology and Software Engineering Center (RITSEC).

According to the 1989 project document, the two centers were to serve the Arab world by transferring state-of-the-art software technology to the region and spawning a home-grown software industry. Both centers would produce advanced software technology and train private and public organizations to become software developers in their own right. The relationship between the two centers would be cooperative. Together they were to create and lead an Arab software industry association, which would have chapters in all countries of the region.

The planners intended to establish the project as a business. The 1989 project document describes the endeavor:

> The Project seeks to establish a self-financing business organization. The organization of the Project follows the analogy of a shareholders body appointing a board of Directors in a multinational corporation. The two funding agencies and the two host countries are the shareholders at the start of the Project. Other countries in the Region or other funding

sources might be invited to become shareholders. The shareholders appoint a "Board of Directors" which assumes the executive powers in the project organization.

Curiously, however, a draft of the articles of association of November 1989 contradicted this set-up. Rather than casting the two centers as businesses, it stipulated that they would have the status of intergovernmental organizations, including tax exemption and diplomatic immunity. This initial confusion later allowed RITSEC to further confound its status by calling itself a nonprofit organization, negating the idea that it was meant to be a profit-bearing multinational company.

UNDP and AFESD agreed to contribute three million dollars each to the project.[6] The host governments promised to provide buildings that would house their respective centers, as well as support personnel, transportation, and office supplies.

The target date for opening the centers was spring 1990, but Iraq's invasion of Kuwait forced a postponement, and the Kuwait center only opened its doors in 1996.[7] RITSEC, however, was established in 1992. It moved into IDSC's old quarters on Hasan Sabry Street in the El Zamalek neighborhood, and El Sherif became its director. He now presided over both IDSC and RITSEC. One of them formed part of the state, the other called itself nongovernmental.

The two organizations complemented each other. While IDSC worked for the Egyptian government, RITSEC's curious status as a regional, intergovernmental, or nongovernmental organization gave it great freedom to maneuver for two reasons. First, unlike IDSC it could draw on financial support from international organizations without raising suspicion with envious government bureaucrats. Second, a number of international funding sources required recipients to have nongovernmental status. IDSC would have been ineligible for these kinds of assistance, but RITSEC could freely tap into them.

Formally there was a strict separation between the two organizations, but in practice the distinction was far from clear. To begin with, IDSC acted on behalf of the Egyptian government when it hosted RITSEC on its premises. Second, RITSEC claimed credit for several IDSC projects.[8] Third, there was a considerable overlap in personnel between the two organizations; this is evident in publications, where authors frequently listed their organizational affiliation as IDSC/RITSEC. Finally, and most importantly, Hisham El Sherif headed both entities. In 2001, when several individuals at IDSC and RITSEC were asked why staff members of IDSC were working for RITSEC, they replied that the hours that IDSC staff members spent on

RITSEC projects were part of the Egyptian government's in-kind contribution to the Regional Software Technology Centers Project.

For El Sherif, the division of labor between the two organizations served a purpose. As IDSC's "international arm" RITSEC could contribute to his goal of making Egypt a globally competitive software exporter. And because IDSC was not considered part of the state, it could openly voice IDSC's vision of the global economy and Egypt's role in it. As the following statement, made at RITSEC's launching seminar, reveals, this vision was far more in line with flexible accumulation than with Egypt's official government policy:

- Governments should encourage exporting regional software products to other countries of the world...
- Countries of the region should encourage large international companies in information technology and software related industries to invest in the region...
- Strategic alliances should be established between RITSEC and leading international software development organizations...
- RITSEC should be capable of articulating strategies that can help the region become a viable global competitor in the software industry and identify advantageous niches in the global market. (RITSEC n.d. a)

RITSEC's interest in opening Egypt to global investment and trade flows made the organization a viable partner for global IT and software companies who pursued the same goal, if from a different vantage point.

Judging by RITSEC's brochures and its website, software development constituted a small fraction of its activities. The organization engaged in systems integration, information systems development in different areas—such as trade, environment, education—web development, multimedia culture preservation, as well as human resource and professional skill development in the area of information technology (RITSEC 2001). It is difficult to tell what the exact nature of the various initiatives was, since different sources provide contradictory information. Unlike IDSC with its award-winning system of project management, RITSEC did not categorize its activities properly and provided inconsistent descriptions of individual projects. This may have been because the organization drew extensively on external funding and implemented projects as money became available. Especially in the area of education, similar resources seem to have been used for different purposes.

Even though RITSEC did not become a specialized software center as intended, it fulfilled at least part of its original purpose, because it helped catalyze a varied IT community in Egypt, comprising Internet service providers (ISPs), providers of IT-enabled services, software developers, training providers, web developers, and others. As given here, a glance at just a few of its many activities shows that political and financial resources from the global economy were offered in abundance.

Connecting Arab Countries

RAITNET, the Regional Arab Information Technology Network, is one of RITSEC's well-publicized but now defunct initiatives. The exact nature of RAITNET is elusive. The network seems to have been different things to different people. Kamel and Abdel Baki (1995) explain that it was launched in December 1994 to bring IT professionals of the Arab world together. As one of its main objectives, the network supported the growth of the software industry in the Arab region by serving IT professionals in governmental and nongovernmental agencies. It offered an e-mail list, gopher and web servers, and discussion groups on IT-related subjects.

UNESCO claims that it initiated the network in 1996, with RITSEC as the lead implementing organization. According to this description, RAITNET included twenty-five Arab organizations working in the field of IT. It offered consultancy to member states and formulation of national and regional projects; training in the field of information and communication technologies and online information dissemination (UNESCO Cairo n.d.). RITSEC offers yet a third account. According to this source, the project sought to develop a framework for a regional information highway for culture and tourism (RITSEC n.d. b).

Web Development for Children

In 1997, RITSEC launched the Arab Child initiative, which comprised a number of activities, such as the establishment of cyber cafés. As part of the initiative, RITSEC created the Little Horus website. Launched in June 1997 in both Arabic and English, the site featured over three hundred pages covering Egypt's history. Little Horus won numerous awards and recognitions: Microsoft founder Bill Gates mentioned the website in his book *The Speed of Thought* as an example of a "web lifestyle [which] is about broadening horizons, not narrowing them."[9] According to RITSEC, the website was a finalist in the 1999 Global Bangemann Challenge, a competition named after the European Commissioner who in 1994 issued the *Bangemann Report* (see chapter three). Additionally, the website won the Childnet International Award of Cable & Wireless in 1999 and several other awards. The Arab Child initiative is a prime example of how RITSEC and IDSC used their projects to establish contacts abroad. It also illustrates how much interest there was in the core economies for projects that showcased the possibilities of IT (RITSEC 1999a,b).

Human Resource Training

RITSEC also engaged in human resource development. For that purpose it founded RITI, the Regional IT Institute, in 1993. It offered IT training to managers, professionals, and technicians in the Arab region, as well as courses in business administration. It included in-person and distance education projects, offered in collaboration with a number of universities in Europe and the United States and with corporations such as Oracle. Thanks to these alliances, Egyptians could obtain an MBA degree from the Maastricht School of Management in the Netherlands without leaving Cairo.

RITSEC was involved in a somewhat confusing array of other distance learning activities, which appear to have been managed by RITI. In 1998, the World Bank's infoDev program funded a feasibility study and pilot implementation for RITSEC's Learnnet in the amount of two hundred and fifty thousand dollars. The project aimed at putting up a video-enabled distance learning network for IT professionals in seven Arab countries. The infoDev pilot connected three training centers in Egypt, Jordan, and Tunisia. Additional nodes were planned (infoDev n.d. a and n.d. d; RITSEC 1999c).

In 2000, RITSEC established the Global Distance Learning Center (GDLC). In cooperation with the World Bank and with USAID support, the center connected Egypt to the World Bank Global Development Learning Network. It intended to link fifty countries around the world into one global network. The content—seminars on best practice in public administration—was administered by the Bank with input from member nodes. Besides working with the World Bank, the Egyptian center developed strategic alliances with organizations such as MIT, the Euro Services' e-Business/e-Excellence in the United Kingdom and ICUS e-Learning in France. As part of the Arab Child initiative, it was also involved in a project called Schoolnet Africa (GDLC Egypt n.d.; RITSEC n.d. c).

A Network of Alliances

Actors from the core and development organizations readily formed alliances with RITSEC. Partners included Advanced Computer Communication, AT&T, Battelle, Microsoft, Motorola, Oracle, Sun, Texas Instruments, and many more. RITSEC was also able to draw on commissions and financial support from numerous donor agencies, including USAID, infoDev, UNESCO, UNDP, and the Arab Fund for Economic and Social

Development. In addition, it was involved in a number of projects sponsored by the European Union as part of the Euro-Mediterranean Partnership (European Commission n.d.; RITSEC n.d. d).

Egypt Gets its Internet Connection

In October 1993, Tarek Kamel from IDSC/RITSEC and Nashwa Abdel Baki from Cairo University established Egypt's first connection to the Internet, using a 9.6 kilobit link that connected the Egyptian Universities Network (EUN) and France. ARENTO, which controlled Egypt's fixed line telecom network and Egypt's connections with the rest of the world, furnished the link. For the first time, Egyptians could communicate using the TCP/IP protocol (Kamel and Abdel Baki 1995; Kelly and Ismail 2001, 6).

The Egyptian government did not understand what the Internet was and what its economic implications were, so it took no notice of the Internet connection. Meanwhile, IDSC continued to expand the network. In 1994, the 9.6 kilobit connection to France was upgraded to 64 kilobit, over the SEMEWE-2 underwater cable that crossed the Mediterranean. By 1997, international connectivity to and from Egypt was provided via satellite links and fiber connectivity to Europe and the U.S. rural areas were connected via VSAT terminals.

In 1994, IDSC made the Internet accessible to the professional public. While educational Internet users dialed up to the university network, IDSC/RITSEC served as the Internet service provider for government organizations and commercial establishments. In order to stimulate interest in the service, IDSC provided companies with free accounts.

Thanks to the free usage policy, demand for Internet access grew quickly, putting strain on the network. Interviewed in 2002, a member of RITSEC remembered those days as difficult:

RITSEC was the first ISP in Egypt, with ARENTO giving it the physical connection. At that time, Tarek Kamel implemented a policy of providing free Internet accounts to companies who wished to access the Internet. Things were quite difficult then. We would sometimes sit for two to three hours dialing up to RITSEC, before we could finally connect to the Internet. The reason was that RITSEC did not have many phone lines, only about 20. At the same time, many users wanted to dial up. So the experience was frustrating, but it was better than nothing. RITSEC also dedicated phone lines to subscribers in other Arab countries, such as Jordan or Syria. In those countries, they did not have Internet access, and dialing up to Egypt, while expensive, was still cheaper than dialing up to France or to the United States. This RITSEC policy was also initiated by Tarek Kamel.

In 1996, IDSC decided to end its monopoly on the provision of Internet services. It allowed private sector companies to lease part of the bandwidth that it had purchased from ARENTO and offer ISP services to the public. As a result, more than sixteen private sector ISPs came into existence between 1996 and 1997 (Kamel 1997; Kelly and Ismail 2001).

ISPs thus leased domestic lines and international connectivity from IDSC, which in turn leased bandwidth from the telecom monopolist. Antagonism between ARENTO and the growing community of Internet professionals grew. Kamel and Abdel Baki complained that while international connectivity was decent, ARENTO charged prohibitively high prices for connecting to the rest of the world. In 1996, the expanding community of IT stakeholders therefore founded the Internet Society of Egypt (ISE). Its function was to protect the circle of ISPs, Internet users, and Web professionals from incursions into their territory by ARENTO, the supervising Ministry of Transport, or another state agency. Kamel (1997) expressed it diplomatically: "The society will protect the newly established Internet community from any unexpected actions by any party."

ISE was located at IDSC. Once again, Hisham El Sherif presided. Tarek Kamel served as secretary general. Beside these two individuals, the board of directors included ISPs and Alaa Mubarak, the older son of President Mubarak. In October 1997, ISE founded an e-commerce committee, and in 1998 it became a chapter of the Internet Society (ESIS 2001; ISE n.d.).

Political Alliances are Consolidated

Throughout the 1990s, IDSC increased its network of alliances in Egypt and abroad. By now, Hisham El Sherif enjoyed a degree of international fame. Thanks to his decade-long efforts to build international alliances, he knew the chief economic officers of global corporations and influential figures at the World Bank. In 1995 he widened his political network even further when he accepted the invitation to join the Global Information Infrastructure Commission (GIIC; see chapter three). As one of GIIC's "Third World representatives," he endowed the views of the organization with legitimacy. The GIIC in turn enabled him to claim association "with its twenty-five top world business leaders" (Third World Summit on Media for Children 2001).

In the mid-1990s, Hisham El Sherif joined several civil society organizations that represented the inner circle of the globalization elite. Egypt's new globalization elite and the network of local IT stakeholders were forming a loose alliance.

Mubarak Takes IT Policy Seriously (Mechanism Six)

By 1996, if not earlier, President Mubarak appointed El Sherif to the U.S.-Egypt's Presidents' Council, and in 1998 Gamal Mubarak invited him to serve on the board of the Future Generation Foundation. Meanwhile Alaa Mubarak, President Mubarak's older son, lent his patronage to the Internet Society of Egypt by serving on its board of directors.

That the globalization elite, the network of IT stakeholders, and the government formed an alliance is not surprising. The state leadership had become convinced that globalization was unavoidable, and it needed domestic partners who supported its policy of integrating Egypt into the world market. The globalization elite were interested in connecting to the core economies. The same was true for Egypt's IT stakeholders. Once the two groups realized that they had similar interests, they began to support one another.

Meanwhile, the IT stakeholders intensified their public relations activities, drawing international attention to Egypt. Starting in 1996, they organized CAINET, a yearly convention on the development of the Internet. CAINET drew eight hundred–twelve hundred participants annually, of whom 15 percent were foreigners. In 1999, Suzanne Mubarak, Egypt's first lady, attended.

In April 1998, the Ministry of Culture, the Supreme Council of Antiquities, IDSC, and RITSEC organized the three-day conference Euromed '98. Its topic was "Using Information Technology to Preserve Cultural Heritage," and it attracted 250 Egyptians and 50 foreigners.

In May 1999, RITSEC and the Internet Society of Egypt held a one-day seminar, which introduced the fundamentals of e-commerce to participants and elaborated on their application to business. The 43 participants came mostly from ISE and the American Chamber of Commerce (ESIS 2001).

Finally, in September 1999 the first National Conference on the Information Revolution in the Era of Mubarak was held. President Mubarak attended the conference in person and launched a national strategy that promised to finally realize IDSC's aspirations and put its ideas of "accelerated development" into practice. A month later he appointed Atef Ebeid to the post of prime minister. IDSC's fortunes were on the rise.

CHAPTER 9

A New Ministry for an Old Country

The enforcement mechanisms described in previous chapters caused the Egyptian state to liberalize its economy, open it to the world market, and adopt the tenets of the IT revolution. But the impact of these mechanisms when operating in conjunction can go well beyond the sum of each working separately. Together they can be transformational, as expressed in the following hypothesis:

> **Hypothesis:** Working in conjunction, enforcement mechanisms that prod the Third World state to comply with its role under flexible accumulation can change the state's composition in a way that improves its ability to carry the requirements of flexible accumulation into the Third World economy.

Regime theorists have long believed that norms and regimes—the sum of which constitutes social structure—can shape state behavior. But this hypothesis states that they can accomplish even more. They have the ability to change the way a state is "put together," which in turn determines how a state perceives itself. The hypothesis given here thus supports the constructivist claim that state identity is a product of socialization.

Martha Finnemore (1996), a constructivist international relations scholar of George Washington University, studied the emergence of science bureaucracies and found that states sometimes imitate their equals in other parts of the world. In contrast to her findings, the hypothesis given earlier suggests that when we observe changes in state composition, a good deal of bullying may have been at work. In those cases, the autonomy of the local citizens has been undermined, because their right to choose their own government institutions has been preempted by outside actors.

The following sections will show that enforcement mechanisms can change the state—not that they necessarily did so in any given country, but that they have the *potential* of doing so. Once again, Egypt presents a clear example.

The President Gives a Speech

On September 13, 1999, at the opening ceremony of Egypt's National Information Technology Conference, President Hosni Mubarak took an unusual measure. He stepped to the podium, glanced at the assembled technology experts, and launched into a speech. It was the first time that he addressed Egypt's IT stakeholders publicly. Well aware of the significance of this gesture, they listened intently. Mubarak said:

> The world imposed an economic system on us that depends on information and science, builds on high-speed information networks and advances by means of creativity and excellence. Globalization brought us an economic order of which transnational corporations are the pillars. They use information and science for their purposes. They build communication networks that connect the world, and they seek to widen their reach and dominate markets.

Access to information and technology, he stated, were distributed unevenly among nations. The industrialized economies possessed vast amounts of these intangible assets; and if Egypt wanted to benefit from them, it needed to expand its national IT community and encourage it to absorb some of these information flows.

Mubarak offered six signposts that would guide IT policy. First, Egypt was to become an IT exporter. Second, the state was to stimulate national demand for information. This would serve the twin goals of rendering domestic industry efficient and creating an export-oriented IT industry. Third, to create an IT industry, the state would train people in the use of IT at all skill levels. Fourth, alliances between members of the Egyptian IT industry and the dominant global players were to lead to technology transfer. Mubarak explained:

> If we want to accelerate the development of this industry, we must build alliances between IT companies in Egypt and their counterparts in the more advanced countries. We also need alliances with those countries that have successfully developed and diversified their IT industry. These

alliances will help us transfer knowledge, reduce production costs, and improve our marketing capacity.

Fifth, to develop the industry, infrastructure had to be upgraded; the government and the private sector needed to cooperate in setting up software plants and labs; and phone rates needed to be low enough to support Egypt's competitive position. Sixth, the regulatory and legislative regime for intellectual property rights had to be reviewed with an eye to encouraging local inventions.

Altogether, the strategy bore the imprint of Egypt's Cabinet Information and Decision Support Center (IDSC). It contained a number of ideas that IDSC had advocated for years, in particular El Sherif's notion that the computerization of individual organizations would bring about macroeconomic growth. In addition, Mubarak referred several times to El Sherif's idea of accelerating development. He furthermore praised the accomplishments of IDSC and the Regional Information Technology and Software Engineering Center (RITSEC) as national achievements on which future IT policy would build.

The conference was a coup for Hisham El Sherif and his colleagues, because they saw their ambitions become reality. By stating that the country was to become IT-driven, President Mubarak signaled to the world that the well-being of the IT stakeholders was central to Egypt's future.

How is the Speech to Be Interpreted?

A casual observer of Egyptian politics might have been perplexed by the address, especially since the president himself was computer illiterate. After a few moments of surprise, the observer might have attributed Mubarak's interest in IT to the influence of his technology-savvy sons, Gamal and Alaa.

Mubarak's personal circumstances may indeed have hastened his attention to technology. However, an analysis of Egypt's political economy suggests that more complex, structural forces were at work, creating a political environment in which a national focus on IT was simply the easiest route to take. To begin with, the Paris Club of creditor nations, together with the World Bank and the IMF, pressed Egypt into a structural adjustment program (mechanism one). It began in 1991 and entailed deep-reaching economic reforms. Through this program, the Paris Club pushed Egypt to replace state capitalism and import substitution with a strategy of private sector and export-led growth. The European Commission supported the thrust of the adjustment program by requiring Egypt to open its borders to European industrial imports (mechanism two).

Here comes the sticking point. The success of an export-led strategy hinges on the development of national expertise in the production of a niche good or service for which there is demand in the world market. For example, China had expertise in producing low-cost garments. Switzerland specialized in providing confidential banking services. In both economies, the state passed macroeconomic, industrial, and regulatory policies that supported these niche sectors; consequently, they produced goods and services that were cheaper or better than those of competitor countries. With this strategy, they generated export revenues. The Egyptian state, therefore, needed to identify a specialty sector capable of exporting profitably. Once this was accomplished, Egypt would need to nurture the sector with an appropriate framework of incentives to boost its global competitiveness.

Meanwhile, with considerable support from the core economies, IDSC directed the government's attention toward the need to introduce IT into the economy (mechanism six). As part of its technology drive, IDSC developed

an export strategy that promised Egypt its own niche in the world market. As seen in chapter eight, this niche consisted of software export.

At the same time, the globalization elite—with support from the core economies—wanted Egypt to pursue a strategy of export-led growth. Elite entrepreneurs had their gaze set on the core for political support and guidance, and core actors called for telecom reform (mechanisms four and five). The globalization elite appropriated this demand, then passed it on to the Egyptian state (mechanism three). In the mid-1990s, the government entered into an alliance with the globalization elite and the IT stakeholders. Together they worked to open the domestic economy to the world market.

In sum, all mechanisms pushed the state toward export-led growth, which depended on a niche that could generate export revenues, and toward a globalization-friendly telecom and IT strategy. By making IT a national priority, the state could hit two birds with one stone: It could satisfy corporate demands for a good communication infrastructure, and satisfy the need for an export specialty. It is therefore plausible to interpret Mubarak's September address as a response to the various enforcement mechanisms that the state faced.

A Ministry is Born

Mubarak's presentation was the first rumbling of something big to come. It happened in October. A month after his speech, the president reshuffled the cabinet. Atef Ebeid, minister of public enterprise and longtime patron of Hisham El Sherif, was elevated to the position of prime minister. Moreover, an old ministry lost influence, and a new one was created.

Ever since the days of Gamal Abdel Nasser, the Ministry of Transport and Communication (MoT) had been in charge of supervising the telecom sector. It had done so in a way that had left the telecom monopolist increasingly unable to upgrade the telecom network. During the 1990s, the Nasserist approach to supervising the telecom sector fell out of favor with corporations, the U.S. Agency for International Development (USAID), the globalization elite, the local IT stakeholders, the state leadership and—quite plausibly—the managers of the telecom monopolist, who felt slighted by the ministry.

Now President Mubarak and Prime Minister Ebeid stripped the ministry of its responsibilities in the areas of postal services and telecom and pushed it into the background of the state. Resistance from the minister would have been futile. The coalition of economic actors that was pitted against him was sufficiently large, and the president was too powerful to entertain protest.

In parallel, the government announced the establishment of the new Ministry of Communications and Information Technologies (MCIT). It took over MoT's telecom-related tasks: The new minister would supervise Telecom Egypt; he would chair the board of the Telecom Regulatory Authority (TRA); and he would be responsible for Egypt's postal service. In addition to inheriting functions from MoT, MCIT also received the new responsibility of implementing the country's IT strategy. If Mubarak's speech of September 1999 represented the state's embrace of the IT revolution, MCIT expressed that embrace in organizational terms.

Only a few months before the reshuffle, Hisham El Sherif had decided to join the private sector. Although he had resigned from IDSC, he remained the leader of RITSEC. When MCIT was created, he expected to be called back into government service. Much to his dismay, however, this did not happen. Instead, Atef Ebeid chose Ahmed Nazif, El Sherif's second in command and a capable man of low profile. He may have had any of several valid reasons. For one thing, while patronage between the government and the private sector is widespread in Egypt, there is no revolving door that allows a person to reenter the government once he or she has joined industry. For another, El Sherif may have been slighted for being a leader, not a team player. Visionary that he was, he liked to be the center of attention and tended to brag. To Ebeid this may have been acceptable as long as El Sherif was in a subordinate position, but had he become a cabinet member, he might have attempted to eclipse his patron. This prospect may have worked against his selection.

When Ahmed Nazif took office, he brought the managers of IDSC and RITSEC with him. Among them was Tarek Kamel, who had established Egypt's first Internet connection in 1993 and now became a senior advisor to the minister. With this transition of personnel, the new ministry inherited IDSC's organizational culture, which had emphasized an orientation toward the private sector and the global economy, as well as an interest in innovation and state-of-the-art technology. IDSC continued to persist, but its staff was reduced and its international profile lowered. It found itself thrown back into its original, purely supportive, function of helping other government agencies with web design and database management.

Soon after its creation, MCIT produced a mission statement, the *National IT Plan*. It called for openness to the global economy, a strong private sector, and norms that would entice both domestic and foreign investors to sink their money into the IT sector. The *National IT Plan* promised the following:

1. MCIT would upgrade the telecom infrastructure.
2. It would help create a legislative environment conducive to private investment in the IT sector.

3. The ministry would create local demand for the IT industry, thus motivating Egyptian and foreign enterprises to enter the sector.
4. It would create an IT industry capable of competing globally. The goal was to achieve a software export volume of $500 million annually by 2005.
5. MCIT would help develop a qualified human resource pool by training IT professionals.
6. It would encourage multinational companies to invest in Egypt's IT sector. (American Chamber of Commerce in Egypt 2002)

What Does It All Mean?

In 1987, Robert Cox, a theorist of Gramscian international political economy, conceptualized the transition from Fordism to flexible accumulation thus:

> First, there is a process of interstate consensus formation regarding the needs or requirements of the world economy that takes place within a common ideological framework (i.e., common criteria of interpretation of economic events and common goals anchored in the idea of an open world economy). Second, participation in this consensus formation is hierarchically structured. Third, the internal structures of states are adjusted so that each can best transform the global consensus into national policy and practice, taking account of the specific kinds of obstacles likely to arise in countries occupying the different hierarchically arranged positions in the world economy. (254)

The process of phasing out MoT and creating MCIT exemplifies the adjustment of state structures that Cox sketched and provides support for the hypothesis introduced at the beginning of this chapter. Here is how the terminology used in this study fits the Coxian model: The IT regime constitutes what Cox calls the "consensus on the needs or requirements of the world economy." Chapters two and three showed that this consensus was generated in a hierarchical fashion, because core actors had a great deal of input into the consensus-making process whereas peripheral actors were relatively excluded. The ideas that trade ought to be freed, that corporations needed the ability to roam, and that Third World economies could leapfrog or accelerate development constitute what Cox calls the "common ideological framework." The process of hierarchical interstate (and corporate) consensus formation produced global social structure in the form of an IT regime and a neoliberal trade regime. Social structure then yielded enforcement mechanisms, which made the Egyptian state opt for IT and create the organizational capacity it needed to implement its new agenda.

The creation of MCIT exemplifies a Coxian state transformation in that its creation was a response to a new, hierarchically derived international consensus. But did the ministry also increase the state's compliance with its role under flexible accumulation? The following sections address this question by following MCIT through the first four years of its existence. They demonstrate that MCIT enhanced state compliance by satisfying four of five principles enshrined in the IT regime:

1. *Increased responsiveness of the fixed line operator.* As chapter two explained, states and corporations in both Europe and the United States had sought an overhaul in telecom ownership rules because they wanted fixed line operators to be more responsive to the demands of corporate customers. The following analysis will demonstrate that under the aegis of MCIT, the responsiveness of Telecom Egypt improved.

2. *A greater number of service providers.* Those actors who helped formulate the IT regime wanted to enhance the provision of communication services by improving quality, increasing quantity, and lowering price. These three goals can be realized by having numerous providers compete for customers because the competitors will try to outperform one another on price and quality; and in the process, the amount of available infrastructure increases. The discussion that follows will show that the number of service providers increased under MCIT.

3. *Regulation that ensures competition and innovation.* Microeconomics textbooks teach students that a sector's level of competition is a function of the number of producers that coexist. In the communications sector, competitive coexistence is difficult to achieve, because communication services are provided over a network that connects customers—via the various operators that own segments of the network—with one another. To maintain the integrity of the network and ensure that every customer can communicate with all other customers, each owner of network segments must connect its infrastructure to that owned by competitors. This means that communication service providers cannot simply compete with one another but must also cooperate. To achieve the proper balance between competition and cooperation, a regulator must supervise service providers in a way that promotes high quality at a low cost. We will see that with respect to regulation, Egypt's Telecom Regulatory Authority did an imperfect job. In the area of regulation, MCIT therefore failed to improve the state's role compliance.

4. Increased network traffic. The function of the IT regime, as stated, is to increase the availability of communication services. Under MCIT, communication services increased in quantity.

5. Adoption of norms. The IT regime contained new norms for electronic commerce (see chapter three). In addition, the trade regime, which was aligned with the IT regime, included new rules for intellectual property rights (see chapter four). The following analysis reveals that MCIT worked to adopt these regime components.

1. Increased Responsiveness of the Fixed Line Operator

Between 1999 and 2003, did Telecom Egypt move toward fulfilling the needs of corporations more responsively? The answer is yes. After the creation of MCIT, the minister put a new management team from the private sector in charge of Telecom Egypt. This changed the character of the monopolist and made it more responsive to business needs.

The board of directors took over in June 2000. Akil Beshir, the new chairman, had been the general manager of Giza Systems Engineering and the vice president of Egyptian Computer Systems. Other board members were Bahaa Hilmy, the former chair of Bank Misr; Ayman Laz, a financial analyst, active member of ECES, and as such a card-carrying member of the globalization elite; and Adel Danish. Danish had spent many years in France leading his company Standardata, which provided software solutions for business applications. He was active in the Africa branch of the Global Information Infrastructure Commission and in the Global Business Dialogue on Electronic Commerce (see chapter three). Akil Beshir appointed Ali Salama from the global accounting firm KPMG to the post of chief financial officer. Between them, the new managers had strong credentials as entrepreneurs who understood how global corporations were run and what they expected of a telecom operator.

The board members strove to turn the operator into a profitable company. To that end, they embarked on several new and profitable ventures, which they organized as subsidiaries to Telecom Egypt. The first subsidiary was TE Mobile.[1] It was to launch cellular operations once the duopoly of MobiNil and Vodafone expired. The second subsidiary was TE Data. Its task was to take over Telecom Egypt's data operations and expand them. TE Data would thus serve as Telecom Egypt's fully owned Internet service provider (ISP). The third subsidiary was Masreyya.[2] It would become Telecom Egypt's brand-new call center arm. It had two main responsibilities: handle the monopolist's customer relations management and lease operator seats to corporations that wanted to outsource their customer service operations (Danish 2002).

Beshir, Hilmy, Laz, and Danish had inherited an organizational culture that they could not easily change. In 2002, Telecom Egypt had fifty-five thousand employees, whose promotions had strictly been based on seniority, not performance. The operator's employee compensation scheme did not create incentives that would have helped Telecom Egypt fulfill its organizational goals and develop the desired customer service mentality. In 2002 a USAID subcontractor complained that this way of remunerating the workforce resulted in poor work and at times sabotage because employees frequently disconnected phone wires and only reconnected them after extorting bribes from customers.

To reduce the workforce by 7 percent, the managers of Telecom Egypt implemented an early retirement scheme. It had two phases. Phase one ended in 2001, when some two thousand employees retired. Phase two ended in June 2002, when another two thousand retired.[3]

Phasing out part of the workforce, however, did not change the culture among the remaining employees. The creation of subsidiaries for Telecom Egypt's new ventures was a second way of dealing with this problem, for it allowed the management to create a separate culture for each of the three subsidiaries and thus avoid "contamination" through the culture of Telecom Egypt's fixed line operations.[4] In 2002, Adel Danish explained that Masreyya, the call center subsidiary, would be staffed by graduates of Egypt's elite school, the American University in Cairo. Since they had better qualifications than workers who owed their jobs to the Nasserist employment guarantee, they would receive a higher salary. Danish said that creating such a distinction among employees within Telecom Egypt was not feasible, because it would cause rancor and resistance. Through the subsidiary, however, a new reward system could be implemented that gave the management tight control over the performance of employees.

All in all, we may conclude that after 1999, the character of the operator changed. Telecom Egypt became more capable of setting and pursuing goals. It became more determined to respond to the demands of high-end customers. But organizational culture continued to work against targets that the management set for the operator.

2. More Service Providers

Did the number of service providers increase under MCIT? The answer is yes. The number of telecom service providers remained constant, but the number of ISPs increased. The telecom service providers were Telecom

Egypt, the sole fixed line carrier, and the two cellular operators, MobiNil and Vodafone. The payphone segment was occupied by three different providers. One was Telecom Egypt. The other two were Nile Telecom and Menatel, whose largest shareholder was France Telecom.

While the telephony segment remained stable with respect to the number of active participants, the ISP segment expanded. The sector had been opened to competition in 1996. Upon its creation in 1999, MCIT introduced a hierarchical categorization of ISPs, with big players (Class A license), medium-sized players (Class B license), and small players (Class C license), each requiring varying degrees of financial commitment.

Class A providers were allowed to co-locate with Telecom Egypt in the telephone exchanges, where they installed their own modems. By allowing these ISPs to co-locate, the ministry sought to ensure that Internet traffic occupied as few voice circuits as possible before being offloaded to the packet-switched data network. In addition to co-locating, Class A ISPs had the permission to sell bandwidth to Class A, B, or C providers.

Class B ISPs invested less in their operations. They received the right to co-locate, but they could only provide bandwidth to end users. Class C providers, also called "virtual ISPs," had sunk the least amount of money into their operations and were not allowed to install their own modems in the exchanges. They leased bandwidth from Class A providers, and they could only provide bandwidth to end users. In 2002, there were four Class A providers: TE Data, which was owned by Telecom Egypt, LinkdotNet, Nile Online, and EgyNet. In addition, there were eight Class B providers and numerous virtual ISPs (Arab Advisors 2002b).

Clearly, the number of companies that provided communication services increased in MCIT's first four years. MCIT thus increased the state's role compliance.

3. Regulation to Support Competition and Innovation

Did MCIT improve the regulatory capacity of the state, especially its ability to rein in the strongest operator? Here, the answer is no. This is mainly because the TRA, which had been established in 1998, was too weak to guarantee competition as envisaged by the global IT regime. The TRA's weakness can be attributed to two factors. First, by 2002, the authority had only 128 employees and hardly any analysts who understood the intricate economics of competitive telecommunications. Second, the TRA was not fully independent but supervised by MCIT, which in turn had stakes in Telecom Egypt. This was a fact that Telecom Egypt leveraged in its dealings with the cellular rivals and ISPs.

Telecom Egypt and the Cellular Rivals

Telecom Egypt chairman Akil Beshir was a feisty manager who wanted to lure customers away from his rivals and played every card in his hand to stay ahead of the cellular competition. He exploited Telecom Egypt's relationship with a weak regulatory authority to the fullest. Because both the TRA and Telecom Egypt were supervised by MCIT and because the TRA executive director Frekreyya Allam had been one of ARENTO's vice chairpersons in the early 1990s, Telecom Egypt hoped that the TRA would make concessions.

The two mobile carriers in turn depended on Telecom Egypt. To reach households that were attached to the fixed line network, they had to interconnect with the old carrier. To connect with telephones located in other countries, they had to hand their traffic off to Telecom Egypt, which monopolized Egypt's international gateways. This power imbalance gave MobiNil and Vodafone, the two cellular operators, an incentive to join forces in their struggle against the mammoth. Since they enjoyed the backing of international investors, they had a certain amount of protection against the fixed line monopolist. Knowing this, they vocally defended their interests.

That the TRA was incapable of keeping the monopolist in check became clear when the question of a third cellular license arose. The 1998 license agreement that MobiNil and Vodafone had signed with the government granted them a duopoly until the end of 2002. Then the state was free to issue a third cellular license, thus increasing the level of competition within the cellular segment. According to a foreign industry observer, the state never intended to sell this third license through a bidding process as a truly competitive regulatory model would have demanded. Instead, it wanted to award Telecom Egypt the license, allowing it to move into a market segment—cellular communications—that was more lucrative than the fixed line network. The fact that Telecom Egypt could win the license without having to enter a competitive bidding process shows that Telecom Egypt enjoyed a privileged relationship with the TRA and MCIT.

That his organization had the first go at the third cellular license did not satisfy Akil Beshir, and he tried to push his privilege as far as he could. To the dismay of MobiNil and Vodafone, he intended to roll out a network without paying the license fee. Beshir argued that Telecom Egypt already possessed the license because it had operated a cellular network before selling it to MobiNil in 1998. This antagonized MobiNil and Vodafone, who charged that Telecom Egypt had forfeited its license when it sold its cellular network.

The controversy tested the TRA's abilities as an impartial arbiter, and the authority failed. Fekreyya Allam remained silent on the dispute. The two cellular carriers, however, did not stand by defenselessly. During a debate aired live on the state-owned television channel Nile TV, the leaders of the two companies threatened to sue the state if it waived the license fee for Telecom Egypt (Samir and Schmitt 2001, 57).

The dispute over the license was resolved only after Prime Minister Atef Ebeid personally intervened and confirmed that Telecom Egypt would pay the fee. Late in 2001, the fixed line operator finally bought the license for the same amount that MobiNil and Vodafone had paid in 1998.

When it was in their mutual business interest, Telecom Egypt and the cellular operators turned from rivals into bedfellows, and the weak TRA stood by rather than safeguarding the presumed best interest of telecom customers. The following episode illustrates this. After acquiring the third cellular license, Telecom Egypt was unable to find a foreign partner for its operations. Seeing that Telecom Egypt had trouble launching the cellular venture, MobiNil and Vodafone suggested in early 2003 that in return for freezing its license for five years they would pay Telecom Egypt a sum roughly equal to the amount it had paid for the license. This arrangement would assure them another half-decade of duopoly (EIU 2003/2). Members of parliament and the local press cried foul, charging that the operators were striking a deal at the expense of the public, which would have to pay the higher prices of a duopoly, rather than enjoying a situation in which three competitors drove down one another's prices. In response, Minister Ahmed Nazif explained that Telecom Egypt had approached more than twenty potential partners without success. To maintain a presence in the market, Telecom Egypt would receive its license fee back and buy a stake in one of the two existing operators, most likely Vodafone. The freed spectrum would be distributed among the existing operators (EIU 2003/3). Once again, the TRA remained silent on a regulatory dispute, and MobiNil had to fear that Vodafone, by becoming closely affiliated with the state, would be privileged in its interaction with Telecom Egypt.

In December 2003, Telecom Egypt bought an 8.6 percent share in Vodafone Egypt. In January 2005, it increased that stake to 25.5 percent and in October 2006 to 48.97 percent (Telecom Egypt 2009). The cellular duopoly continued until 2006, when a consortium under the leadership of Etisalat of the United Arab Emirates bought a new cellular license and established Etisalat Egypt. Since 2007, all three cellular providers hold 3G licenses and are thus capable of providing their users with advanced services such as mobile television or video conferencing (WDR 2007).

In conclusion, the institutional setting in which Telecom Egypt and its cellular rivals were embedded allowed for a degree of competition, but also a good deal of state patronage. It was not the commercial model that had been the vision behind the IT regime.

Telecom Egypt and the Internet Service Providers

The relationship of the local ISPs with Telecom Egypt contained friction. Like the two cellular operators they were, to a certain degree, at the mercy of Telecom Egypt. Not only did they lease their infrastructure from the monopolist; they were also in competition with Telecom Egypt's data subsidiary, TE Data, and Telecom Egypt had incentives to favor its subsidiary, thus impairing the profitability of the other ISPs. Once again, the TRA turned out to be a weak arbiter.

For international connectivity, Telecom Egypt bought bandwidth on the FLAG cable, a high-capacity undersea cable owned by an international private consortium that ran from Alexandria to New York. If a class A or B ISP wanted to connect to a counterpart in the United States, it purchased some of this bandwidth from Telecom Egypt. Interviewed in 2002, a manager of a class A ISPs complained that the purchase of bandwidth occurred at a high mark-up:

Q: Regarding international capacity, you said that Telecom Egypt has a de-facto monopoly. How do you get your international bandwidth?
A: We get it all from Telecom Egypt. We cannot buy directly from a carriers' carrier [i.e., a wholesaler of international bandwidth]. It is Telecom Egypt who sells it to us.

Q: Can you tell Telecom Egypt you want a piece on such-and-such a route and Telecom Egypt is obliged to buy it for you? Does the TRA make sure that Telecom Egypt purchases whatever you want?
A: No, Telecom Egypt is not obliged to purchase anything. It does what it wants. What happens is that Telecom Egypt buys capacity from FLAG. FLAG rips Telecom Egypt off. Then Telecom Egypt turns around and charges us twice the price it paid, so it gets a hefty mark-up. Telecom Egypt takes advantage of [this ISP]. They charge us this high mark-up, and there's no value added. I went to one of the managers at Telecom Egypt and told her that no matter how I make my calculations, amortization of the cable cost etc., I never arrive at the price Telecom Egypt is charging. She told me: "That's the price, I don't have to tell you where it comes from. If you don't like it, you can jump into the Nile."

As late as 2002, ISPs were unable to build their own infrastructure. Even though various sources claimed that class A providers had the right to do so,[5] this possibility was purely theoretical. Khaled Bichara (2002), the chief executive officer of LinkdotNet, a class A ISP, pointed out that ISPs had to lease all wiring from Telecom Egypt. The only infrastructure elements they owned were the modems they installed in exchanges. Hisham Abdel Rahman, an analyst at the TRA, confirmed this statement.

ISPs therefore depended on Telecom Egypt. Unlike the cellular operators, they did not have international investment in their networks, so their visibility was lower. This meant that they had less leverage when they dealt with Telecom Egypt and the state. It would have been the task of the regulator to ensure that Telecom Egypt did not exploit its market position as the sole owner of infrastructure, but the TRA was unable to cope with its task. According to Hamdy El-Sissi of the ISP Nile Online, the reason for this was the tremendous complexity of the new technologies, which exceeded the expertise of TRA analysts.

In conclusion, MCIT appears to have made efforts to lead the communication sector toward competition, but a conflict of interest kept it from doing so effectively. On the one hand, MCIT supervised the regulatory agency charged to serve as an impartial arbiter between the various competitors and regulate their interaction in the best interest of consumers. On the other hand, MCIT owned Telecom Egypt and therefore had an interest in helping it obtain the best possible conditions from the regulator. Minister Nazif clearly had trouble reconciling the two roles he was playing.

In addition, the TRA lacked the know-how to regulate a sector that was becoming increasingly complex. In that respect, the agency simply mirrored the fact that it was located in a Third World economy. Egypt had few resources to spare for true industry experts, who commanded steep salaries on the international market.

4. Increased Network Traffic

Did connectivity increase under MCIT? The answer is yes. Egypt's communication infrastructure improved, and Internet and high-speed services became more and more available. Telecom Egypt worked hard to improve the fixed line telecom infrastructure. Between 1997 and 2002, it doubled the number of mainlines from 3.7 million to 7.5 million. Due to Egypt's high population growth rate, the jump in teledensity rates was less dramatic, but it was respectable nonetheless, increasing from 6.24 percent in 1997 to 10.92 in 2002. Telecom Egypt also raised the number of international circuits, from 160 in 1981, to 5,309 in June 1998, to 9,532 in 2001. At the same time, international traffic increased greatly, from 28 million minutes in 1981, to 811 million minutes in 2001 (American Chamber of Commerce in Egypt 2002).

The cellular competitors were also fast in rolling out their service, and as a result cellular penetration rates grew from 0.14 percent in 1997 to 7.62 in 2002. In 2002, the ratio of cellular subscribers to mainline subscribers was 70 percent (Arab Advisors 2002a, 3).

Within the payphone segment similar improvements were visible. While there were 250 public payphone stations in 1981, there were 5,000 in 1998, and 32,000 in 2001. Similarly, Internet traffic was rising. Egypt's international Internet bandwidth increased from 20 Mbps in 1999 to 450 Mbps at the end of 2001. However, this increase in bandwidth supply was not sufficient to meet demand, and Egyptian webpages often loaded at a snail's pace. Arab Advisors explain that for this reason many Egyptian companies maintained their web content in either the United States or in Europe where backbone was redundant. The majority of websites were hosted abroad, mainly in the United States with companies (Arab Advisors 2002b; American Chamber of Commerce in Egypt 2002).

These numbers show that in the first four years of its operations, MCIT brought Egypt into compliance with flexible accumulation by increasing the country's connectivity. Since then, the ministry has continuously improved the country's IT infrastructure. Table 9.1 provides comparative data for 1999, 2005, and 2009.

Table 9.1   Egypt's IT indicators over the years

	October 1999	December 2005	July 2009
Fixed telephone lines per 100 inhabitants	7.6	14.6	13.6
Proportion of households subscribing to fixed line telephony	No data available	No data available	54.76%
Cellular subscribers per 100 inhabitants	1	19.11	67.48
Internet subscribers per 100 inhabitants	0.58	12.27	18.22
Proportion of households with Internet access at home	No data available	No data available	47.69%
Broadband subscribers per 100 inhabitants	0.001	0.2	1.26
International Internet bandwidth (in Megabits/second)	No data available	4,432	53,578
International Internet bandwidth per inhabitant (in Megabits/second)	0.000038	62.13	703.45

Source: www.egyptictindicators.gov.eg

5. Adoption of Norms

Did MCIT promote the adoption of specific elements of the IT regime? The answer, once again, is yes. The *National IT Plan* stipulated that MCIT would assist the government in creating a legislative environment that would nurture an export-oriented IT industry. The key to developing such an industry was attracting foreign investment. That, in turn, meant that the government would have to create a regulatory framework that supported global electronic commerce, adhered to the intellectual property rights definitions of potential investors from the core economies, and incorporated global industry standards.

While MCIT explained the needs of the IT industry to lawmakers, the actual task of developing legislation fell to other agencies: The Ministry of Finance was in charge of the banking regulations that determined companies' access to loans, the Ministry of Trade was responsible for reviewing existing regulations for exports, and so forth. Therefore, MCIT's support for regulations that assisted communication flows across borders, encouraged electronic commerce, and promoted investment has to be examined in the broader context of governmental policy adoption.

To begin with, MCIT was eager to create e-commerce opportunities, and it did so with strong support from the IT stakeholders, who had organized themselves as the e-commerce committee of the Internet Society of Egypt (ISE).[6] However, this touched on the political responsibilities of the Ministry of Trade, which had been examining e-commerce policies for at least a year. In March 1998, the ministry made a well-informed submission on the topic to the World Trade Organization (WTO, Committee on Trade and Development 1998). In August 1998, it initiated a government committee to look into issues related to e-commerce. Many government entities were represented, including the Central Bank of Egypt and IDSC. Thus, when MCIT came into existence, an organizational support network for promoting e-commerce was already in place. Because of this, MCIT left the lead to the Ministry of Trade, the Central Bank of Egypt, and the e-commerce committee of the Internet Society of Egypt.

In 2002, the National Assembly passed law 82/2002, which moved the country closer to the intellectual property rights definition that prevailed at the international level. The law assigned MCIT the responsibility for monitoring and curbing software piracy. Perhaps as a result of the attention the government paid to the phenomenon, piracy dropped considerably, from 85 percent in 1998 to 52 in 2002 (IPRC 2003). But the International Intellectual Property Alliance (IIPA), a U.S.-based organization representing companies that owned copyrights on motion pictures, music, and software, remained dissatisfied. In 2004, it complained that MCIT was not yet in charge of enforcing the law:

> Egypt has long been noted as a market essentially closed to most U.S. right holders, due to major barriers to legitimate business—piracy being the chief one. There was little change to this situation in 2003. While copyright protection on the books improved with passage of a new [intellectual property rights] Code in 2002, implementing regulations issued in the fall of 2003 did not implement the copyright law provisions, leaving in doubt when purview over business and entertainment software would move to the Ministry of Communications and Information Technology (MCIT)—a badly needed development for the business and entertainment software industries. The move to MCIT, which is dictated by the law, is necessary because it ensures that enforcement officials with the necessary expertise would be handling software cases. It is hoped that the new IPR Code is implemented and the new mandate of MCIT is fully exercised without further delay.

In 2002, the government worked on an e-commerce law that was to govern taxation, security, and digital signatures (American Chamber of Commerce in Egypt 2002). Two years later, on April 7, 2004, a law was enacted. It was narrower in scope than the legislative proposals originally under discussion, because it did not cover taxation and touched only briefly on intellectual property rights issues. The law established an authority that made the technical specifications for electronic signatures and supervised the process of administering these signatures. The authority was to be managed by a board of directors chaired by MCIT. It included representatives of the Ministry of Defense and the Ministry of Interior. Presumably, these latter would ensure that the encryption technology that would be used did not impair the surveillance of opposition forces.

To promote the software industry, the government offered a five-year tax holiday to all software companies. In addition, in 2001 a software engineering certification center was established, which certified Egyptian companies using the Capability Maturity Model. This model offered an internationally recognized standard for quality management in the software industry (American Chamber of Commerce in Egypt 2002).

All in all, we can conclude that MCIT was part of a multi-agency effort to adapt Egypt's laws and standards to IT rules that existed at the global level. Adaptation was not complete. This may have been due to countervailing pressures from older state agencies bent on protecting their turf or domestic constituencies that depended on illegally copied software. It may also have been due a lack of analytical resources needed by the government for comprehending and implementing the increasingly complex rules of the game.

In sum, MCIT moved the state toward role compliance. Under its aegis, Telecom Egypt became more responsive to customer needs, the number of service providers increased, the volume of network traffic increased, and the government adopted a number of IT norms that existed at the global level. MCIT's weakest point was the regulation of the sector. Here the TRA was too close to the fixed line operator to be impartial. Moreover, it was under-staffed and underfunded, which kept it from regulating the communication sector in a manner that did justice to its complexity.

This evidence supports the hypothesis, advanced at the beginning of this chapter, that enforcement mechanisms can change state composition and hence state identity. It also demonstrates that the power shift between MoT and MCIT constitutes a state transformation as sketched by Robert Cox (1987).

Conclusion

Under the aegis of MCIT, Egypt's IT landscape became more sophisticated. Egypt's IT stakeholders succeeded partially in their plan to turn the country into a software exporter. In addition to negotiating the relationship between Telecom Egypt, the cellular operators, and the ISPs, MCIT took a host of measures to strengthen and advertise Egypt's nascent IT industry. Ahmed Nazif wooed investors; he led Egyptian IT delegations to Virginia, Ireland, and other locations. His ministry opened Internet cafés and IT clubs. It provided training to technology neophytes and to those who wanted to become professional programmers. For a small ministry, MCIT accomplished an astonishing lot. The agency did not reach its 2005 target of exporting five hundred million dollars by the year 2005. In January of 2006, the ministry issued a press release estimating the export of software programs at two hundred million dollars (MCIT 2006).

Software outsourcing expert Erran Carmel of American University con-firmed in a 2008 email to the author that the Egyptian software export industry was expanding and that many Egyptian firms enjoyed high vis-ibility in trade shows. MCIT states that in 2008, Egypt's IT sector exported goods and services in the sum of eight hundred million dollars (MCIT 2009).

In July 2004 another cabinet reshuffle took place. This time, Minister Ahmed Nazif, a modest man who believed in the opportunities of globaliza-tion, became prime minister. His senior advisor Tarek Kamel succeeded him as minister of communication and information technologies. Two individuals who had been reared at IDSC now occupied cabinet posts. This advancement further strengthened the coalition between actors from the core, the globalization elite, the local IT stakeholders, and the Egyptian state. In making Ahmed Nazif prime minister President Mubarak signaled to the world that his intention to "leapfrog into the information age" and embrace globalization was a long-term commitment. Meanwhile, average Egyptians such as Hisham, the young Cairene student in chapter one, continue to be without influence over the rules constraining their society or the creation of ministries that govern their country.

PART III

Lessons

CHAPTER 10

Inferences from the Egyptian Case

The previous chapters have attempted to show that the negotiation and implementation of IT rules were part and parcel of the world's transition to flexible accumulation or, in shorthand, globalization. States and corporations from the core economies sought to capture the most lucrative niches in the global economy. With that intention, they forged an IT regime that emphasized rapid information and communication flows. State and nonstate actors from the world's periphery played minor parts in this process.

This had profound implications for the right of the human being to participate in forging the rules that constrain his or her life. Those individuals with ties to states and companies of the core economies could, if they chose to inform themselves, provide their small input into regime formation, for instance, by writing to their senators, joining specialized civil society groups, making their voices heard in shareholder assemblies, investing their retirement portfolio through socially responsible mutual funds, voting in elections, or using their purchasing power to send politically motivated market signals. Of course, none of these core citizens could expect to have a significant individual impact on the global rules of the game. But they could expect to have as much influence as a member of a 5.2 billion strong electorate *should* have had.[1]

Those individuals with ties to state and nonstate actors from the periphery had far fewer possibilities for providing input into global decision-making. In comparison to their counterparts from the core, peripheral states had little say when it came to global regime formation. So no matter how often Third World citizens wrote to their parliamentarians, they could not expect that their opinions would get the hearing at the international level that they deserved. And because on average, their purchasing power was much weaker than that of core citizens, they had fewer opportunities to influence corporations through their participation in shareholder assemblies, reallocations of their retirement portfolios, or politically motivated buying decisions. This is why the marginalization of peripheral organizations from global rule-making processes is tantamount to disrespecting the autonomy of Third World citizens.

In a second step, this study examined the case of Egypt and found that core actors, through numerous enforcement mechanisms, imposed the IT regime on the peripheral state. Faced with the social fall-out from structural adjustment, the Mubarak administration nurtured those privileged segments of the population that agreed with adjustment and supported the strategy of private sector and export led growth: the globalization elite and the local IT stakeholders. The narrow alliance between these domestic actors, the Egyptian state, the World Bank, and core creditors worked to shape the country's economy in a way that made it more compatible with flexible accumulation. Their politics culminated in the establishment of MCIT, the Ministry of Communications and Information Technologies.

The process that led up to the creation of MCIT had significant consequences for the autonomy of Egyptians. Egypt had an authoritarian political system, which meant that citizens had little influence over the country's economic strategy to begin with. But when the state attempted to comply with the mandates of the World Bank and the International Monetary Fund (IMF), it tightened the screws on the domestic opposition beyond the usual, cracking down on the Islamist movement, bringing the mosques under government control and subjecting the nongovernmental organizations (NGOs) to a new, repressive NGO law. Needless to say, the overwhelming majority of Egyptians had no say when it came to creating MCIT.

The study contends that while it was the state that actively disenfranchised the Egyptian population, creditors, corporations, and international development organizations played the part of accomplices. To clarify, imagine this scenario: Convinced that by turning to Islam Americans will achieve salvation, King Abdullah of Saudi Arabia approaches the U.S. government and demands that it promote Muslim values. He also offers financial assistance for that purpose. Meanwhile, Egypt's Azhar University, an organization renowned for its expertise in Sunni Muslim doctrine, provides the U.S. government with advice on how to regulate relations among its religious communities. In addition, the Organization of the Islamic Conference promises to eliminate half of America's external public debt if the U.S. government adjusts the American value system by introducing religious education in elementary schools.

Seeking the goodwill of these organizations, the government decides to put some of their suggestions into practice. Then it realizes that to properly do so, it needs to establish a department of religion. How would Americans react to this?

It is easy to imagine that Americans would be outraged—not only because government proselytism violates the constitutional separation between religion and state, but also because foreign actors have usurped a decision-making process that according to democratic theory should be left to the American people.

If it is inappropriate for outsiders to intervene in America's domestic affairs, then why do we think nothing of usurping the political rights of Egyptians? Autonomy implies that citizens wield collective control over a country's economic and political path. By that standard, every enforcement mechanism that bore down on the state and preempted the citizens' collective right to control their country's future represented a violation of Egyptians' autonomy.

What Inferences Can a Single Case Yield?

The question that needs to be answered now is whether Egyptians were unique in their disempowerment, or whether other world citizens experienced similar forms of coercion. For that, it is necessary to determine if the enforcement mechanisms detected for Egypt apply to other peripheral economies.

Chapter four laid down the procedure for this. According to Berger and Luckmann (1966), social structure creates roles not for individual actors, but for types of actors. Consequently, it addresses individuals not as unique beings but as members of types, and through enforcement mechanisms it prods them to comply with the role expectations that are associated with those types. In light of this, we can draw causal inferences from the Egyptian case by applying the following four steps:

1. Study one single actor, and glean the enforcement mechanisms that are at work. In this study, the actor in question is the Egyptian state. The period under study extends roughly from 1990 to 2000.
2. Ask yourself: As a member of what *type* is the enforcement mechanism addressing the actor?
3. Ask yourself: What other members does the identified type contain? Once again, the period under study extends approximately from 1990 to 2000.
4. Draw the inference that the specific enforcement mechanism gleaned from the one case you studied will apply to the other social actors whom you have identified as members of the same type.

This procedure should not be applied mechanically. Berger and Luckmann's framework allows for incongruities between actors and roles that render generalization more complex than the aforementioned steps let on. Consider the following three.

First, an individual actor may only be a partial member of a type. In that case, the role expectation that is associated with the type will target the actor only imperfectly. To explain, think of a type as a set, that is, a category. "Mother," "democratic country," "middle class citizen," "grocery store" are examples of sets.

A set can be crisp or fuzzy (Ragin 2000). When a type forms a crisp set, each actor that is to be categorized is marked either as a member of the type or as a nonmember. There are no transitional categories. An example is the set, or type, of "low income country." The World Bank has created this type for use in development research. It defines a country as a low income country if its gross national income (GNI) per capita lies below a specified dollar amount, say US$ 635. Low income country forms a crisp set, because at any given time, it is possible to qualify each country in the world as a member or a nonmember of the set. It is not possible for a country to be merely a partial member of the set.

Many types, in contrast, form fuzzy sets. Here, actors that are to be categorized have varying degrees of membership in the type. An actor can be fully in the set, on the border between being in and out of the set, fully out of the set, or anything in between. The type "state presiding over an indebted economy" exemplifies the idea of a fuzzy set. Obviously there are degrees of indebtedness—in some countries, overall debt amounts to 70 percent of GNI. In other countries, it amounts to a mere 20 percent of GNI. Dealing with a type that constitutes a fuzzy set requires awareness that actors who are only partial members of the type will experience the associated enforcement mechanism only imperfectly. Actors who are not members of the type, of course, should not experience the enforcement mechanism at all.

Second, each social actor belongs not only to one but to several types, and their role prescriptions may be incompatible. Assume that Petra belongs to the types of "mother" and "college professor." The role prescription for the former type demands that she devote a good deal of time to nurturing, raising, and socializing her children. The prescription that goes with the latter type expects her to devote much time to research that yields professional publications. Petra's two roles make competing claims on her time. Even if Petra is put under great pressure to "do her duty," she may be unable to fulfill the expectations that are associated with both roles. In her case, social structure is exercising two competing causal powers on Petra. Its causal power to demand that Petra be a good mother competes with its power to demand that she be a good professor. Petra may resolve the conflict by yielding to the stronger power and devote much of her time to her children. Meanwhile, she will bear the cost of defying the weaker power, perform poorly in her role of professor, and forego merit raises.

Third, a state's resistance to enforcement mechanisms will depend on the extent of countervailing pressure it faces from domestic constituencies. What a state ends up doing is thus a compromise between these conflicting commitments.

Now that the basic concerns have been addressed, it is time to examine the background factor that was discussed in chapter six and the enforcement mechanisms of chapters six through eight.

The Background Factor

The demise of the Soviet Union, which occurred between 1989 and 1991, changed the relationship between the Egyptian state and the core actors in two ways. First, it eliminated a source of Cold War rent for Egypt. Second, it discredited socialism and to a lesser extent state capitalism as economic paradigms. Altogether, it increased Egypt's ideological and financial dependence on the core states. It therefore acted as a background factor that increased the causal powers of the creditors from the core vis-à-vis the Egyptian state.

This background factor applied not only to Egypt, but to the periphery in general. In concluding their edited volume *The Global Crisis in Foreign Aid* (1998), Richard Grant from Syracuse University and Jan Nijman from the University of Miami find that during the Cold War, the United States used foreign aid to win clients in its struggle against the USSR. In the 1990s, however, the ideology of the market and market access became hegemonic, and donor states made the disbursement of assistance funds contingent on economic liberalization in recipient countries.

Enforcement Mechanism One: Structural Adjustment

Step One: Glean the Enforcement Mechanism
Chapter six explored the following enforcement mechanism: The World Bank, in cooperation with the Paris Club of creditor states and the IMF, imposed a structural adjustment program on the Egyptian state.

Step Two: As a Member of What Type Did this Mechanism Address the Egyptian State?
The Paris Club, the World Bank, and the IMF addressed the Egyptian state as a member of the type "state presiding over an indebted low or middle

income economy." The first two organizations used different schemes for typifying states: The World Bank offered its services only to those states that it had categorized as presiding over a low or middle income economy; the Paris Club addressed those states that presided over an economy that suffered from a high level of external debt. Meanwhile, the IMF acted as the agent of the Paris Club in monitoring the country's performance.

The type state presiding over an indebted low or middle income economy consists of two components—income level and level of indebtedness. Consequently, it constitutes a two-dimensional fuzzy set of the following kind: Those states that presided over a poor economy *and* suffered from a severe external debt burden were fully inside the set. They should have experienced the full brunt of the enforcement mechanism.[2] In 1991, the year in which Egypt began its structural adjustment, this applied to Zambia. Those states that fulfilled only *one* of the two conditions were partially inside the set. They should have experienced the enforcement mechanisms with less strength. In 1991, this applied to Gabon. Those states that fulfilled *none* of the two conditions were outside the set. They should not have been exposed to the enforcement mechanism at all. In 1991, this applied to Switzerland.

Figure 10.1 portrays this relationship graphically, using the examples of Zambia, Egypt, Gabon, and Switzerland. The shading of the box denotes

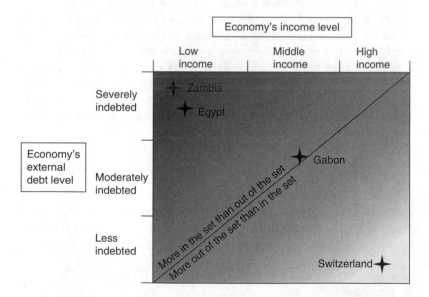

Figure 10.1 The type "state presiding over a low or middle income economy" depicted as a fuzzy set.

the extent to which a data point is inside the set. The area that is shaded dark grey (upper left corner) is the area that is fully in the set. The area in white (lower right corner) is the area that is fully outside the set.

Step Three: What Other Members Did the Identified Type Contain?
For each state that applied for an adjustment loan, the Bank determined whether it was eligible for loans at all and, if so, whether it was entitled to low interest loans and World Bank guarantees. The crucial measure was a state's level of GNI per capita in US$. On this basis, the Bank distinguished between low, middle, and high income countries (World Bank 2008a,b).

In 1991, the year in which Egypt began with its adjustment program, low income countries were those with a per capita GNI of less than 635 US$. Their states had access to particularly low interest rate loans, but not to World Bank guarantees. They were also allowed to use preferential treatment for its contractors in procurement decisions.

The category of middle income country contained several income brackets:

- States with a per capita GNI between 635 US$ and 1,235 US$. They were eligible for loans that took twenty years to mature and had limited access to World Bank guarantees.[3]
- States with a per capita GNI between 1,236 US$ and 2,555 US$. They qualified for loans that matured after seventeen years and had access to World Bank guarantees.
- States with a per capita GNI between 2,556 US$ and 4,465 US$. They were eligible for fifteen-year loans and had access to Bank guarantees.

The World Bank also provided loans to states with 4,466–7,910 US$ per capita. However, it considered these states so wealthy that upon repayment of the loan they were to join the ranks of the donor states.

For the purposes of this study, the type "state presiding over a low- or middle income economy" therefore comprised states with a per capita GNI of up to 4,465 US$. "Upper middle income countries" with 4,466–7,910 US$ per capita were on the cusp between being in the set and out of the set. Finally, states with over 7,910 US$ per capita were fully out of the set.

Box 10.1 applies this scheme for the year 1991, when Egypt experienced this particular enforcement mechanism. It also assigns asterisks to those countries that according to the World Bank were moderately or severely indebted.

Box 10.1 World Bank classification of countries by income level and level of indebtedness (year: 1991)

States with less than 635 US$ per capita:
Afghanistan, Bangladesh*, Benin**, Bhutan, Burkina Faso, Burundi**, Cambodia, Central African Republic*, Chad, China, Comoros**, Congo (Dem. Rep.)**, Egypt**, Equatorial Guinea**, Ethiopia*, Gambia*, Ghana**, Guinea**, Guinea-Bissau**, Guyana**, Haiti, Honduras**, India, Indonesia*, Kenya**, Lao PDR, Lesotho, Liberia**, Madagascar**, Malawi**, Maldives, Mali**, Mauritania**, Mozambique**, Myanmar**, Nepal, Nicaragua**, Niger**, Nigeria**, Pakistan*, Rwanda, São Tomé and Principe**, Sierra Leone**, Solomon Islands, Somalia**, Sri Lanka*, Sudan**, Tanzania**, Togo**, Uganda*, Vietnam, Yemen, Rep.*, Zambia**, Zimbabwe*.

States with 635–1,235 US$ per capita:
Angola, Bolivia**, Cameroon*, Cape Verde*, Congo (Rep.)**, Côte d'Ivoire**, Dominican Republic*, Ecuador**, El Salvador, Guatemala*, Jordan, Kiribati, Mongolia, Morocco**, Namibia, Papua New Guinea, Paraguay*, Peru**, Philippines**, Samoa, Senegal**, Swaziland, Syrian Arab Republic*, Tajikistan, Tonga, Vanuatu.

States with 1,236–2,555 US$ per capita:
Albania, Algeria*, Armenia, Azerbaijan, Belize, Bulgaria, Chile**, Colombia*, Costa Rica**, Dominica, Fiji, Georgia, Grenada, Jamaica*, Kazakhstan, Kyrgyz Republic, Lebanon, Malaysia, Mauritius, Moldova, Panama, Poland**, Romania, St. Lucia, St. Vincent and the Grenadines, Thailand, Tunisia, Turkey*, Turkmenistan, Ukraine, Uzbekistan.

States with 2,556–4,465 US$ per capita:
Argentina**, Belarus, Botswana, Brazil**, Estonia, Gabon*, Hungary**, Latvia, Libya, Lithuania, Mexico**, Russian Federation, South Africa, St. Kitts and Nevis, Suriname, Trinidad and Tobago, Uruguay**, Venezuela**.

States with 4,466–7,910 US$ per capita:
Antigua and Barbuda, Barbados, Korea (Rep.), Malta, Oman, Portugal, Puerto Rico, Seychelles.

States with over 7,910 US$ per capita:
Andorra, Australia, Austria, Bahamas, Bahrain, Belgium, Bermuda, Brunei Darussalam, Canada, Channel Islands, Cyprus, Denmark, Faeroe

Islands, Finland, France, French Polynesia, Germany, Greece, Greenland, Hong Kong, Iceland, Ireland, Israel, Italy, Japan, Kuwait, Luxembourg, Macao (China), Netherlands, New Caledonia, New Zealand, Norway, Qatar, Saudi Arabia, Singapore, Spain, Sweden, Switzerland, Taiwan, United Arab Emirates, United Kingdom, United States, Virgin Islands (U.S.), San Marino.

Notes:
** denotes countries that the World Bank classified as severely indebted in 1991. Severely indebted means either: present value of debt service to GNI exceeds 80 percent or present value of debt service to exports exceeds 220 percent.
* denotes countries that the World Bank classified as moderately indebted in 1991. Moderately indebted means either of the two key ratios exceeds 60 percent of, but does not reach, the critical levels.
Note that if a country does not have a star, this means *either* that the World Bank categorized it as less indebted, *or* that it did not classify it by indebtedness.
Source: World Bank (2008b), World Development Indicators database.

This overview makes it possible to determine which states were full members of the type "state presiding over an indebted low or middle income economy," which states were partial members of the type, and which states were outside the type. The lower a country's level of income, and the greater its number of asterisks, the further it was inside the set.

Step Four: Draw an Inference
Full members of the type were especially likely to face the enforcement mechanism of structural adjustment. The brochure *World Bank Lending Instruments: Resources for Development Impact*, published by the Bank in 2001, lays out what this implied:

Adjustment operations now generally aim to promote competitive market structures (for example, legal and regulatory reform), correct distortions in incentive regimes (taxation and trade reform), establish appropriate monitoring and safeguards (financial sector reform), create an environment conducive to private sector investment (judicial reform, adoption of a modern investment code), encourage private sector activity (privatization and public-private partnerships), promote good governance (civil service reform), and mitigate short-term adverse effects of adjustment (establishment of social protection funds). (World Bank, Operations and Country Services 2001a, 13)

The deeper inside the set a country was, the stronger the pressure on its state to undergo structural adjustment and adopt the tenets of the Washington Consensus.

Enforcement Mechanism Two:
The Euro-Mediterranean Partnership

Step One: Glean the Enforcement Mechanism
Chapter six revealed the following enforcement mechanism: The European Commission made the Egyptian state sign an association agreement that opened the Egyptian market to European industrial exports.

Step Two: As a Member of What Type Did This
Mechanism Address the Egyptian State?
The Egyptian state and the EU signed the association agreement in the context of the Euro-Mediterranean Partnership. The driving force behind the Partnership was the European Commission. It wanted to tie the EU's southern periphery closer to Brussels. To achieve this goal, it devised a multilateral cooperation track, in which the EU interacted with all members of this periphery at the same time, and a bilateral track, which consisted of bilateral trade agreements between the EU and each Mediterranean partner. Here, the Commission drew up a template trade agreement, applied it to each individual partner and then modified it to suit that state's particular circumstances. In making Egypt sign an association agreement, the Commission thus addressed the Egyptian state as a member of the type "Southern Mediterranean partner" of the EU.

Step Three: What Other Members Did the Identified Type Contain?
Besides Egypt, the type "Southern Mediterranean partner" contained the following members: Algeria, Jordan, Lebanon, Morocco, Syria, and Tunisia. Table 10.1 lists the date at which each bilateral association agreement was signed and the date it entered into force.

In 1995, Cyprus and Malta participated as partner states in the multilateral aspect of the Euro-Mediterranean Partnership, but because they were en route to joining the EU, which they did in 2004, they did not sign a bilateral association agreement. This means that they were only partial members of the type, and since the association agreement is the more "profound" component of the partnership, they were more outside than

Table 10.1 Signature and entry into force of the Euro-Mediterranean association agreements

Country	Date agreement is signed	Date agreement enters into force
Algeria	April 2002	September 2005
Egypt	June 2001	June 2004
Israel	November 1995	June 2000
Jordan	November 1997	May 2002
Lebanon	June 2002	April 2006
Morocco	February 1996	March 2000
Palestinian Authority	February 1997	July 1997*
Syria	October 2004 (first draft agreement initialed), December 2008 (second draft agreement initialed) **	After ratification
Tunisia	July 1995	March 1998

*Note that this is an interim association agreement as the Palestinian Authority is not a sovereign state.
** "Initialing" occurs at the ambassadorial level and precedes formal signature by the heads of state.

inside the type. Something similar applies to Turkey, which is seeking EU membership. Instead of a typical association agreement, it signed a customs union agreement with the EU.

Israel is a full participant in the Partnership. But as it is the only Jewish state in the otherwise Muslim Middle East and many of its older citizens once experienced persecution at the hands of European governments, the EU has a special relationship with Israel. It is therefore possible that the EU addressed Israel as a unique, individual state rather than as a member of a type.

In 1997, the EU signed an interim association agreement with the Palestine Liberation Organization, which acted on behalf of the Palestinian Authority. As the Palestinian Authority is not a sovereign state, its association agreement is by necessity of a different quality than that of, say, Morocco.

Step Four: Draw an Inference
By signing the bilateral association agreements, the southern partners of the EU agreed to open their economies to competitive industrialized exports

and expose their weak industrial sectors to foreign competition. Because this competition could be expected to create social disruption in the Southern Mediterranean economies, it is unlikely that their states opened the national markets willingly. Instead, it is likely that the Commission applied its superior bargaining power to open these markets. Thus, the states that signed association agreements (with the exception perhaps of Israel) probably did so in response to an enforcement mechanism.

Enforcement Mechanism Three: The Globalization Elite

Step One: Glean the Enforcement Mechanism
Chapter six revealed the following enforcement mechanism: The World Bank and the U.S. Agency for International Development (USAID) raised the causal power of the globalization elite to authoritatively demand flexibility and IT connectivity from the state.

The World Bank and USAID supported Egypt's globalization elite in a number of ways. First, both organizations launched research that investigated private sector needs. This signaled to the state that the private sector enjoyed high priority in the thinking of both USAID and the Bank. It also helped the members of the private sector understand their own interests, formulate strategies, and make demands on the state.

Second, both the Bank and USAID financed conferences that examined the needs of the private sector and helped establish connections between government ministries and businessmen. Last, USAID funded civil society organizations that were designed to promote the interests of the wealthier segments of the private sector.

Step Two: As a Member of What Type Did This
Mechanism Address the Egyptian State?
The Bank and USAID used different schemes for categorizing the Egyptian state. For USAID, Egypt was a member of the type "state presiding over a peripheral economy that receives USAID funds." The private sector analyses that the World Bank wrote and the local conferences that it sponsored complemented Egypt's structural adjustment program. The Bank thus addressed the Egyptian state as a member of the type "state presiding over an economy that undergoes structural adjustment."

Step Three: What Other Members Did the Identified Type Contain?
Identifying the members of the type requires determining how the World Bank and USAID constructed their respective types. USAID determined who belonged to the type "state presiding over a peripheral economy that

receives USAID funds" by consulting the annual breakdown of funding that it received from Congress and by reviewing the special programs that the executive branch assigned to it. Who belonged to the type therefore depended on congressional and presidential foreign policy priorities. The World Bank, on the other hand, constructed the type "state presiding over an economy that underwent structural adjustment" by reviewing the list of adjustment operations it administered.

The next step is to combine these two types into a two-dimensional fuzzy set of the following kind:

- States that received USAID funds *and* underwent structural adjustment were fully inside the set and experienced the brunt of the enforcement mechanism.
- States that *either* received USAID funds *or* underwent structural adjustment were partial members of the set and experienced the mechanism less fully.
- States that *neither* received USAID funds *nor* underwent structural adjustment were outside the set and did not experience the enforcement mechanism.

Step Four: Draw an Inference
In conclusion, those states that received both USAID funds and underwent structural adjustment experienced the enforcement mechanism most fully. In those countries the globalization elite should have received a great deal of support from USAID and the Bank.

Enforcement Mechanism Four: USAID and Telecom Reform

Step One: Glean the Enforcement Mechanism
Chapter seven revealed the following enforcement mechanism: USAID prodded the state step by step toward telecom sector reform.

Step Two: As a Member of What Type Did This
Mechanism Address the Egyptian State?
For USAID, Egypt was a member of the type "state presiding over a peripheral economy that receives USAID funds."

Step Three: What Other Members Did the Identified Type Contain?
It contained other states that received USAID funds. As we saw when examining mechanism three, the list of USAID recipients depended on the foreign policy priorities of the U.S. president and the U.S. Congress.

Step Four: Draw an Inference
For this mechanism, drawing an inference is less straightforward than it was for the previous mechanisms. Telecommunications is only one of many economic sectors on which USAID's experts provide development advice. Whether or not a state that received USAID funding experienced a sector reform project therefore depended on whether USAID and the state in question agreed to funnel the allocated economic assistance into the telecom sector. Moreover, the specific content of the project was unlikely to resemble that of the Egyptian project, because content is largely a function of the monetary allocation a project receives, and in Egypt, which is the largest recipient of USAID assistance, this allocation was unusually high.

However, those recipients of USAID funds who did opt for a telecom-related program could be sure that USAID would promote sector reform. The following 1999 statement by U.S. trade representative Charlene Barshefsky, which speaks to the agency's commitment to shaping telecom policy in the periphery, supports this claim:

> USAID, together with the Federal Communications Commission and other agencies, undertakes technical assistance efforts in telecommunications worldwide. One prominent example is USAID's Southern Africa Regional Telecommunications Restructuring Program (RTRP), which helps promote modern telecommunications laws and regulation in six southern African nations through technical advice, seminars for regulatory officials and suggestions on legislation.[4]

An online search of USAID publications for the term "telecommunications" indicates that between 1990 and 2000 USAID conducted telecommunications-related activities in at least thirty-three countries: Armenia, Benin, Botswana, Bulgaria, Croatia, Czech Republic, El Savador, Ghana, Guatemala, India, Indonesia, Jordan, Madagascar, Mali, Moldova, Mongolia, Morocco, Mozambique, Namibia, Nicaragua, Niger, Pakistan, Panama, Philippines, Poland, Romania, Russia, Tanzania, Thailand, Togo, Tunisia, Zambia, and Zimbabwe. Presumably, in all these countries USAID counseled sector reform.

Enforcement Mechanism Five:
The EU Supports Sector Reform

Step One: Glean the Enforcement Mechanism
Chapter seven revealed the following enforcement mechanism: The European Commission prodded the state to consider sector reform.

Step Two: As a Member of What Type Did This
Mechanism Address the Egyptian State?
The Commission addressed Egypt as a member of the type "Southern Mediterranean partner" of the EU. As explained with respect to enforcement mechanism two, the Commission used a standardized approach to negotiating the bilateral association agreements with its Southern Mediterranean partners. As discussed in chapter seven, this template contained specific provisions designed to improve the provision of telecom in the countries of the Southern Mediterranean.

Step Three: What Other Members Did the Identified Type Contain?
It contained the other Southern Mediterranean partners of the EU (see mechanism two).

Step Four: Draw an Inference
The Commission supported sector reform in all Southern Mediterranean economies, not only in Egypt.

Indeed that the Commission wanted its Southern neighbors to adapt their telecom sectors to the needs of flexible accumulation becomes clear when we examine the multilateral track of the Euro-Mediterranean Partnership. It contained an "Action Plan for the Development of the Euro-Mediterranean Information Society." One of its three components consisted in devising "new approaches to telecom policy" (ISPO 1998). In 2000, the EU provided € 2.5 million for the endeavor. This money was spent on regional telecommunications fora, technical workshops, study tours, on-the-job training, training seminars for regional policymakers, and the collection of information on the telecommunication sector by creating a virtual Mediterranean telecommunications observatory. The thematic foci were sector reform, competition, and the regulatory implication of reform.

Enforcement Mechanism Six: The IT Stakeholders

Step One: Glean the Enforcement Mechanism
Chapter eight revealed the following enforcement mechanism: Through their support for the IT stakeholders, core actors helped prod the state to move IT policy to the top of the political agenda.

Step Two: As a Member of What Type Did This
Mechanism Address the Egyptian State?
This mechanism worked through the country's IT stakeholders. Core actors provided funding for IT projects that demonstrated the viability of

globalization. The recipient IT stakeholders could use the funding to show off their expertise and improve their status in Egypt's society. This, in turn, increased their causal power to demand that the state adopt the tenets of the IT revolution and embrace globalization.

The ultimate target of this enforcement mechanism was therefore the Egyptian state. Determining what type the state embodied requires knowing what countries core actors and development organizations targeted when they funded IT projects. Even though every individual sponsor of IT projects had distinct guidelines for choosing target locations, their various criteria can be aggregated into the simple requirement that a site be located in a peripheral economy.

In support of this contention, consider the IT funding landscape. By the mid-1990s states and nongovernmental organizations from the core, corporations, and international development organizations such as the World Bank realized that IT could greatly enhance international trade, and they believed that it offered additional possibilities in fields such as education and health care. Seizing this insight, they devised funding opportunities for IT stakeholders in peripheral countries, who would show what the new technologies could do and spread IT acceptance. The number of funding opportunities for such projects was large. Peripheral IT stakeholders who sought funding could find it if they understood the English language, had project management skills, knew where to look for funding sources, and possessed the skill of navigating the jungle of donor bureaucracies. Here is a small sample of funding sources. Not all of them applied to Egypt or were tapped by Hisham El Sherif and his colleagues.

infoDev. In 1995, the World Bank created a small subsidiary organization by the name of infoDev. Its mission was to "actively encourage the use of [information and communication technologies] to provide better goods and services benefiting the poor more efficiently through pilot, demonstration, and best practices projects" (infoDev 2001, 7). Peripheral economies were the target sites. The organization received grants from the World Bank and core states. Smaller contributions came from Motorola, IBM, Cisco and Telecom Italia (infoDev 2003). A donor committee of those core actors who contributed funds to infoDev's operations supervised the organization's annual work program. Predictably, infoDev's operations contained a commitment to market liberalization. Its prospectus states that infoDev "channels policy advice and other technical assistance to governments in developing economies on privatization, private entry and competition in the communications and information sectors, and on improving the policy, regulatory and business environment for investment" (infoDev n.d. b).

Activities fell into the following areas: consensus building, information infrastructure development, telecommunications reform and market access, and demonstration projects. Any source could submit suggestions for infoDev activities. Project funding was in the range of one hundred thousand dollars (infoDev n.d. b and n.d. c).

Internet for Economic Development. Vice President Al Gore announced this initiative on October 12, 1998, when he gave a speech to the Plenipotentiary Conference of the International Telecommunication Union (ITU). The initiative was to showcase successful models for development using the Internet in a small number of USAID-assisted countries (USAID n.d.). It generated various studies that took stock of the development of the Internet in client countries.[5] The focus of the initiative was on integrating economies into the global e-commerce network. The assessment for Morocco, for instance, stated:

> Commerce on the Internet could total tens of billions of dollars by the turn of the century. For this potential to be realized fully, governments will need to adopt a nonregulatory, market-oriented approach to electronic commerce, one that facilitates the emergence of a transparent and predictable legal environment to support global business and commerce. (USAID n.d.)

In 1999, U.S. trade representative Charlene Barshefsky commented in a similar vein: "Our recently introduced Internet and Development Project seeks to assist in policy reform that is aimed at liberalization, open competition and universal access."[6]

Leland Initiative. Administered by USAID, a smaller program of the Clinton-Gore administration was the Leland Initiative, with a fifteen-million-dollar budget spreading over five years. Its goal was to extend full Internet connectivity to twenty or more African countries, including Madagascar, Mali, Mozambique, Côte d'Ivoire, Benin, Rwanda, Senegal, and Guinea.[7]

USAID. Beyond implementing flagship initiatives such as the Leland Initiative, USAID made IT a theme in its overall work. Its strategy document of 2000 demanded that development programs were to include IT components (USAID 2003).

EUMEDIS. As part of the multilateral track of the Euro-Mediterranean partnership, the European Commission launched the "Action Plan for the

Development of the Euro-Mediterranean Information Society" (ISPO 1998). One of its components was the EUMEDIS initiative. Approved by the Commission in 1999, it aimed to reduce the informational and technological gap that separated the Southern Mediterranean region from neighboring countries. The initiative pursued its goal by interconnecting Euro-Mediterranean research communities and launching pilot projects in five sectors: information and communication technologies applied to education; electronic commerce and economic cooperation; health care networks; multimedia access to cultural heritage and tourism; information and communication technologies applied in industry and innovation (ISPO 2000).

This overview captures only a minute fraction of the funding opportunities that were available for peripheral IT stakeholders. So how did these initiatives and organizations address the states with whom they interacted?

- infoDev addressed states as a member of the type "state presiding over a peripheral economy."
- The Internet for Economic Development Initiative addressed a state as a member of the type "state presiding over a peripheral economy that President Clinton chose to include."
- The Leland Initiative addressed a state as a member of the type "state presiding over an economy of Sub-Saharan Africa."
- The EUMEDIS initiative addressed a state as a member of the type "state presiding over a Southern Mediterranean economy."

All these initiatives, therefore, addressed their state as a member of the type "state presiding over a peripheral economy," or some variant thereof.

Step Three: What Other Members Did the Identified Type Contain?
In the decade of the 1990s, IT stakeholders in peripheral economies had abundant access to funding opportunities. This warrants the conclusion that all peripheral states fall into the type of state that is addressed by enforcement mechanism six.

Step Four: Draw an Inference
Mechanism six targeted all peripheral states. However, the strength of the mechanism depended on the ability of IT stakeholders to tap the available sources. Egypt's Information and Decision Support Center (IDSC) and its subsidiary, the Regional Information Technology and Software Engineering Center (RITSEC), were experts in that regard. They understood how to

search for donors and write proposals. If IT stakeholders in other economies possessed the same acumen, they had access to similar resources.

Unexamined Enforcement Mechanisms

The discussion so far shows that the mechanisms of the Egyptian case can be extrapolated to a number of other, unexamined cases. Importantly, the Egyptian case does not exhaust the range of enforcement mechanisms that originated in social structure and prodded Third World states toward role compliance. For example, in 1995 the World Bank adopted operational policy 4.50 that stated any Bank loans for telecom sector were predicated on sector reform. Its text was:

> Bank lending to state enterprises [in the telecom sector] is contingent on firm government commitment to sector reform. Such lending is tied to (a) a clear and sustainable strategy to reduce government involvement in the ownership and management of telecommunications operations, or (b) specific progress in reform, for example, along the following lines: restructuring along commercial lines with increased financial and administrative autonomy from government; ensuring competent management, including (when necessary) support from more experienced operators; revising tariffs to reflect financial and efficiency objectives; containing the scope of operations to avoid preempting competition; removing barriers to entry; making equitable arrangements to interconnect new entrants; and, when appropriate, establishing a plan and timetable for transferring ownership control to the private sector. (World Bank 1995b)

Operational policy 4.50 thus represents an enforcement mechanism as defined by Berger and Luckmann: it grew out of social structure, sought to make peripheral states abide by the new best practice for sector administration, and contained sanctions—the withholding of funds from states that rejected sector reform. If this policy constituted an enforcement mechanism, why did it not operate in the Egyptian case? The answer is that the Egyptian state did not ask the Bank for a project loan in the telecom sector. Consequently, the Bank had no opportunity to make its demands known.

The Egyptian case therefore did not exhibit the full range of mechanisms at work, and many more of them crisscrossed the world system. Studying additional cases, perhaps in other world regions, would therefore enrich the picture of globalization set forth in this book. For example, a study of the

Asian periphery could flesh out whether Japan as a core economy attempted to cajole regional states into role compliance.

Conclusion

In conclusion, the Egyptian state is not unique in experiencing enforcement mechanisms, and Egyptian citizens are not unique in suffering autonomy violations. Globalization and the IT revolution had a disempowering impact on many Third World citizens.

CHAPTER 11

Epilogue

A World Full of Enforcement Mechanisms

The previous chapter showed that the world is filled with enforcement mechanisms. Those that accompany globalization create a systemic bias in the world economy, which makes it relatively easy for Third World states to comply with neoliberal norms but renders defiance difficult. Consequently, more states will comply than resist. This, in turn, means that more and more economies will be integrated into the neoliberal world economy, and all those indicators that scholars have found to be a mark of globalization increase in their numeric value: There will be greater volumes of cross-border communication, greater mobility of capital, and stronger flows of goods from country to country. At the same time, large parts of the world population find themselves incapable of shaping their institutional surroundings and subjected to rules that were not of their making. As much as we privileged First World citizens greet the ability to communicate with distant peers, download music at the push of a button, or upload our life's story to Facebook, and as much as we appreciate that computing technology eases workflows in Third World countries, we should also recognize that the IT revolution has had a darker, crippling side.

This book holds that globalization has not simply "happened," but that it has been made. Actors created norms; norms shaped role expectations; role expectations generated enforcement mechanisms; enforcement mechanisms biased the system toward globalization and, at its end point, flexible accumulation.

In this assessment this account differs markedly from optimistic best seller treatments such as Thomas Friedman's (2000) *The Lexus and the Olive*

Tree. Friedman treats globalization as a system that miraculously came into being when the Cold War ended. Since then, he says, it has been a fact to which actors can only adapt. The book advises Third World states to don the "golden straitjacket" as quickly as they can, give up their old function as economic planners, dismantle barriers to trade, and open their markets to foreign investors. The promise is that once states follow this path, they will receive economic dividends. In a nutshell, Friedman counsels Third World states to give in to the enforcement mechanisms identified in this study.

It is true that no one has globalization under control. However, some control it more than others, and by failing to tell their audiences where the rules of globalization originated, popular authors such as Friedman intensify the phenomenon that they purport to explain.

Why is There So Little Resistance to Corporate Globalization?

Since the transition to flexible accumulation disempowers Third World citizens, we should expect them to oppose this process. Confirming this expectation, Richard Kahn and Douglas Kellner of the University of California explain that in the 1990s and 2000s a sizable movement against corporate globalization emerged, which involved participants from both core and peripheral societies. The two authors point out that corporate globalization has elicited resistance from actors as diverse as the Zapatistas in Mexico and the Taliban in Afghanistan (Kahn and Kellner 2007). In addition, at the World Trade Organization's Doha round of trade negotiations Third World states negotiated more aggressively than they had in the past. As a consequence, the round collapsed in 2003 and again in 2008.

Nevertheless, given the degree of disempowerment that this study described, the number of people involved in resistance activities is surprisingly small. Why is this? Chapter four took a first stab at this question, when it explained that ideology—specifically the leapfrogging promise—helped minimize resistance.

Additional answers may lie in the complexity of globalization, which makes it difficult to trace globalization's effects on autonomy in the periphery back to its origins in Paris, Washington, or Punta del Este. Remember that the process by which the rules for IT were made and implemented moved through various fora in different world regions, most notably the United States and Europe, before being carried into the Egyptian setting, where the state mediated between actors from the core and the majority of the country's population. Only after the state responded to the enforcement mechanisms did the coercive impact of social structure hit the Egyptian economy in the form of structural adjustment programs, new labor relations, and a new state agency for IT. Egypt's citizens may have realized that they had nothing to do with the creation of Egypt's new ministry, but they likely did not know who was responsible for it. It is therefore conceivable that marginalized peripheral citizens are unable to trace their sense of disenfranchisement back to a specific source.

What is To Be Done?

Despite its critical examination of the IT revolution, this book is not directed against technology per se. Instead, it targets the procedures by which rules regarding the ownership, sale, and deployment of technology are made, and it calls these procedures unjust. The solution is therefore not to abolish technology and catapult the world back into the 1970s. Instead, decision-making at all levels of communal interaction needs to be democratized. In the present case, this applies especially to domestic and global procedures. If the process by which rules are created is just—that is, if every human being that is subject to rules has a part in their making—the rules themselves will be just (Young 2000). So will be their enforcement mechanisms.

It is important to stress that it does not suffice to democratize *either* the national level *or* the global level. Instead, democratization must occur at both levels simultaneously. To see why, imagine a situation in which the national level of decision-making is democratic, but the global level is not. In that case, citizens of a Third World country might be able to negotiate a political strategy that they would like their state to advance at the international level, but the state would not be able to do so, and global regimes would not adequately reflect the input of that country's population. Next, imagine another situation in which the global level of decision-making is democratic but the national level is not. In this case, the Third World state could influence global decision-making, but the input it provides would not reflect the desires of its citizens. Creating a world order that is just therefore necessitates democratization in authoritarian societies such as Egypt. At the same time, it requires that fora such as the World Trade Organization be made participatory.

The first task has been a concern of core states. The government of President George W. Bush, for example, was very vocal about the need to bring democracy into authoritarian political systems. However, the administration's rhetoric legitimized imperial intentions. Nowhere is this clearer than in the case of Iraq. When the government claimed that war was necessary, it cited the presence of weapons of mass destruction as its main motive. In addition, it insisted that the country's residents ought to be liberated from their dictatorial state. The administration's neoconservative friends reasoned that once Iraq was turned into a democracy, other Arab countries would follow suit, benefitting at once these countries' citizens and the United States, which would gain a strong foothold in the region. Although the American government claimed to worry about human rights in Iraq, its war effort was likely motivated by a desire for control of the country's oil reserves. Considering the fact that the Iraq invasion caused the deaths of well over one hundred thousand residents,[1] the stated desire to enhance Iraqis' autonomy appears as a mere fig leaf for hegemonic ambitions. The instrumental embrace of democratization rhetoric is not what is needed. A world order that respects the autonomy of human beings requires that a commitment to autonomy trumps self-serving political goals.

The second task of democratizing global governance has been tackled by scholars of cosmopolitanism. They have begun to debate what a commitment to human autonomy worldwide means for the status of national borders and whether First World societies are ethically obliged to allocate part of their wealth for poverty alleviation in poor nations (Pogge and Horton 2008). They have also begun to examine how works of democratic theory, which were written for the national level, speak to the problem of global decision-making. If we truly believe that all human beings are equal, and if, moreover, the concept of the nation state is losing its relevance, does it make sense to confine demands for democracy to the national level and bracket the consideration of global regime formation? On the basis of what moral or philosophical principles can such confinement be justified? To tackle some of these questions, Daniele Archibugi of the Italian National Research Council in Rome published the volume *Debating Cosmopolitics* (2003), in which a number of scholars explored ways to enhance human input into global governance processes. Then he followed up with the study *The Global Commonwealth of Citizens: Towards Cosmopolitan Democracy* (2008). In it he examined, among others, the possibilities of creating a world parliament and endowing it with similar functions as the European Parliament.

All in all, political philosophers have begun to push the ideas of liberalism and democratic theory beyond the nation state and open them up to people from countries outside the traditional cradles of liberalism. This is a welcome and much needed development.

But fascinating as it is, this area of research is in its initial stages, and many questions still lack answers. Two such questions arise directly from this study. First, assuming that universal consensus about the necessity to democratize governance has been achieved, what ways are there to represent citizens at the international level whose states fail to aggregate citizen demands? And second, what rights should corporations have in a national or worldwide democracy? Traditional democratic theory has insisted that governments receive their mandates from citizens on a one-person-one-vote basis. Where does the corporation fit in? What human beings, exactly, does a corporation represent? What rights, if any, does a corporation have to sway decision processes that are designed for humans? Should steps be taken to curb corporate influence? Given the political significance that large companies nowadays have, it is surprising to find that few democratic theorists have engaged these questions.

This brief discussion shows that even as a pure thought experiment, designing a governance system that respects human autonomy is a great challenge. It will be equally difficult to bring these thoughts—once they have matured into a complete normative framework—to implementation. After all, for corporate actors and their beneficiaries, enormous amounts of money are at stake, and they will surely resist such efforts. In fact, because of the enormous power of large companies, and because core states are captive to their concerns, democratization can happen only if the grassroots call for it loudly enough. Only then will those states move.

This difficulty should not deter those who believe in autonomy from researching ways to implement the idea. It also must not keep them from bringing it to the attention of the public. The contradictions of globalization may be difficult to see for those who sit inside Joel Osteen's rotating globe. These "insiders" may find alluring advantages in the hegemonic vision of flexibility, capitalism, and wealth creation and therefore assume that flexible accumulation benefits the rest of humanity as well. But to many who live in the world's periphery, globalization is a dubious proposition. If we believe that all humans are equally valuable and that they have a need for autonomy, we should act on that conviction.

Notes

Chapter 1

1. In this work, I use "rules" and "institutions" interchangeably. Explicit rules may also be referred to as "regulations," while implicit rules may be termed "norms." Moreover, the expression "standards" refers to technical rules that govern the production of goods and services (for instance, rules that govern how the various web browsers recognize and display a webpage).
2. In that regard, I follow the same route as Franda (2001) and Cogburn (2005, 57).
3. Bradley et al. (1999, 30) refer to this complex accountability thread as "cascading agency problem."

Chapter 2

1. "International settlements regime" is a technical term that telecom experts, states, and carriers used to describe the specific procedure by which carriers settled their accounts with each other. The ITU was in charge of overseeing the settlements regime, which formed part of the telecom regime.
2. The economic paradigm governing telecom under Fordism was the "natural monopoly" paradigm. See Mitchell and Vogelsang (1991).
3. Terminal equipment includes devices that end users attach to the phone network. Examples are telephone sets, fax machines, and computer modems.
4. Value-added services were services that the network itself could provide beyond simple circuit-switched telephone service. Examples are call waiting and voice-mail. Technological developments have made it possible for terminal equipment to take over many of these functions.
5. It is important to note that the EC's legislative branches only wanted to open European telecom to European competitors. U.S. carriers had to wait for the GATS negotiations on basic telecom to get access to the European market.
6. The Commission issued its first telecom-related report in 1984. See European Commission (1984).

7. It specifically cited articles 37 (1), 86, and 90 (1) and (2).
8. Knowledge-intensive services are service activities that, for their completion, require a considerable investment in technology. According to the OECD (2006), typical examples are research and development, management consulting, legal services, accounting, finance, and marketing-related service activities (7).
9. "Body shopping" means that service workers travel in person to those locations that are to be serviced.
10. According to the World Trade Organization, there is no standard international definition for "basic telecommunications." At the outset of the WTO negotiations, participants agreed to set aside the different definitions they used domestically, and negotiate all telecommunications services except those considered to be "value-added" or "enhanced" (WTO 1996).

Chapter 3

1. These were the University of California at Los Angeles, Stanford, the University of California at Santa Barbara, and the University of Utah.
2. It also added a node at RAND (Zakon 2002).
3. All RFCs can be found at http://tools.ietf.org/html/.
4. Unlike the Internet BITNET did not transmit messages in real time, as segments of the network were only in service during certain periods. Instead, every node on the path toward the destination stored the messages until the next segment of the route became available.
5. That TCP/IP gained such currency was not only due to NSF support, but also to its flexibility and reliability. Unlike other protocols, such as the older network control protocol and the OSI protocol advanced in Europe, the TCP/IP protocol suite enabled the internetworking approach, which "enables system designers and implementers to provide network users with a single, highly available, highly reliable, easily enlarged, easily modifiable, virtual network" (Martillo 1989).
6. All RFCs can be found at http://tools.ietf.org/html/.
7. There had been a few commercial networks as early as the 1950s. SABRE, for instance, came into being in 1957 as a cooperative effort between IBM and American Airlines. It was a real-time airlines reservations system, which sent messages, processed wait-lists, and prepared boarding passes (Evans 1967).
8. For an overview of the various networks, see Quarterman and Hoskins (1986).
9. Individuals interested in computing could afford to purchase these small machines, use them for computation, and make them communicate remotely. Hobbyists created networks to "electronic bulletin boards" and by 1983 a network among personal computers running Microsoft's MS-DOS operating system emerged, called FidoNet, which extended the store-and-forward model of BITNET beyond research institutions (Wimmer 1997, 73; Zakon 2002).

10. Like the American BITNET, EARN was a store-and-forward network, running the IBM Network Job Entry protocol.
11. *The Economist*, October 16, 1993, 101.
12. Information technologies were computers that, on a stand-alone basis, turned data into usable information. Communication technologies were network technologies such as the telecom network or the Internet. Thanks to the convergence that has taken place since the early 1990s, information and communication technologies are now frequently referred to as "IT," as they are in this book.
13. In 2004 the fee for full membership was fifty-seven thousand dollars.
14. See Krechmer (2000) for a discussion of the pitfalls such market-driven standardization presents for small companies that are not industry leaders.
15. In November 2009, the organization adopted the new name "Global Business Dialogue on e-Society."
16. IANA's leader Jon Postel had been in charge of numbering ARPANET hosts ever since the 1970s. See RFC 433.

Chapter 4

1. See chapter one.
2. See also Franda (2001) and Cogburn (2005).
3. Those services that required a heavy investment in technology were easily digitized and sold over the Internet and created largely in core economies.
4. Whether or not the object exercises its power thus depends on external, contingent events.
5. For details, see the World Bank's operational policy 4.50 in chapter ten.
6. For details on infoDev, see chapter ten.
7. It is important to note that each social actor fills not only one role, but several. For example, my acquaintance Erin plays the following roles simultaneously: student, woman, Irish American. Similarly, the Egyptian state plays the following roles: "state presiding over a Muslim country," "state presiding over a world heritage site," "Southern Mediterranean partner of the EU."
8. At the same time it is entirely possible that certain enforcement mechanisms are not actualized in the specific case we studied. Studying a number of cases may therefore yield additional enforcement mechanisms. Such additional study is especially fruitful if the new cases occupy different positions in the social structure. For example, the European Union might pursue a regional policy for Latin America that differs in a number of ways from the Euro-Mediterranean Partnership. Consequently, the states in Latin America will experience different enforcement mechanisms than the states located in the Mediterranean.

Chapter 5

1. Parastatals are state-owned enterprises.

Chapter 6

1. "Preferential trade" refers to trade where Egypt had access conditions to the EU market that were better than the access conditions that non-EU countries enjoyed under the minimum standards for openness set by the General Agreement of Tariffs and Trade.
2. In May 1991 the government concluded an eighteen-month stand-by agreement with the IMF for 278 special drawing rights ($372 million) to support the economic reform and structural adjustment program of the World Bank (Weiss and Wurzel 1998, 24).
3. Moreover, most of EU exports into the Southern Mediterranean did not occur under preferential terms but under regular WTO most favored nations terms.
4. The U.S.-Egypt's Presidents' Council represents both U.S. and Egyptian private sector interests and is therefore not a truly Egyptian organization. However, for the purposes of this book, the Council qualifies as an Egyptian civil society organization because it provided a political venue to Egyptian private sector interests.
5. The Gore-Mubarak Partnership was officially named the "U.S.-Egypt Partnership for Growth and Development."
6. This section on labor-state relations is based on Pripstein Posusney (1997, 220–243).
7. In 1994, the town Mallawi in the governorate of Minya in Upper Egypt was subjected to a twelve-hour dusk-to-dawn curfew. It was kept in place for two years (EIU 1996/2, 12).
8. For the difference between inclusionary and exclusionary authoritarianism, see O'Donnell (1973, 53–114).

Chapter 7

1. The only other entities that controlled telecom infrastructure for their own specialized needs were the Suez Canal Authority, defense service, railways, broadcasting and television, and civil aviation authorities (World Bank 1981, 1).
2. Expressed demand is the sum of direct exchange line and the waiting list.
3. For more information about the organizational culture of paternalism see, for instance, Palmer et al. (1988).
4. Under monopoly conditions these might be companies operating under license from ARENTO.
5. In 1996, the Ministry had funneled £E 2.8 billion of ARENTO's profits into subsidizing development of the Cairo metro (EIU 1997/2, 31).
6. It is article 52. Additional examples of the way in which the EU affected the decision-making environment of the Egyptian state in the area of telecom and IT are conferences such as the Euro-Med Net 98 Conference in Cyprus. This conference launched a survey of the Mediterranean information societies. In addition, the EU funded a number of regional activities in the areas of telecom and IT. All this happened in the context of the Euro-Mediterranean Partnership

(ENCIP 2003; European Commission, Information Society Project Office n.d.; NECTAR 1998).

7. For a fuller discussion of the conference, see chapter six.
8. Like the first operator, this operator would use the GSM standard.
9. Law 19/1998.
10. The original stockholders of ECMS protested. They had purchased their stock in the belief that the company already owned a license, and they did not want to see their dividends vanish under the impact of the license fee. The government's action caught Misrfone by surprise as well. When it had submitted the bid for its cellular license, it had assumed that it would compete against the inefficient state operator, not against a well-funded consortium with international expertise. In the end, Misrfone shrugged the blow off, because the Egyptian market was large enough for two competitors.
11. Over two-thirds of these had been put in place by Menatel (6,793) and Nile Telecom (4,288) (Arab Advisors 2002a, 36).

Chapter 8

1. For example, Huntington (1968).
2. By that time UNDP had supported computerization in countries such as India, to support the institutional capacity of public administration.
3. This performance-driven human resource policy may have been an arrangement with Atef Ebeid, whose position as minister of administrative development put him in charge of government employment. Very likely, IDSC's performance-oriented approach to human resource management entailed not only temporary contracts, but also a pay scale that offered much better monetary incentives than those applied to the rest of the state bureaucracy.
4. This sum excludes costs borne by the Ministry of Cabinet Affairs.
5. See IDSC, TDP (1994).
6. This sum was for both centers.
7. It was created under the name of Redsoft.
8. To mention only one example, RITSEC (2001) indicated that it had implemented the governorates decision support project (20).
9. Bill Gates quoted in RITSEC (1999b).

Chapter 9

1. Another name for this subsidiary was Wataneyya.
2. Masreyya is now called Xceed.
3. In June 2001, the workforce numbered fifty-three thousand employees.
4. In addition the creation of subsidiaries was to make it easier to attract foreign investors (Danish 2002).
5. For example, Arab Advisors (2002b, 9).
6. In 1999 ISE ceased to convene, but the e-commerce committee continued its activities.

Chapter 10

1. The figure 5.2 billion denotes the size of the world population in 1990.
2. Even if a country was fully inside the set, it may not have experienced the enforcement mechanism, because it may have violated a necessary condition for World Bank investment. One such condition is relative political stability. If a country is torn by civil war, the Bank will not invest in it, no matter how poor or indebted it is.
3. These guarantees allowed states to raise additional money on the international financial market.
4. Charlene Barshefsky's statement to the High-level Symposium on Trade and Development at the World Trade Organization on March 17, 1999. Quoted in U.S. Embassy Tel Aviv (1999).
5. Examples are USAID (1999) on Bulgaria, and SETA (2000) on the Czech Republic.
6. Charlene Barshefsky's statement to the High-level Symposium on Trade and Development at the World Trade Organization on March 17, 1999. Quoted in USIS (1999).
7. Charlene Barshefsky's statement to the High-level Symposium on Trade and Development at the World Trade Organization on March 17, 1999. Quoted in ibid.

Chapter 11

1. One of the conservative estimates comes from the *Associated Press*, which in 2009 estimated the number of Iraqi casualties to be at 110,600 (Gamel 2009).

Works Cited

Abelson, Donald. 2000. The FCC's International Agenda, Accomplishments and Challenges: Remarks of Donald Abelson, Chief, International Bureau, Federal Communications Commission, at the Center for Strategic and International Studies, February 10, 2000. Retrieved on January 22, 2003, from http://www. csis.org/ics/fcc.html.

Ajami, Fouad. 1982. The Open-Door Economy: Its Roots and Consequences. In *The Political Economy of Income Distribution in Egypt*, ed. Gouda Abdel-Khalek and Robert Tignor, 469–516. New York, NY: Holmes & Meier Publishers.

American Chamber of Commerce in Egypt. 2002. *Information Technology in Egypt*. Cairo, Egypt: American Chamber of Commerce in Egypt.

———. 2003. Egypt-U.S. Trade. http://www.amcham.org.eg/BSAC/ustrade/ Trade.asp. Accessed May 22, 2004.

Amin, Galal A. 1995. *Egypt's Economic Predicament: A Study in the Interaction of External Pressure, Political Folly and Social Tension in Egypt, 1960–1990*. New York, NY: E.J. Brill.

Anderson, N.L. 1995. ITS America and the National/Global Information Infrastructure: A Strategic Report. Retrieved on November 30, 2002, from http://www.itsa.org/committe.nsf/4773c5ec712911ba8525 65d4005423ad/383d 370508d1941b8525629600642125?OpenDocument.

Arab Advisors. 2002a. Egypt Communications Projections Report. Amman, Jordan: Arab Advisors Group.

———. 2002b. Egypt Internet and Datacomm Landscape Report. Amman, Jordan: Arab Advisors Group.

Archibugi, Daniele (ed.). 2003. *Debating Cosmopolitics*. New York, NY: Verso.

———. 2008. *The Global Commonwealth of Citizens: Towards Cosmopolitan Democracy*. Princeton, NJ: Princeton University Press.

Awad, Ibrahim. 1991. Socio-Political Aspects of Economic Reform: A Study of Domestic Actors' Attitudes towards Adjustment Policies in Egypt. In *Employment and Structural Adjustment: Egypt in the 1990s*, ed. Heba Handoussa and Gillian Potter, 275–294. Cairo, Egypt: The American University in Cairo Press.

Berger, Peter L., and Thomas Luckmann. 1966. *The Social Construction of Reality: A Treatise in the Sociology of Knowledge.* New York, NY: Anchor.

Bhaskar, Roy. 1979. *The Possibility of Naturalism: A Philosophical Critique of Contemporary Human Sciences.* Brighton, UK: Harvester Press.

Bianchi, Robert. 1989. *Unruly Corporatism: Associational Life in Twentieth-Century Egypt.* New York, NY: Oxford University Press.

Bichara, Khaled, Chief Executive Officer, LinkdotNet. 2002. Interview by author, February 25. Cairo, Egypt.

Bradley, Michael, Cindy A. Schipani, Anant K. Sundaram, and James P. Walsh. 1999. The Purposes and Accountability of the Corporation in Contemporary Society: Corporate Governance at a Crossroads. *Law and Contemporary Problems* 62 (3): 9–86.

Brenner, Neil. 1999. Beyond State-Centrism? Space, Territoriality, and Geographical Scale in Globalization Studies. *Theory and Society* 28: 39–78.

Brock, Gillian, and Harry Brighouse. 2005. Introduction. In *The Political Philosophy of Cosmopolitanism*, ed. Gillian Brock and Harry Brighouse, 1–9. New York, NY: Cambridge University Press.

Cairo Times. [1999]. NGO Law Passed in Full. Retrieved on December 8, 2003, from http://www.cairotimes.com/content/issues/hurights/ngolaw3.html.

Carré, Olivier. 1984. *Mystique et Politique: Lecture Révolutionnaire du Coran par Sayyid Qutb, Frère Musulman Radical.* Paris, France: Les Editions du Cerf.

Christman, John. 2009. Autonomy in Moral and Political Philosophy. In *The Stanford Encyclopedia of Philosophy (Fall 2009 Edition)*, ed. Edward N. Zalta. Retrieved on February 2, 2010, from http://plato.stanford.edu/archives/fall2009/entries/autonomy-moral/.

Clinton, William, and Albert B. Gore. 1997. A Framework for Global Electronic Commerce. Retrieved on March 21, 2004, from http://www.technology.gov/digeconomy/framewk.wpd.

Coalition of Service Industries. 2006. About CSI. Retrieved on May 1, 2006, from http://www.uscsi.org/about/.

Cogburn, Derrick. 2003. Governing Global Information and Communications Policy: Emergent Regime Formation and the Impact on Africa. *Telecommunications Policy* 27 (1–2): 135–153.

———. 2004. Elite Decision-Making and Epistemic Communities: Implications for Global Information Policy. In *The Emergent Global Information Policy Regime*, ed. Sandra Braman, 154–178. New York, NY: Palgrave Macmillan.

———. 2005. Partners of Pawns? The Impact of Elite Decision-Making and Epistemic Communities in Global Information Policy on Developing Countries and Transnational Civil Society. *Knowledge, Technology & Politics* 18 (2): 52–81.

Collier, Andrew. 1994. *Critical Realism: An Introduction to Roy Bhaskar's Philosophy.* New York, NY: Verso.

Communet. 1995. G-7 ministerial conference on the global information society: Making way for the new by destroying the old civilization—FINS special report February 21, 1995 (report posted by International Association of Library

Federations and Institutions). Retrieved on November 29, 2002, from http://www.ifla.org/documents/infopol/intl/g7/g7fins01.txt.

Comor, Edward. 1998a. Governance and the "Commoditization" of Information. *Global Governance* 4: 217–233.

———. 1998b. *Communication, Commerce and Power: The Political Economy of America and the Direct Broadcast Satellite, 1960–2000*. New York, NY: St. Martin's Press.

———. 1999. Governance and the Nation-State in a Knowledge-Based Political Economy. In *Approaches to Global Governance Theory*, ed. Martin Hewson and Timothy J. Sinclair, 117–134. Albany, NY: State University of New York Press.

Cook, Gordon. 1992. A National Network that Isn't. *Computerworld* 26 (10): 91–95.

Council of the European Communities. 1988. Council Resolution of 30 June 1988 on the Development of the Common Market for Telecommunications Services and Equipment up to 1992 (88/C 257/01).

———. 1990. Council Directive of 28 June 1990 on the Establishment of the Internal Market for Telecommunications through the Implementation of Open Network Provision (90/387/EEC).

———. 1993. Council Resolution of 22 July 1993 on the Review of the Situation in the Telecommunications Sector and the Need for Further Development in that Market (93/C 213/01).

Cowhey, Peter. 1990. The International Telecommunications Regime: The Political Roots of Regimes for High Technology. *International Organization* 44 (2): 169–199.

Cox, Robert. 1987. *Production, Power, and World Order: Social Forces in the Making of History*. New York, NY: Columbia University Press.

———. 1996. The Global Political Economy and Social Choice. In *Approaches to World Order*, ed. Robert W. Cox and Timothy J. Sinclair, 191–208. Reprint, *The New Era of Global Competition: State Policy and Market Power*, ed. Daniel Drache and Meric S. Gertler. Montreal, Canada: McGill-Queen's University Press, 1991. New York, NY: Cambridge University Press.

Danish, Adel, Board Member, Telecom Egypt; Chairman and CEO, Masreya Information Systems. 2002. Interview by author, April 2. Cairo, Egypt.

Dataquest. 1991. The Egypt High Technology Industry: Inward Investment Strategy Plan. Final report prepared for the Cabinet Information and Decision Support Center. San Jose, CA: Dataquest.

Davies, Andrew. 1994. *Telecommunications and Politics: The Decentralised Alternative*. New York, NY: St. Martin's Press.

Dessouki, Ali Eddin Hillal. 1991. The Public Sector in Egypt: Organization, Evolution, and Strategies of Reform. In *Employment and Structural Adjustment: Egypt in the 1990s*, ed. Heba Handoussa and Gillian Potter, 259–274. Cairo, Egypt: The American University in Cairo Press.

Dooley, Tara. 2007. At Home in the World: Lakewood's Congregation is America's Largest, but Joel Osteen's Following is Far Larger. *Houston Chronicle*, October 17.

Retrieved on February 2, 2010, from http://www.chron.com/disp/story.mpl/life/religion/5209200.html.

Drahos, Peter. 1998. The Universality of Intellectual Property Rights: Origins and Developments. Presentation delivered at the panel discussion to commemorate the 50th anniversary of the Universal Declaration of Human Rights, organized by the World Intellectual Property Organization in collaboration with the Office of the United Nations High Commissioner for Human Rights, Geneva, November 9, 1998. Retrieved on July 23, 2006, from http://www.wipo.int/tk/en/hr/paneldiscussion/papers/pdf/drahos.pdf.

EB refers to the yearly "Egypt" entries of the *Britannica Book of the Year* published by Encyclopedia Britannica. The full citation for "EB 1992" would be: Encyclopedia Britannica. 1992. *Britannica Book of the Year: 1991*. Chicago, IL: Encyclopedia Britannica.

Egypt's International Economic Forum.1999. Egypt's International Economic Forum: Committed to Egypt's Economic Prosperity. Information brochure. Cairo, Egypt: Egypt's International Economic Forum.

Egypt-U.S. Presidents' Council. 1996. Egypt-USA Presidents' Council: A Report Prepared for: The Middle East/North Africa Economic Conference III. Cairo, Egypt, November 12, 1996. Cairo, Egypt: Archives of the Egypt field office of the U.S. Agency for International Development.

EIEF. *See* Egypt's International Economic Forum.

EIU refers to the quarterly country reports on Egypt issued by the Economist Intelligence Unit. The full citation for "EIU 1997/3" would be: Economist Intelligence Unit. 1997. *Country Report Egypt 1997 (Third Quarter)*. London, UK: Economist Intelligence Unit.

El Sherif, Hisham. 1983. An Accelerated Development Strategy for Developing Countries: An Informatics, Decision Support Systems Approach. PhD dissertation, Massachusetts Institute of Technology.

———. 1990. Managing Institutionalization of Strategic Decision Support for the Egyptian Cabinet. *Interfaces* 20: 97–114.

El Sherif, Hisham, and Omar A. El Sawy. 1988. Issue-Based Decision Support Systems for the Egyptian Cabinet. *MIS Quarterly* 12: 551–567.

El-Nahhas, Mona. 2003. Brotherhood at the Bar. *Al-Ahram Weekly*, March 13–19, 2003. Retrieved December 6, 2003, from http://weekly.ahram.org.eg/2003/629/eg8.htm.

Embassy of the United States, Tel Aviv. 1997. FCC Chairman Hundt on WTO Basic Telecom Agreement. Retrieved on January 12, 2008, from http://www.usembassy-israel.org.il/publish/press/fcc/archive/1997/march/fc10320.htm.

———. 1999. Barshefsky Statement for WTO Symposium on Development. Retrieved on July 11, 2008, from http://www.usembassy-israel.org.il/publish/press/ustr/archive/1999/march/ot1318.htm.

ERCIM. *See* European Research Consortium for Informatics and Mathematics.

ESIS. *See* European Survey on the Information Society.

European Commission. 1984. Communication from the Commission to the Council on Telecommunications: Progress Report on the Thinking and Work done in the Field and Initial Proposals for an Action Programme (COM (84) 277).

————. 1987. Towards a Dynamic European Economy. Green Paper on the Development of the Common Market for Telecommunications Services and Equipment (COM (87) 290).

————. 1988. Directive of 16 May 1988 on Competition in the Markets in Telecommunications Terminal Equipment (88/301/EEC).

————. 1990. Commission Directive of 28 June 1990 on Competition in the Markets for Telecommunications Services (90/388/EEC).

————. 1993. White Paper on Growth, Competitiveness, and Employment: The Challenges and Ways forward into the 21st Century (COM (93) 700 final).

————. 1996. Commission Directive of 13 March 1996 Amending Directive 90/388/EEC with Regard to the Implementation of Full Competition in Telecommunications Markets (96/19/EC).

————. 1997a. A European Initiative in Electronic Commerce. Communication to the European Parliament, the Council, the Economic and Social Committee and the Committee of the Regions (COM (97) 157).

————. 1997b. Communication from the Commission of 15 July 1997 on the Information Society and Development: The Role of the European Union (COM/97/0351 final).

————. n.d. Euromed Heritage: Regional Programme in Support of the Development of Euro-Mediterranean Cultural Heritage. Retrieved December 31, 2003, from http://europa.eu.int/comm/external_relations/euromed/euromedheritage-proj_en.pdf.

European Commission, Directorate General External Relations. 1996. Conférence de Rome sur la Coopération Euro-Mediterranéenne dans le Domaine de la Société de l'Information: Conclusions de la Présidence. Retrieved on December 8, 2003, from http://europa.eu.int/comm/external_relations/euromed/conf/sect/si.htm.

————. 1998. Euro-Mediterranean Partnership. Brussels, Belgium: European Commission.

European Commission, Information Society Project Office. 1998. The Action Plan for the Development of the Euro-Mediterranean Information Society. PowerPoint presentation. Retrieved on January 12, 2001, from http://europa.eu.int/ISPO/eumedis/hyperlink/EUMEDIS_gb.ppt.

————. 2000. Mediterranean Countries: EUMEDIS initiative—Euro-Mediterranean Information Society. Retrieved on January 12, 2001, from http://europa.eu.int/ISPO/intcoop/i_med.html.

European Parliament. 1993. Resolution on the Commission's 1992 Review of the Situation in the Telecommunications Services sector (Resolution A3-0113/93).

European Research Consortium for Informatics and Mathematics. 1995. The Development of the Internet in the Mediterranean Countries and the Co-Operation with the European Union (study carried out for the European Commission). Sophia Antipolis, France, European Research Consortium for Informatics and Mathematics.

European Survey on the Information Society. 2001. IS Promotional Activities: Egypt Summary Report: 1999–2000. Retrieved December 31, 2003, from http://www.eu-esis.org/esis2prom/EGprom7.htm.

Evans, George J. 1967. Experience Gained from the American Airlines SABRE System Control Program. In *Proceedings of the 22nd National Conference of the Association for Computing Machinery*, 77–83. Retrieved June 19, 2004, from http://delivery.acm.org/10.1145/810000/805977/p77-evans.pdf?key1=805977 &key2=5124767801&coll=portal&dl=ACM&CFID=22033424&CFTOKE N=65394995.

Fahmy, Ninette. 2002. *The Politics of Egypt: State-Society Relationship*. New York, NY: Routledge.

FCC. *See* Federal Communications Commission, International Bureau.

Federal Communications Commission, International Bureau. 1995. Report and Order in the Matter of Market Entry and Regulation of Foreign-Affiliated Entities. IB docket no. 95-22, FCC 95-475.

Finnemore, Martha. 1996. *National Interests in International Society*. Ithaca, NY: Cornell University Press.

Franda, Marcus. 2001. *Governing the Internet: The Emergence of an International Regime*. Boulder, CO: Lynne Rienner.

Friedman, Thomas L. 2000. *The Lexus and the Olive Tree: Understanding Globalization*. New York, NY: Anchor Books/Random House.

Froomkin, A. Michael. 1999. Semi-Private International Rulemaking: Lessons Learned from the WIPO Domain Name Process. Retrieved February 8, 2010, from http://osaka.law.miami.edu/~froomkin/articles/tprc99.pdf.

Gabr, Shafik. 1998. Globalization of the Arab Middle East and Maghreb economies. Presentation given to the emerging economies of the Arab world Euromoney conference, September 15–17. http://www.artoc.com.eg/Document/ artglob.doc. Accessed June 25, 2004.

Gamel, Kim. 2009. AP Impact: Secret Tally Has 87,215 Iraqis Dead. *ABCNews*, April 23. Retrieved February 6, 2010, from http://abcnews.go.com/International/ WireStory?id=7411522.

Garrison, William, Director, ICT Program, Kenan Institute of Private Enterprise, 2001a. Interview by author, June 5, Washington, DC.

———. 2001b. Interview by author, July 18, Washington, DC.

GBDe. *See* Global Business Dialogue on Electronic Commerce.

GDLC Egypt. *See* Global Distance Learning Center Egypt.

GIIC. *See* Global Information Infrastructure Commission.

Gill, Stephen, and David Law. 1993. Global Hegemony and the Structural Power of Capital. In *Gramsci, Historical Materialism and International Relations*, ed. Stephen Gill, 93–124. New York, NY: Cambridge University Press.

Giugale, Marcelo M., and Hamed Mobarak. 1996. Preface. In *Private Sector Development in Egypt*, ed. Marcelo M. Giugale and Hamed Mobarak, i–ii. Cairo, Egypt: The American University in Cairo Press.

Global Business Dialogue on Electronic Commerce. 2002. About the GBDe. Retrieved November 11, 2002, from http://www.gbde.org/acrobat/bro-churesm.pdf.

———. n.d. GBDe Origins. Retrieved November 28, 2002, from http://www. gbde.org/origins.html#.

Global Distance Learning Center Egypt. n.d. About GDLC-Egypt. Retrieved December 31, 2003, from http://www.gdlcegypt.org.eg/about.html.

Global Information Infrastructure Commission. 2002a. Homepage. Retrieved November 25, 2002, from http://www.giic.org.

Grant, Richard, and Jan Nijman (eds). 1998. *The Global Crisis in Foreign Aid.* Syracuse, NY: Syracuse University Press.

Grier, David, Professor at George Washington University, 2001. Interview by author, March 7. Washington, DC.

Hamelink, Cees. 1983. *Finance and Information: A Study of Converging Interests.* Norwood, NJ: ABLEX Publishing Corporation.

Handy, Howard et al. 1998. Egypt: Beyond Stabilization, toward a Dynamic Market Economy. IMF occasional paper series, no. 163. Washington, DC: International Monetary Fund.

Harb, Imad. 2003. The Egyptian Military in Politics: Disengagement or Accommodation. *Middle East Journal* 57 (2): 269–291.

Harvey, David. 1990. *The Condition of Postmodernity: An Enquiry into the Origins of Cultural Change.* Cambridge, MA: Basil Blackwell.

Hasenclever, Andreas, Peter Mayer, and Volker Rittberger. 1997. *Theories of International Regimes.* New York, NY: Cambridge University Press.

Hauben, Michael. 1997. *Netizens: On the History and Impact of Usenet and the Internet.* Los Alamitos, CA: IEEE Computer Society Press.

Hedblom, Milda K., and William B. Garrison. 1997. European Information Infrastructure Policy Making in the Context of the Policy Capacity of the European Union and Its Member-States: Progress and Obstacles. In *National Information Infrastructure Initiatives: Vision and Policy Design*, ed. Brian Kahin and Ernest J. Wilson III, 490–507. Cambridge, MA: The MIT Press.

Heikal, Mohamed. 1983. *Autumn of Fury: The Assassination of Sadat.* London, UK: Andre Deutsch.

Held, David. 2005. Principles of Cosmopolitan Order. In *The Political Philosophy of Cosmopolitanism*, ed. Gillian Brock and Harry Brighouse, 10–27. New York, NY: Cambridge University Press.

Heywood, Peter. 1992. Internet Europe: Is Commercial Traffic in the Stars? *Data Communications* 21 (11): 104–109.

High-Level Group on the Information Society. 1994. Recommendations to the European Council: Europe and the Global Information Society. Retrieved August 22, 2002, from http://europa.eu.int/ISPO/ docs/basics/docs/bangemann.pdf.

Huntington, Samuel P. 1968. *Political Order in Changing Societies.* New Haven, CT: Yale University Press.

ICANN and U.S. Department of Commerce. *See* Internet Corporation for Assigned Names and Numbers and U.S. Department of Commerce.

IDSC and Central Bank of Egypt. *See* Information and Decision Support Center of the Egyptian Cabinet and Central Bank of Egypt.

IDSC. *See* Information and Decision Support Center of the Egyptian Cabinet.

IDSC. TDP. *See* Information and Decision Support Center of the Egyptian Cabinet. Technology Development Program.

IETF. *See* Internet Engineering Taskforce.

IIPA. *See* International Intellectual Property Alliance.

ILPF. *See* Internet Law and Policy Forum.

infoDev. *See* World Bank. infoDev.

Information and Decision Support Center of the Egyptian Cabinet. [1988]. *The Cabinet Information and Decision Support Center: An Overview.* Cairo, Egypt: IDSC.

———. [1990]. *The Cabinet Information and Decision Support Center (IDSC): An Overview.* Cairo, Egypt: IDSC.

Information and Decision Support Center of the Egyptian Cabinet. Technology Development Program. 1994. *Hi-Tech-Companies in Egypt.* Cairo, Egypt: Cabinet Information and Decision Support Center.

———. 1996. *Hi-Tech Companies in Egypt: 1995–1996.* Cairo, Egypt: Cabinet Information and Decision Support Center.

Information and Decision Support Center of the Egyptian Cabinet and Central Bank of Egypt. [1989]. *Debt Management Project.* Cairo, Egypt: IDSC.

Information Infrastructure Taskforce. 1994. U.S. Goals and Objectives for the G7 GII Conference: Provided to European Commission Secretariat on September 14 for Input in the Development of the G7 Conference. Retrieved November 29, 2002, from http://www.ifla.org/documents/infopol/intl/g7/g7us.txt.

International Intellectual Property Alliance. 2004. 2004 Special 301 Report: Egypt. Retrieved June 13, 2004, from http://www.iipa.com/rbc/2004/2004SPEC301EGYPT.pdf.

International Planning and Research Corporation. 2003. Eighth Annual BSA Global Software Piracy Study: Trends in Software Piracy 1994–2002. Retrieved February 9, 2004, from http://global.bsa.org/globalstudy/2003_GSPS.pdf.

Internet Corporation for Assigned Names and Numbers and U.S. Department of Commerce. 1998. Memorandum of Understanding between the U.S. Department of Commerce and Internet Corporation for Assigned Names and Numbers. November 25, 1998. Retrieved on February 3, 2010, from http://www.icann.org/en/general/icann-mou-25nov98.htm.

Internet Engineering Taskforce. n.d. Participating in the Efforts of the IETF. Retrieved November 27, 2002, from http://www. ietf.org/join.html.

Internet Law and Policy Forum. [2002]. About ILPF. Retrieved March 21, 2004, from http://www.ilpf.org/about/.

Internet Society. 1996. Press Release: New International Committee Named to Resolve Domain Name System Issues. November 12, 1996. Retrieved February 3, 2010, from http://www.isoc.org/isoc/media/releases/iahcmembers.shtml.

Internet Society of Egypt. n.d. Board of Directors. Retrieved December 31, 2003, from http://www.ise.org.eg/BOD.htm.

IPRC. *See* International Planning and Research Corporation.

ISE. *See* Internet Society of Egypt.

ISPO. *See* European Commission, Information Society Project Office.

K&M Engineering and Consulting Corporation. 1994. Policy Reform and Institutional Development Assessment. Final Report Performed for the Arab

Republic of Egypt National Telecommunications Organization (ARENTO) and the United States Agency for International Development (USAID) under Contract no. 263-0177-3-8890. August. Washington, DC: K&M Engineering and Consulting Corporation.

Kahn, Richard, and Douglas Kellner. 2007. Resisting Globalization. In *The Blackwell Companion to Globalization*, ed. George Ritzer, 662–674.Malden, MA: Blackwell.

Kamel, Sherif. 1993. Decision Support in the Governorates Level in Egypt. In *Challenges for Information Management in a World Economy: Proceedings of the 1993 Information Resources Management Association International Conference in Salt Lake City, Utah, May 24–26*, ed. Mehdi Khosrowpour, 390–398. Harrisburg, PA: Idea Group Publishing.

Kamel, Tarek. 1997. Internet Commercialization in Egypt: A Country Model. Proceedings of the 1997 INET Conference, Kuala Lumpur, Malaysia, June 25–27. Retrieved February 4, 2010, from http://www.isoc.org/inet97/proceedings/E6/E6_2.HTM.

Kamel, Tarek, and Nashwa Abdel Baki. 1995. The Communication Infrastructure and the Internet Services as a Base for a Regional Information Highway. Proceedings of the 1995 INET Conference, Honolulu, United States, June 27–30. Retrieved February 4, 2010, from http://www.isoc.org/inet95/proceedings/PAPER/006/html/paper.html.

Kedzie, Christopher. 1997. The Third Waves. In *Borders in Cyberspace: Information Policy and the Global Information Infrastructure*, ed. Brian Kahin and Charles Nesson, 106–128. Cambridge, MA: The MIT Press.

Kellner, Douglas. 2002. Theorizing Globalization. *Sociological Theory* 20 (3): 285–305.

Kelly, Girardet, and Magda Ismail. 2001. *Internet on the Nile: Egypt Case Study.* Geneva, Switzerland: International Telecommunication Union.

Keohane, Robert, and Joseph S. Nye. 2000. Globalization: What's New? What's Not? (And So What?) *Foreign Policy* Spring: 104–119.

Khalil, Nevine. 2001. Hisham El-Sherif: Live and Learn - a Passion for Success, a Mission to Conquer Time and Knowledge. *Al Ahram Weekly*, October 25–31. Retrieved December 31, 2003, from http://weekly.ahram.org.eg/2001/557/profile.htm.

Khare, Rohit. 1998. The Evolution of the World Wide Web Consortium. Retrieved March 21, 2004, from http://www.ics.uci.edu/~rohit/w3c-evol.

Khattab, Mokhtar. 1999. Privatization in Egypt: Constraints and Resolutions. In *Partners for Development: New Roles for Government and Private Sector in the Middle East and North Africa*, ed. Samiha Fawzy and Ahmed Galal, 95–116. Washington, DC: The World Bank.

Kleiman, Kathryn. 2003. Internet Governance: A View from the Trenches. Retrieved March 21, 2004, from http://www.acm.org/usacm/PDF/ACM-IGP_Ford_Foundation_White_Paper.pdf.

Kleinwächter, Wolfgang. 2001. Global Governance in the Information Age. Papers from the Center for Internet Research. Aarhus, Denmark: University of Aarhus.

Retrieved March 21, 2004 from http://cfi.imv.au.dk/pub/skriftserie/003_klein-waechter.pdf.

Komiya, Megumi. 1990. Intelsat and the Debate about Satellite Competition. In *The Political Economy of Communications: International and European Dimensions*, ed. Kenneth Dyson and Peter Humphreys, 58–76. New York, NY: Routledge.

Krasner, Stephen D. 1982. Structural Causes and Regime Consequences: Regimes as Intervening Variables. *International Organization* 36 (2): 185–205.

Krechmer, Ken. 2000. Market-Driven Standardization: Everyone Can Win. *Standards Engineering* 52 (4): 15–19. Retrieved March 21, 2004, from http://www.csrstds.com/fora.html.

Land Center for Human Rights. 1999. Violence in the Egyptian Countryside 1998–1999. Retrieved December 6, 2003, from http://www.derechos.org/human-rights/mena/lchr/violence.html.

Lehman, Howard. 1993. *Indebted Development: Strategic Bargaining and Economic Adjustment in the Third World*. New York, NY: Palgrave Macmillan.

Lerner, Daniel. 1958. *The Passing of Traditional Society*. Glencoe, IL: The Free Press.

Levinson, Charles. 2003. Free to Preach. *Cairo Times*, August 14–20. Retrieved December 6, 2003, from http://www.cairotimes.com/news/Khutba0723.html.

LivingInternet. n.d. Internet History: TCP/IP. Retrieved June 19, 2004, from http://livinginternet.com/i/ii_tcpip.htm.

Loutfi, Osman, Professor at Cairo University, 2002. Interview by author, January 10. Cairo, Egypt.

Mann, Catherine L., Sue E. Eckert, and Sarah Cleeland Knight. 2000. *Global Electronic Commerce: A Policy Primer*. Washington, DC: Institute for International Economics.

Martillo, Joachim Carlo Santos. 1989. Round Two in the Great TCP/IP versus OSI Debate. Retrieved June 19, 2004, from http://www.cs.appstate.edu/-khj/that/cs/area/net/tcpvsosi.html.

May, Christopher. 2004. Capacity Building and the (Re)Production of Intellectual Property Rights. *Third World Quarterly* 25 (5): 821–837.

MCIT. *See* Ministry of Communications and Information Technology Egypt.

McKenney, James L., and H. Edward Nyce. 1989. The Role of the Large Corporation in the Communications Market. In *Future Competition in Telecommunications*, ed. Stephen P. Bradley and Jerry A. Hausman, 225–252. Boston, MA: Harvard Business School Press.

Migdal, Joel S. 1988. *Strong Societies and Weak States: State-Society Relations and State Capabilities in the Third World*. Princeton, NJ: Princeton University Press.

Miliband, Ralph. 1969. *The State in Capitalist Society: An Analysis of the Western System of Power*. New York, NY: Basic Books.

Mills, David L., and Hans-Werner Braun. 1987. The NSFNET Backbone Network. In Proceedings of the ACM SIGCOMM 87 Symposium in Stoweflake, Vermont, 191–196. Retrieved June 18, 2004, from http://portal.acm.org/ft_gateway.cfm?id=55502&type=pdf&coll=portal&dl=ACM&CFID=22033424&CFTOKEN=65394995.

Ministry of Communications and Information Technology Egypt. 2006. News: Dr.Kamel: Egypt's Software Exports Reach $200 Million, January 4. Retrieved May 6, 2008, from http://www.mcit.gov.eg/NewsDetails.aspx?id=GEFREILTor8= .

———. 2009. *Information and Communications Technology Indicators Bulletin. June 2009.* Cairo, Egypt: Ministry of Communication and Information Technology. Retrieved December 27, 2009, from http://www.egyptictindicators.gov.eg/NR/rdonlyres/2A1CBF8E-0455-432A-BDE9-476AD1C68EF3/0/ICTIndicatorsBulletinQ109English2009712133157.pdf.

Mitchell, Bridger, and Ingo Vogelsang. 1991. *Telecommunications Pricing: Theory and Practice.* New York, NY: Cambridge University Press.

Momani, Bessma. 2003. Promoting Economic Liberalization in Egypt from U.S. Foreign Aid to Trade and Investment. *Middle East Review of International Affairs (MERIA)* 7 (3). Retrieved December 3, 2003, from http://meria.idc.ac.il/journal/2003/issue3/jv7n3a6.html.

Mosco, Vincent. 1993. Free Trade in Communication: Building a World Business Order. In *Beyond National Sovereignty: International Communication in the 1990s,* ed. Kaarle Nordenstreng and Herbert Schiller, 193–209. Norwood, NJ: Ablex Publishing Corporation.

Narayan, Deepa (ed.). 2002. *Empowerment and Poverty Reduction: A Sourcebook.* Washington, DC: The World Bank.

Nassar, Heba, Wafaa Moussa, Amin Kamel, and Ahmed Miniawi. 1992. Review of Trends, Policies and Programmes Affecting Nutrition and Health in Egypt (1970–1990). UN ACC/SCN country case study for the XV Congress of the International Union of Nutritional Sciences, September 26 to October 1, 1993, Adelaide, New Zealand. Retrieved June 1, 2006, from http://www.unsystem.org/scn/archives/egypt/begin.htm.

National Science Foundation 1992. NSF9224—Network Information Services Manager(s) for NSFNET and NREN. Program guideline of March 19. Retrieved on February 3, 2010, from http://www.nsf.gov/pubs/stis1992/nsf9224/nsf9224.txt.

Network Working Group. 1990. Commercialization of the Internet: Summary Report. Request for comments no. 1192. Retrieved April 22, 2003, from http://www.cis.ohio-state.edu/cgi-bin/rfc /rfc1192.html.

Nicolaïdis, Kalypso. 1995. International Trade in Information-Based Services: The Uruguay Round and Beyond. In *The New Information Infrastructure: Strategies for U.S. Policy,* ed. William J. Drake, 269–302. New York, NY: The Twentieth Century Fund Press.

Nidumolu, Sarma R., Seymour E. Goodman, Douglas R. Vogel, and Ann K. Danowitz. 1996. Information Technology for Local Administration Support: The Governorates Project in Egypt. *MIS Quarterly* 20: 197–224.

NSF. *See* National Science Foundation.

NTIA. *See* U.S. Department of Commerce. National Telecommunications and Information Administration.

O'Donnell, Guillermo. 1973. *Modernization and Bureaucratic-Authoritarianism: Studies in South-American Politics*. Berkeley, CA: University of California, Institute of International Studies.

OECD. *See* Organization for Economic Cooperation and Development.

Organization for Economic Cooperation and Development. 2006. *Innovation and Knowledge-Intensive Service Activities*. Paris, France: OECD Publishing.

Orts, Jorge. 2001. Cyber Crime and the Private Sector: The Global Business Dialogue on Electronic Commerce. Powerpoint presentation in contribution to the "workshop on cybercrime," held on January 11–12, 2001, in Seville, Spain, and organized by the JRC Institute for Prospective Technological Studies. Retrieved November 12, 2002, from .http://www.jrc.es/pages/events/docs/Cibercrimen.ppt.

Packenham, Robert A. 1992. *The Dependency Movement: Scholarship and Politics in Development Studies*. Cambridge, MA: Harvard University Press.

Paik, Gina, and P.-R. Stark. 2000. The Debate over Internet Governance: A Snapshot in the Year 2000. Retrieved March 21, 2004, from http://cyber.law.harvard.edu/is99/governance/introduction.html.

Palmer, Monte, Ali Leila, and El Sayed Yassin. 1988. *The Egyptian Bureaucracy*. Syracuse, NY: Syracuse University Press.

Panitch, Leo. 1996. Rethinking the Role of the State. In *Globalization: Critical Reflections*, ed. James H. Mittelman, 83–113. Boulder, CO: Lynne Rienner.

Patomäki, Heikki. 2002. *After International Relations: Critical Realism and the (Re) Construction of World Politics*. New York, NY: Routledge.

Petri, Peter A. 1997. Trade Strategies for the Southern Mediterranean. OECD Development Centre Working Paper No. 127. Paris, France: OECD. Retrieved March 2, 2008, from http://titania.sourceoecd.org/vl=1604334/cl=20/nw=1/rpsv/cgi-bin/wppdf?file=5lgsjhvj7cq4.pdf.

Pincus, Andrew J. 2000. Toward a Uniform Commercial Legal Framework for Global Electronic Transactions. *Economic Perspectives* 5 (2): 11–13.

Pogge, Thomas, and Keith Horton (eds). 2008. *Global Ethics: Seminal Essays*. St. Paul, MN: Paragon House.

Pool, Ithiel da Sola. 1983. *Technologies of Freedom*. Cambridge, MA: Belknap Press.

———. 1990. *Technologies without Boundaries: On Telecommunications in a Global Age*. Cambridge, MA: Harvard University Press.

Power, D.J. 2003. A Brief History of Decision Support Systems, Version 2.8, May 31. Retrieved December 31, 2003, from http://DSSResources.COM/history/dsshistory.html.

Pripstein Posusney, Marsha. 1997. *Labor and the State in Egypt: Workers, Unions, and Economic Restructuring*. New York, NY: Columbia University Press.

Pye, Lucian (ed.). 1963. *Communications and Political Development*. Princeton, NJ: Princeton University Press.

Quarterman, John S., and Josiah C. Hoskins. 1986. Notable Computer Networks. *Communications of the ACM* 29 (10): 932–971.

Radwan, Raafat, Chairman of IDSC, 2002. Interview by author, March 18. Cairo, Egypt.

Ragin, Charles. 2000. *Fuzzy Set Social Science.* Chicago, IL: University of Chicago Press.

Regional Information Technology and Software Engineering Center. 1999a. Programs: Little Horus. Retrieved December 31, 2003, from http://www.ritsec. net/html/little_horus.html.

———. 1999b. Awards. Retrieved December 31, 2003, from http://www.ritsec.net/ html/awards.html.

———. 1999c. Regional Study: Establishing a Regional Distance Learning Network "Pilot Project." Retrieved August 19, 2000, from http://www.infodev. org/projects/25.pdf.

———. 2001. Regional Information Technology and Software Engineering Center (RITSEC): Profile. Cairo, Egypt: RITSEC.

———. n.d. a. Recommendations from RITSEC's Launching Seminar. Retrieved December 31, 2003, from http://www.ritsec.org.eg/ritsec-dec/launch_table.htm.

———. n.d. b. Cultureware, Using Modern Technology to Preserve the Past: Other Cultureware Activities. Retrieved December 31, 2003, from http://www.ritsec. org.eg/ritsec-dec/cultureware_05.htm.

———. n.d. c. Arab Child initiative: Investing in the Future: Schoolnet Africa. Retrieved December 31, 2003, from http://www.ritsec.org.eg/ritsec-dec/arab_05.htm.

———. n.d. d. Alliances. Retrieved December 31, 2003, from http://www.ritsec. org.eg/ritsec-dec/agreement.htm.

Reuter/Tabor Griffin. 1995. Counter Summit to Explore Problems in GII Development. G7 Live in the News, February 24, 1995 (report posted by the University of Torino). http://www.di.unito.it/mail_archive/G7/0001.html. Accessed 11/29/02.

Richmond, Riva. 1997. Multiplying Mobile Phones: A Surprise Move Will Bring Competition—Not Just Private Sector Participation—to the Mobile Phone Network. *Cairo Times,* November 27. Retrieved February 16, 2004, from http:// www.cairotimes.com/content/issues/ecref/ mobile20.html.

RITSEC. *See* Regional Information Technology and Software Engineering Center.

Roberts, Lawrence G. 1999. Internet Chronology. Retrieved June 19, 2004, from http://www.ziplink.net/~lroberts/ InternetChronology.html.

Rostow, Walt Whitman. 1960. *The Stages of Economic Growth: A Non-Communist Manifesto.* Cambridge, UK: Cambridge University Press.

Roudart, Laurence. 2001. Analyse Microéconomique de l'Impact sur les Revenues Agricoles et de la Liberalization des Prix du Fermage. In *Land Reform Bulletin* (2001/1), ed. P. Groppo. Rome, Italy: Food and Agriculture Organization of the United Nations.

Saleh, Nivien. 2007. Europe in the Middle East and Northern Africa: the Subtle Quest for Power. *Mediterranean Quarterly* 18 (1): 75–88.

———. 2009. Philosophical Pitfalls: The Methods Debate in American Political Science. *Journal of Integrated Social Sciences,* 1 (1): 141–176. Retrieved February 4,

2010, from http://www.jiss.org/articles/documents/JISS20091_1_141-176PhilosophicalPitfalls.pdf.

Samir, Said, and Paula Schmitt. 2001. Telecom Egypt: A Break-In or Breakthrough? *Pharaos*, June: 54–59.

Saunders, Robert J., Jeremy J. Warford, and Björn Wellenius. 1994. *Telecommunications and Development*. Baltimore, MD: Johns Hopkins University Press.

Sayer, Andrew. 1994. *Method in Social Science: A Realist Approach*. New York, NY: Routledge.

Schiller, Dan. 1996. *Theorizing Communication: A History*. New York, NY: Oxford University Press.

———. 1999. *Digital Capitalism: Networking the Global Market System*. Cambridge, MA: MIT Press.

Schiller, Herbert. 1970. *Mass Communications and American Empire*. New York, NY: Augustus M. Kelley Publishers.

Sinclair, Scott, and Jim Grieshaber-Otto. 2002. *Facing the Facts: A Guide to the GATS Debate*. Ottawa, Canada: Canadian Centre for Policy Alternatives.

Singh, J.P. 1999. *Leapfrogging Development? The Political Economy of Telecommunications Restructuring*. Albany, NY: State University of New York Press.

Spiwak, Lawrence J. 1998. From International Competitive Carrier to the WTO: A Survey of the FCC's International Telecommunications Policy Initiatives 1985–1998. *Federal Communications Law Journal* 51 (1): 111–228.

Springborg, Robert. 1989. *Mubarak's Egypt: Fragmentation of Political Order*. Boulder, CO: Westview Press.

SRI International. 1998. Egyptian Center for Economic Studies: External evaluation. Study carried out on behalf of the U.S. Agency for International Development Egypt: Economic Growth Office. Project no. 263–0264. Cairo, Egypt: U.S. Agency for International Development.

Stehmann, Oliver. 1995. *Network Competition for European Telecommunications*. New York, NY: Oxford University Press.

Sterling, Christopher. 2005. *Shaping American Telecommunications: A History of Technology, Policy, and Economics*. Mahwah, NJ: Lawrence Erlbaum Associates.

Sunsonline. 1982a. US Move on "Services" and "Investment" Misfires. October 28. Retrieved January 22, 2003, from http://www.sunsonline.org/trade/process/during/82/10280082.htm.

———. 1982b. Third World Cannot Accept GATT Rules, Principles and Framework for Services and Investment. November 26. Retrieved January 22, 2003, from http://www.sunsonline.org/trade/process/ during/82/11260082.htm.

———. 1998. Telecommunications: ITU vs. WTO Contest over Telephone Revenues. November 25. Retrieved January 22, 2003, from http://www.sunsonline.org/trade/process/followup/1998/ 11250298.htm.

Taubman, Geoffrey. 1998. A Not-So World Wide Web: The Internet, China, and the Challenges to Nondemocratic Rule. *Political Communication* 15: 255–272.

Telecom Egypt. 2009. Company Milestones: 150 Years of Telecommunications. Retrieved December 27, 2009, from http://ir.telecomegypt.com.eg/Company%20 Milestones.asp.

Thimm, Alfred L. 1992. *America's Stake in European Telecommunication Policies.* Westport, CT: Quorum Books.

Third World Summit on Media for Children. 2001. Dr. Hisham El Sherif. Retrieved December 31, 2003, from http://www.3rd-ws.org/speech/SHERIF.htm.

Titus, James P. 1967. ARPA: A Visible Means of Support. *Communications of the ACM* 10 (8): 519–520.

Tormey, Simon, and Jules Townshend. 2006. *Key Thinkers from Critical Theory to Post-Marxism.* Thousand Oaks, CA: Sage.

U.S. Agency for International Development. 1993. Egypt Telecommunications Sector Support 263-0223 Project Paper (PP), Dated Signed: 07/26/93. Washington, DC: USAID.

————. 2003. Our Work: Economic Growth and Trade—Information Technology. Retrieved April 5, 2004, from http://www.usaid.gov/our_work/economic_ growth_and_trade/info_technology/index.html.

————. n.d. Internet for Economic Development Initiative: Description of USAID/ Morocco Participation. Retrieved December 3, 2002, from http://www.usaid. gov/info_technology/ied/reports/iedmorocco1.html.

U.S. Agency for International Development, Center for Development Information and Evaluation. 1994. Capital Projects: U.S. Aid and Trade in Egypt. AID Technical Report No. 8. Arlington, VA: USAID Development Information Services Clearinghouse.

U.S. Agency for International Development. Egypt Field Office. 1992. Country Program Strategy FY 1992–1996: Telecommunications. Cairo, Egypt: USAID.

U.S. Agency for International Development. Inspector General. Regional Inspector General for Audit, Cairo. 1986. Audit of Telecomunications I, II, and III. USAID/ Egypt Project Nos. 263-0054, 263-0075 and 263-0117. Audit Report No. 6-263-86-5. May 11. Washington, DC: USAID.

U.S. Congress. House. Committee on Energy and Commerce. Subcommittee on Telecommunications and Finance, and Subcommittee on Commerce, Consumer Protection, and Competitiveness. 1993. Joint Hearing before the Subcommittee on Telecommunications and Finance and the Subcommittee on Commerce, Consumer Protection, and Competitiveness of the Committee on Energy and Commerce. 103rd Congress, First Session, August 3. Serial No. 103-50.

U.S. Congress. Senate. Committee on Commerce, Science, and Transportation. Subcommittee on Communications.1988. International Telecommunications Issues: Hearing before the Subcommitee on Communications of the Committee on Commerce, Science, and Transportation. 100th Congress, Second Session, April 19. S. Hrg. 100-716.

U.S. Department of Commerce. National Telecommunications and Information Administration. 1993. The National Information Infrastructure: Agenda for Action. Retrieved February 2, 2003, from http://www.ibiblio.org/nii/NII-Agenda-for-Action.html.

U.S. Department of Commerce. 1995. *Global Information Infrastructure: An Agenda for Cooperation.* Washington, DC: U.S. Government Printing Office. Retrieved January 22, 2003, from http://www.ntia.doc.gov/reports/giiagend.html.

U.S. Embassy Tel Aviv. *See* Embassy of the United States, Tel Aviv.

U.S. General Accounting Office. 1985. Report to the Administrator Agency for International Development: The U.S. Economic Assistance Program for Egypt Poses a Management Challenge for AID. Gaithersburg, MD: U.S. General Accounting Office Document Handling and Services Facility.

UNESCO Cairo. *See* United Nations Educational, Scientific and Cultural Organization. Cairo Office.

United Nations Educational, Scientific and Cultural Organization. Cairo Office. n.d. Major Programme Area IV: Communications, Information and Informatics. Retrieved December 31, 2003, from http://unesco-cairo.org/Publications/AR-96/area4000.htm.

United Arab Republic, Ministry of Communications. 1960. *Seven Years of Transport and Communications in the Egyptian Region of the U.A.R.* Cairo, Egypt: Ministry of Communications. Document is available at the archives of the Centre d'Etudes et de Documentation Economiques, Juridiques et Sociales (CEDEJ), Cairo, Egypt.

USAID Egypt. *See* U.S. Agency for International Development. Egypt Field Office.

USAID. *See* U.S. Agency for International Development.

USAID. Center for Development Information and Evaluation. *See* U.S. Agency for International Development. Center for Development Information and Evaluation.

USAID. Inspector General. *See* U.S. Agency for International Development. Inspector General

Villani, Michele, first secretary, trade matters, Delegation of the European Commission in Egypt. 2002. Interview by author, March 25.

W3C. *See* World Wide Web Consortium.

WDR. *See* World Dialogue on Regulation for Network Economies.

Webster, Frank. 1995. *Theories of the Information Society.* New York, NY: Routledge.

Weinbaum, Marvin G. 1986. *Egypt and the Politics of U.S. Economic Aid.* Boulder, CO; Westview.

Weiss, Dieter, and Ulrich Wurzel. 1998. *The Economics and Politics of Transition to an Open Market Economy: Egypt.* Paris, France: Organization for Economic Co-operation and Development.

Wheatley, David. 1990. *The March.* Produced by the British Broadcasting Company, directed by David Wheatley. 95 min. British Broadcasting Company. Videocassette.

Wheelock, Keith. 1960. *Nasser's New Egypt: A Critical Analysis.* New York, NY: Frederick A. Praeger.

Williamson, John. 1990. What Washington Means by Policy Reform. In *Latin American Adjustment: How Much Has Happened?* ed. John Williamson, 5–20.

Washington, DC: Institute for International Economics. Retrieved February 1, 2008, from http://www.petersoninstitute.org/publications/papers/paper. cfm?ResearchID=486.

Wimmer, Helmut. 1997. Zur Konvergenz von Technologie und Denken: Hypertext und Internet. Diplomarbeit zur Erlangung des akademischen Grades Magister der Sozial- und Wirtschaftswissenschaften, Universitaet Wien. Retrieved April 22, 2003, from http://mitglied.lycos.de/rapidwien/KOMPLETT.PDF.

World Bank. 1981. Staff Appraisal Report—Egypt—Arab Republic of Egypt National Telecommunications Organization (ARENTO)—Third Telecommunications Project—June 26, 1981. Washington, DC: The World Bank.

———. 1989. Project Completion Report—Egypt—Second and Third Telecommunications Projects (Credit 774-EGT and Loan 2041 EGT), June 22, 1989. Washington, DC: The World Bank.

———. 1994. Private Sector Development in Egypt: The Status and the Challenges. Prepared for the Conference "Private Sector Development in Egypt: Investing in the Future," Cairo, October 9–10, 1994. Cairo, Egypt: The World Bank.

———. 1995a. Economic Policies for Private Sector Development. Volume 1: A Policy Action Plan for Private Sector Development. Report available at USAID Egypt, Development Information Center, Call number DA 40-WB.

———. 1995b. Operational Policy 4.50: Telecommunications Sector, May 1995. Retrieved August 5, 2000, from http://wbln0018.worldbank.org/Institutional/ Manuals/OpManual.nsf/toc1/6A7634BEFEF4E8D88525672C007D0801?Ope nDocument.

———. 2002. *Information and Communication Technologies: A World Bank Group Strategy*. Washington, DC: The World Bank Group.

———. 2006. PovertyNet: Empowerment. Retrieved March 25, 2006, from http:// web.worldbank.org/WBSITE/EXTERNAL/TOPICS/EXTPOVERTY/EXTE MPOWERMENT/0,,contentMDK:20245753~pagePK:210058~piPK:210062~ theSitePK:486411,00.html.

———. 2008a. Data and Statistics: A Short History. Retrieved May 26, 2008, from http://go.worldbank.org/0CO1RKFBP0.

———. 2008b. Data and Statistics: Historical Classifications (Excel spread-sheet). Retrieved May 26, 2008, from http://siteresources.worldbank.org/ DATASTATISTICS/Resources/OGHIST.xls.

World Bank. GICT. *See* World Bank. Global Information and Communication Technologies Department.

World Bank. Global Information and Communication Technologies Department. 2000. The Networking Revolution: Opportunities and Challenges for Developing Countries. infoDev working paper. Washington, DC: The World Bank.

World Bank. infoDev. 2001. *Information for Development Program: 2000 Annual Report*. Washington, DC: The World Bank. Retrieved April 22, 2003, from http://www.infodev.org/library/AR/ann00.pdf.

———. 2003. *Information for Development Program: 2002 Annual Report*. Washington, DC: The World Bank. Retrieved April 22, 2003, from http://www. infodev.org/library/AR/ann02.pdf.

World Bank. infoDev. n.d. a. Regional Distance Learning Network for Information Technology. Project ID Number 025-950924. Retrieved December 7, 2002, from http://wbln0018.worldbank.org/ict/projects.nsf/ 9ab8b92c7ab711d385256b1800 57ba4c/72d2ccf0ce78a4e085256b10005b7d46?OpenDocument.

———. n.d. b. Prospectus. Retrieved April 23, 2003, from http://www.infodev.org/ about/prospectus.htm.

———. n.d. c. Projects by Region. Retrieved April 23, 2003, from http://wbln0018. worldbank.org/ict/projects.nsf/5.

———. n.d. d. Regional Distance Learning Network for Information Technology. Project Number: 025-950924. Retrieved January 23, 2002, from http://wbln0018. worldbank.org/infodev/infodev.nsf/ 43b9454e703ede5f85256922005478a5/b43 6877dab688e428525661e004e2d46?OpenDocument.

World Bank. Operations Evaluation Department. 1993. The Bank's Experience in the Telecommunications sector: An OED Review. Washington, DC: The World Bank.

World Bank. Operations Policy and Country Services. 2001a. World Bank Lending Instruments: Resources for Development Impact. Washington, DC: The World Bank. Retrieved May 26, 2008, from http://siteresources.worldbank.org/ INTBULGARIA/Resources/Lending_Instr_Eng.pdf.

World Development Indicators Database. Online: www.worldbank.org/data.

World Dialogue on Regulation for Network Economies. 2007. Egypt: Mobinil acquires 3G license. Retrieved December 27, 2009, from http://www.regulateon-line.org/content/view/1069/79/.

World Trade Organization. 1996. Press Brief: Basic Telecoms. Retrieved January 22, 2003, from http://www.wto.org/english/thewto_e/minist_e/min96_e/telecoms. htm.

———. 1997a. The WTO Negotiations on Basic Telecommunications. Retrieved January 22, 2003, from http://www.wto.org/english/news_e/pres97_e/summary. htm.

———. 1997b. Data on Telecommunications Markets Covered by the WTO Negotiations on Basic Telecommunications. Retrieved January 22, 2003, from http://www.wto.org/english/ news_e/pres97_e/data3.htm.

———. n.d. Uruguay Round Decision on Negotiations on Basic Telecommunications. Retrieved January 22, 2003, from http://www.wto.org/english/tratop_e/serv_e/ telecom_e/tel22_e.htm.

World Trade Organization. Committee on Trade and Development. 1998. Global Electronic Commerce in Goods and Services—Communication from the Delegation of Egypt, WT/COMTD/W/38, March 3.

World Trade Organization. Council for Trade in Services. 1998. Presence of Natural Persons (Mode 4): Background Note by the Secretariat. Internal document, S/C/W/75, December 8 (98-4927). Retrieved January 22, 2003, from http:// www.wto.org/english/tratop_e/ serv_e/w75.doc.

World Wide Web Consortium. 2001. The World Wide Web Consortium: Prospectus. Retrieved November 27, 2002, from http://www.w3.org/Consortium/Prospectus/ Overview.html.

————. 2002. World Wide Web Consortium Members. Retrieved November 27, 2002, from http://www.w3.org/ Consortium/Member/List.

WTO. *See* World Trade Organization.

WTO. Committee on Trade and Development. *See* World Trade Organization. Committee on Trade and Development.

Young, Iris Marion. 2000. *Inclusion and Democracy*. New York, NY: Oxford University Press.

Zakon, Robert Hobbes. 2002. Hobbes' Internet Timeline V. 5.6. Retrieved November 25, 2002, from http://www.zakon.org/robert/internet/timeline/.

Zaytoun, Mohaya A. 1991. Earnings and the Cost of Living: An Analysis of Recent Developments in the Egyptian Economy. In *Employment and Structural Adjustment: Egypt in the 1990s*, ed. Heba Handoussa and Gillian Potter, 219–258. Cairo, Egypt: The American University in Cairo Press.

Zielinski, Marek. 1987. Founding member of the EARN-Poland link discussion group, 2001. Phone interview by author, April 2, New York, NY.

Index

262 • Index